Susie, Sadly, and the
Black Torpedo of Doom

Susie, Sadly, and the Black Torpedo of Doom

John S. Littell

NEW AMERICAN LIBRARY

New American Library
Published by New American Library, a division of
Penguin Putnam Inc., 375 Hudson Street,
New York, New York 10014, U.S.A.
Penguin Books Ltd, 80 Strand,
London WC2R 0RL, England
Penguin Books Australia Ltd, Ringwood,
Victoria, Australia
Penguin Books Canada Ltd, 10 Alcorn Avenue,
Toronto, Ontario, Canada M4V 3B2
Penguin Books (N.Z.) Ltd, 182–190 Wairau Road,
Auckland 10, New Zealand

Penguin Books Ltd, Registered Offices:
Harmondsworth, Middlesex, England

First published by New American Library, a division of Penguin Putnam Inc.

First Printing, August 2002
10 9 8 7 6 5 4 3 2 1

Library of Congress Cataloging-in-Publication Data:
Littell, John S.
Susie, Sadly, and the black torpedo of doom / John S. Littell.
p. cm.
ISBN 0-451-20636-3 (alk. paper)
1. Littell, John S. (John Smith)—Childhood and youth.   2. United States—Social
life and customs.   I. Title.

CT275.L479 A3 2002
973.91'092—dc21
[B]   2002069210

Set in Garamond Book
Designed by Ginger Legato

Printed in the United States of America

For Susie and Sadly—but not the Black Torpedo of Doom

Contents

PART ONE

FEVER

"**M**y froat hurts," a little voice said in my ear.

I opened one eye and focused on the alarm clock. It was 7:01 A.M.

"It's the middle of the night," I groaned. "Go back to bed."

"I fink I'm going to frow up," Susie said.

At the ripe old age of five, my sister had reverted to baby talk, but I wasn't listening. I was almost fifteen years old and sleeping was my hobby, as well as my vocation. With nine minutes of sack time rudely ripped away from me, I was steamed.

"Go tell Mom," I croaked.

"She's sleepin'," Susie said.

"What do you think I'm doing?" I asked, annoyed beyond endurance.

"Talkin'," she said.

"Go!"

As she scuttled out of my room, I caught the flash of something startlingly red in the dim light.

"Wait a minute," I said. "Come back here."

Susie turned around and slowly approached my bed. She was wearing a flannel nightie with pink-and-blue teddy bears printed on it, a pink quilted bathrobe, and what had originally been white bunny slippers. After a hard year's wear, however, the bunnies looked suspiciously like brown water rats.

What startled me was not her ratty footwear—it was her face. Usually, Susie had a pale little face framed by a brown pageboy haircut. That morning her face looked like a ripe, plump tomato.

"What have you been into?" I asked, figuring that she had smeared some of Mom's makeup all over her face—a not uncommon occurrence at our house.

"Nuffin'," she said.

I put out a hand and touched her forehead. It was hot and dry to the touch. No makeup came off on my fingers.

I climbed out of bed and led her back to her room.

"You stay there," I said. "I'll get Mom."

"She won't like being waked up," Susie said, her blisteringly red face crumpled with worry.

"Stay," I said, covering her up. "I'll be right back."

I found my father having breakfast in the dining room. When he ate breakfast, which was rarely, he always ate in formal splendor, shunning the kitchen table, which was good enough for the rest of us. He was wearing a dark suit, starched white shirt, and a tie at seven a.m.

That morning he was engaging in a particularly disgusting ritual. Once a month or so, he would fix himself calves' brains in cream sauce for breakfast. The brains came in a can from France, where presumably calves were much smarter than they were in the United States— their brains being in demand and all. I never did know if he actually enjoyed chomping down on such repulsive fare or if he simply did it to annoy my mother. Mom was horrified by cooking in general, so the sight of calves' brains in the morning must have driven her over the edge.

"The brains are delicious," my father said, raising a forkful of the cauliflower-like substance to his mouth. "Would you like to try some?"

If I had accepted his invitation, he would have keeled over in a dead faint.

"No, thanks," I said. "I'll stick to corn flakes. But you'd better go look at Susie. She says she's sick."

"Not again," my father said. "Your mother kept her home all last week with that terrible sore throat."

"She looks like a boiled lobster," I added.

"Lobster," my father said. "I wonder if lobster would go with calves' brains?"

A responsible parent, however, he left his brains on the table and went to inquire about his daughter's health. He returned moments later, ashen faced, and directed me to wake my mother because he was too cowardly to do it himself. Nobody wanted to be responsible for waking my mother prior to seven-fifteen in the morning. This was a suicide mission, but I could tell by my father's face that this was a mission worth dying for.

"Mom," I whispered from the doorway of my parents' bedroom. "Mom, wake up."

She opened one eye and stared at me balefully.

"It's the middle of the night," she mumbled. "Go back to bed."

She must have inherited that trait from me.

"It's Susie," I said. "She's really sick and Dad says for you to come."

"Why can't you children stay healthy?" my mother groaned.

She had already been cooped up with a sick child for a week and she wasn't relishing a repeat performance. Her repertoire of games, puzzles, songs, and stories was woefully depleted.

I quickly retreated, sidling warily past the congealing brains, and headed for the safety of my room, in case the emergency turned out to be a false alarm. On the way, I encountered my eleven-year-old brother, Stephen. He was wearing spaz pajamas: blue flannel, cowboys slaughtering Indians, knit cuffs and sleeves.

"Have you seen Susie?" he asked me. "She's as red as a beet."

Always filled with good cheer in the morning, I answered, "Beets are purple, stupid."

"Well, she's almost purple," he said.

"No, she's—"

"Please," my father said, appearing from the dining room. "Her exact hue is immaterial. The child is suffering."

"What's wrong with her?" I asked.

"I'll be damned if I know," my father said. "But I'm calling Dr. Alexander right now."

Our physician, Dr. Alexander, was that rarest of species today: a general practitioner. He set broken bones, removed unwanted appendixes and tonsils, prescribed the latest antibiotics, gave shots and vaccinations, and delivered babies on the side—or, more likely, from the front. And for nostalgia buffs—he made house calls. A tall, distinguished man with sparse white hair and thin wire-rim glasses, Dr. Alexander inspired confidence. His slight British accent made him seem suave and knowledgeable about almost everything to almost everyone—except my mother. Mom always felt she got the short end of the stethoscope from him.

That feeling dated back to a time when the entire family had come down with the flu. After he patiently and thoroughly examined my father, my brother, and me, all the while expressing his sympathy and concern for us, Dr. Alexander wrote out a prescription and handed it to my mother.

"You'll have the same," he said and left without so much as taking her pulse.

"He looks like Gregory Peck's father," my mother complained later. "He sounds like Ronald Colman. And if he ever got drummed out of the medical corps, he could make a fine living as an actor playing a doctor. Why then do I keep thinking about Dr. Frankenstein?"

Still, in an emergency, no one else would do.

Neither my father nor my mother was an alarmist when it came to their children's health. They had been through chicken pox, mumps, measles—both German and otherwise—flu, strep throat, colds, fevers, chills, burns, cuts, bruises, scrapes, sprains, and broken bones. I thought nothing could faze them, but they seemed fazed, all right— real fazed. Dr. Alexander must have sensed it, too, because he was at our door within a half hour, just as I was getting ready to leave for school.

He and my mother disappeared into Susie's room for a few minutes. When they returned, my father said, "Well?"

"Truly remarkable," Dr. Alexander said, removing his glasses and rubbing his eyes as if he couldn't believe what he had just seen. "As you know, I've been a physician for forty years and this is the first case I've ever seen in America—though when I was a child in England it was quite common."

"What the hell is it?" my father demanded. "What's wrong with her?"

"Well, you won't believe it," Dr. Alexander said. "I didn't either at first, but all the symptoms are present. It is a fortunate thing that I am so—"

"Old?" I asked, caught up in the suspense.

"John!" my mother said sharply.

"Experienced, shall we say," Dr. Alexander said with a tight smile. "I recognized it right away. It used to be called scarlatina. But Susie has what they now call scarlet fever."

From the look on my father's face, the doctor might as well have said bubonic plague or typhus. I had never heard of scarlet fever, but it sounded bad, very bad. I didn't know it then, but it would get a whole lot worse.

However, to understand the full impact of this diagnosis you have to understand a few things about Susie, me, and the rest of the family. And to do that we have to return to the thrilling days of yesteryear: specifically, 1955.

Chapter 1

BEFORE THE DELUGE. Globe-trotting reporter
Mary W. Littell in 1941, pre-husband, pre-children,
and pre-pillbox hats.

Annunciation

In the spring of 1955, my mother was a satisfied woman. And she had a right to be. She had been married for twelve years; she had two children, mercifully both in school and neither one headed for a career in ax murdery; she had begun to sell the stories she had written; and she had survived—barely—a memorable year in the south of France. Further, she could look back on a life that was filled with accomplishments. She had overcome the economic deprivation caused by the premature death of her father; she had graduated from college; and she had worked as a newspaper reporter in Texas. She had even hosted a radio show before she married my father during World War II.

At the age of forty, with all that behind her, Mom had been working part-time for *Life* magazine, which she considered the ne plus ultra of publications. For a small-town reporter, originally from St. Louis, the allure of big-time journalism in New York City was overwhelming. Working for *Life* was the most glamorous thing she could imagine. Even if her job was lowly, she got to hobnob with famous writers, editors, and photographers—the kind of stars who would have filled an auditorium if they had deigned to visit Texas or Missouri. Every year we attended the *Life* picnic held in Connecticut at the estate of Henry and Clare Boothe Luce. Mom thought that eating hot dogs in such august company was tantamount to being a star herself. My father was more impressed by the open bar.

I suppose Mom's job had caused some tension between her and my father. Husbands were loath to let their wives work in those days. But trying to stop Mom from working at *Life* would have been like prohibiting Joe DiMaggio from joining the major leagues. He would get there somehow, even if he had to be the clubhouse janitor. Mom was just as determined, though I doubt she could have hit for average.

She didn't know it then, but her comfortable, if rather predictable, life was about to come to an end. It all started on a bright, sunny morning in May. My mother was standing on the platform waiting for the train to Grand Central Station. She was wearing a pleated skirt with a matching pink jacket and a white blouse. Her hat was also pink, as were her high heels. She was wearing white gloves, which were de rigueur for ladies traveling to New York City in those days. Mom wasn't looking for trouble, but she was about to find it.

It was just after nine, and her favorite train, the nine-fifteen, was due shortly. This was the first non-rush-hour train, and it catered to company presidents, retired Wall Street attorneys, eager shoppers, and people like Mom who had such bad jobs nobody cared what time they got to work. Earlier trains were filled with rising young executives trying to get to the office to do a bit of bootlicking and corporate ladder scaling. While they were nervous, the people on Mom's train were relaxed; they were either too rich or too poor to have anything to lose.

During the summer, I used to ride my bike past the station and gawk at the twitchy early-morning commuters standing in formation on the platform. They were mostly men, mostly wearing dark suits and carrying briefcases. Between Memorial Day and Labor Day, a majority of them sported straw boaters. They stood there reading their papers and I learned early on how to identify their political affiliation. Republicans read the *Herald Tribune,* Democrats read the *New York Times,* and dangerous subversives like my mother read books. Actually, once Mom boarded the train, she put away her book, pulled out a sheaf of paper, and began working on whatever story she was writing at the time. A long train ride and laptop computer would have made her as prolific as P. G. Wodehouse.

But on that particular May morning, Mom's hope of doing any work was thwarted by the unusual appearance of her friend Gloria Anderson. Mrs. Anderson (as I knew her) was a statuesque blond lady who seemed to peer down at me from Mount Olympus, and like that mountain, her face was perpetually wreathed in clouds—clouds of smoke emanating from a foot-long gold cigarette holder. I admired her cigarette holder so much, I asked my father if I could take up smoking at the age of ten. He said no, I had to wait a year.

"Gloria!" my mother exclaimed. "You look terrible."

"Thanks, Mary. What a nice compliment so early in the morning," Gloria said.

"But what's wrong?" my mother asked.

Gloria was usually charming, funny, and dressed as if she were about to be presented at the Court of St. James. But without makeup, her dress wrinkled, and her face haggard, she looked positively frumpy—for Gloria.

"Oh, nothing much is wrong," Gloria said. "My life is ruined, that's all."

When the train arrived, they got on together, and my mother sat next to her.

"Come on, give," my mother said when the train jolted into motion.

"Well, let's see. I'm forty-two years old, I'm the editor of one of America's top magazines, I have a husband who loves me, one child in college, and another one about to graduate from high school. I'm moderately attractive, well read, a Cordon Bleu chef, and if I do say so myself, I'm a genius when it comes to interior decorating."

"Sounds dreadful," my mother said, laughing.

"It is," Gloria whispered. "I'm pregnant."

"Oh, my God," my mother said, shocked to her soul.

"God had nothing to do with it," Gloria said. "This is the devil's work. I'm sure of it. What am I going to do?"

For most of the bumpy ride to New York City, they discussed various options, but they found no satisfactory solution.

"I suppose I could fly to Sweden or someplace for the, uh, operation," Gloria said as they neared Grand Central. "But it seems so . . . sordid."

My mother agreed. In those days women pretty much had to play the hand they were dealt—even rich and successful women like Gloria Anderson.

"But what about your job?" my mother asked. Mom envied Gloria's editorial success.

"I guess I'll have to quit," Gloria said. "And after ten years of back-breaking toil."

"That's so unfair," Mom said.

"Yeah, and what else is new?"

A few days after her disturbing talk with Gloria, my mother had lunch with our neighbor Helen Thompson.

"Have you heard about Gloria?" Helen asked.

That simple question set my mother off like a volcano, according to Helen, who told me the story some thirty years later.

"You know I love Gloria," my mother sputtered. "But how stupid can she be? What about the danger? Women over forty can have all sorts of problems. I mean this could actually kill her. Or she might deliver a deformed baby. It makes me so mad how smart people can be so dumb!

"And what about her husband? What could he have been thinking? How could he let this happen? Why wasn't he more careful? I swear, Helen, this is one of the most imbecilic things I ever heard in my life. Her kids will be embarrassed, she will lose her job—and what a job!— all because she's pregnant. Stupid! Stupid! Stupid!"

A week later my mother discovered that she had two things in common with Gloria Anderson—they were both stupid and they were both pregnant.

Chapter 2

AUTOMANIA. Stephen (left), John (center), our old car (right), prior to the advent of the Chevy station wagon.

Autosuggestion

I was nine years old in 1955, a third grader with a smart mouth and a penchant for doing dumb things. I had a six-year-old brother named Stephen and a hamster named Ginger, and believe me, the hamster was a lot less trouble than Stephen.

My life in those days was divided into three parts: school, home, and friends. I never really thought much about school because I had figured out early on how to scam the system. The way to get along, as Sam Rayburn famously said, was to go along. I knew exactly how much work I needed to do to keep my parents and teachers off my back. But I refused to do one iota more. Of course, sometimes my behavior drifted dangerously beyond the pale and that would initiate a flurry of parent-teacher conferences. But generally I was a well-behaved child—not because I wanted to be, but because being evil was just too much hard work. In short, I was not exactly a candidate for massive doses of Ritalin—even if it had existed back then.

I lived with my parents in a suburb of New York City—not a brash new suburb, but an old, established village that could trace its roots back to Colonial times.

The suburbs? Ewwwww! That's the usual response I get from people who want to know where I grew up. And it's true: Suburbs can be intolerant and stultifying—especially if you are a Maoist revolutionary, a Lesbian Avenger, or a Hollywood screenwriter. From *Main Street* to *American Beauty,* the burbs have been battered, blasted, and brutalized. But for people with kids, the suburbs were a quiet, safe place to live. Those who crave sexual perversity, drugs, pornography, and fast times should stop complaining and move to New York City.

I did.

Historically, though, the suburbs have gotten a bad rap. In 1955 my family could go away for the weekend and not bother locking the doors or closing the windows. We knew everybody in town or at least had heard their names. The police, presumably hired for their intimidating size, gave speeding tickets to out-of-towners, not local residents. Crime was an aberration, not an absolute. You could go out at night and not wonder if you would make it back alive. A house would be burgled every three years or so, and that would cause a furor. Mistakes had been made; measures would be taken. Then it would all blow over for another three years.

In all the time I lived in the suburbs, no one was ever murdered. Hell, none of my friends' parents even got divorced. They may have hated each other, but they stayed together for the sake of the children. That seems a quaint notion today, but that was what the suburbs were about then: kids. We had almost unlimited freedom from fear. We went where we wanted to go and did the usual goofy kid things.

Best of all, there was no structure. Our little league team had no uniforms or miniature stadia. Somebody's long-suffering father gave you a hat and told you to play second base and that was it. Today, a child's activities are closely monitored and scheduled down to the last millisecond. Parents have to organize and coordinate a child's day with the care and precision of the landing at Normandy. That's because they are scared—rightly—to let their kids out of their sight.

My parents were glad to see the back of me, but I suppose I liked them well enough. Or at least I can say that they never intentionally embarrassed me in public. Some of my friends had much cooler parents, but mine were satisfactory most of the time. Of course, they could be a pain when they exercised their parental authority, insisting, for example, that I not fling myself off the roof pretending to be Superman. Small-minded of them, but in those days parents took their jobs seriously. They didn't want to be pals, mentors, facilitators, or role models; they didn't feel compelled to discuss their sexual and financial affairs with their nine-year-olds. They just wanted to be parents. They told you what to do and you did it—unless you could find a way to weasel out of it. That was enough for them—and more than enough for me.

My parents, it seemed to me, were a part of the background noise, subtly insinuating themselves into my affairs, but allowing me to make my own mistakes and live my own life. I never had any doubt about who I was or what I did. That was a huge disappointment to me later in life because I never developed a raging case of teenage angst or had the compulsion to dress Goth and off my classmates at school. Worse, I was denied the pleasure of wallowing in self-pity and I missed out on the sheer indulgence of "finding myself" at college. I already knew who I was. Unfortunately, there was not much I could do about it.

Throughout the summer of 1955, I was obsessively engaged in playing kick baseball at a nearby playground, so I failed to detect any changes at home. My brother, Stephen, however, wasn't fooled. With his usual exquisite sensitivity, he asked my mother one day, "How come you're so fat?"

I hadn't noticed. Mom was Mom, fat or thin. But he was right.

"Well," she said slowly, "I'm going to have a baby."

"Why?" Stephen asked.

"A good question," my mother said, rolling her eyes heavenward.

"Well, why?" he demanded.

Mom took a deep breath and went into her "I am serious" voice. She sat us down and explained the details in terms that would have been considered excessively prudish by the Victorians.

"When a man loves a woman, and they get married, sometimes they have a baby," she began, probably reciting from something called *A Modern Mother Discusses Life with Her Children,* no doubt published by *Reader's Digest*.

"Why would they do that?" Stephen asked.

"A baby is an expression of love between a man and a woman," Mom said.

"Like a Christmas present?" I asked.

My mother sighed audibly and launched into a carefully contrived speech, something about planting seeds and wombs and the joys of motherhood. I wasn't much interested in either the coming baby or the mechanical details of how one was produced. The entire project seemed much too distant and theoretical for my taste. Besides, it was a hot, sunny day and the kids were waiting for me at the playground. So

I was grateful when the whole hideous affair screeched to a halt, thanks to Stephen. He held up his hand and said flatly, "I don't think this is a good idea."

"But don't you want a little brother or sister?" my mother asked piteously.

"No, I'd rather have a dog," Stephen said.

"Neat-o, a dog," I chimed in. "Keep the baby. I got to go."

That was the last time my mother tried to convince my brother and me that babies were wonderful. And because children have an attention span of less than thirty seconds, Stephen and I promptly forgot about the whole squalid business—just as we forgot about other parental concerns, such as washing our hands, brushing our teeth, and doing our homework.

That fall I was interested in far more glamorous things than babies: the 1956 cars. In those days, the new models were presented to the public in September. Beautiful girls in sequined ball gowns and elbow-length gloves lounged seductively on the bright paintwork and sparkling chrome, daring you to step closer to the car of your dreams. I liked the girls okay, but those cars . . . now they were sexy.

For a full month, I pored over the ads in the *Saturday Evening Post, Life, Collier's,* and any other magazines I could get my hands on. I memorized the makes and models and could spot a Plymouth Fury or a Pontiac Bonneville from a mile away. Had all this enthusiasm been directed toward my schoolwork, I would have won a scholarship to Harvard. But studying the brand-spanking-new 1956 cars wasn't work at all—it was pure pleasure.

That was why I was almost beside myself with excitement when my father announced he was buying a new car. I knew exactly the make and model he wanted—the Ford Thunderbird. In my estimation, the T-bird was tied with the Corvette as the coolest car on the road. But what sold me was Thunderbird's continental kit. That tire on the rear end looked neat-o, I told my father.

"Sounds agreeably racy," he said. "Rather like the '39 Lincoln."

The what?

But when I showed him a picture of the Thunderbird, my father frowned.

"Why, it has only two seats," he said, astonished.

Everyone knew that.

"We could take turns riding in it," I suggested. "Or Stephen could ride in the trunk."

"Practical as well as durable, I see," my father said cryptically.

Needless to say, that was the last I heard about Thunderbirds, Corvettes, and any car that was remotely cool. My father was not a car nut like I was. He thought that "automobiles," as he usually called them, should be reliable and inexpensive. He was (auto) immune to the slick ads. In fact, I was amazed to discover that he knew practically nothing about cars. That was a real shock because he knew so much about so many other things.

Though his vehicular virtuosity was nil, my father seemed to have an interest in the subject, and that fed my obsession. We would drive down the street in the family Oldsmobile and he would point out various cars for me to identify.

"What's that red one?" he would ask.

And I would blurt out, "Chevy Impala, convertible, V8, whitewalls, dual exhaust, three on the column. They call it 'The Hot One' on TV."

"Hot, indeed," my father would say; then, unaccountably, he would launch into a tirade about the vacuousness of television.

I didn't know why he was anti-TV. I liked television, and about the only thing that would drag me away from the tube were the piles of new car brochures that my father brought home. They were lushly produced on slick, heavy paper that felt sensuous in my hand. I enjoyed fondling them—and memorizing the contents. I spent hours considering the benefits of two-tone paint jobs, AM/FM radios, deluxe interiors, sports packages, and convertible tops. I learned the word *option,* but not its implications.

"Come on, John," my father said one glorious autumn afternoon. "Let's go kick a few tires."

I wasn't sure what was required of me, but it was a nice day for a ride, even in your father's Oldsmobile. To my delight, we pulled into a Ford dealer's lot and I shot out of the car to get my hands on all those shiny new models.

"This one, Dad!" I shouted, throwing my arms around the hood of a black-and-white Crown Victoria. It was wearing a diadem of chrome that stretched, a foot wide, across the roof. This was a massive, totally cool car that made me forget the tiny Thunderbird.

"Nice," my father said. "But let's kick a few more tires."

Dutifully, I kicked every tire in the dealer's lot, but that didn't seem to tell me much. My foot aching, I questioned my father about the efficacy of this practice.

"If the tire falls off," he said, "then it's not a very good car."

That made sense, so I kicked harder, but no cars came crashing to the ground. The reason for that, I suppose, was that Ford had a first-class product that year. Unfortunately, it was not good enough to tempt my father. He held out for a month; then he finally chose the car he wanted: a 1956 Chevrolet station wagon, gold and white, blackwalls, AM radio, and not much else, not even phony wood sides. For a kid like me, who was in love with the sizzle, that car was one big, dumb steak.

My father claimed he had gotten a good deal on the wagon because the colors were so hideous. He was right about that, but the clunky Chevy did have that blissful new car smell and an enormous red steering wheel, which partially made up for the fact that it wasn't a Thunderbird. Partially. Who could imagine a gorgeous model draping herself over the grille of our bizarrely colored station wagon? I was disappointed that all my hard work studying the automotive market had resulted in such a dud and I complained bitterly.

"A car is a car is a car," my father said, "though I believe Miss Stein has a chauffeur."

That put me in my place—whatever it meant. And although I was as confused as usual, I knew when to shut up.

So that was 1955, a year that had begun with visions of T-birds and 'Vettes dancing in my head and ended with a lousy Chevy sitting in the driveway. It was a year that held great promise and great disappointment.

And by the way, that was the same year my kid sister was born. I know that for a fact because we got her the same year we got the station wagon.

Chapter 3

PONY BOY. John, age two, at a birthday party featuring girls and pony rides. Although he wanted a horse desperately, he was constantly thwarted by recalcitrant parents who thought, unreasonably, that a horse stabled in his bedroom was unsuitable.

The Black Torpedo of Doom

Summer slipped into fall, and I was busy with school, sports, and helping my father buy a new car. I hadn't heard about the baby for some time, and I suppose my mother had, sensibly, given up trying to explain the facts of life to my brother and me. Then, as the due date neared, Mom went nuts. Dr. Alexander had told her the baby would be born on Christmas Day. He thought that was cute; she was horrified.

As a Christmas Eve baby herself, Mom had never had a proper birthday party when she was a child. She had been told by her parents that she would receive both Christmas and birthday presents on December 25, a reasonable arrangement that adults would have found efficient and satisfactory. My mother, however, was crushed. She wanted to be the center of attention, dress up, and invite all her friends over to celebrate her special day. But all she ever got on her natal day was a Lady Baltimore cake. When she finally worked up the nerve to complain, much later in life, her mother was amazed. "Why didn't you tell me?" my grandmother asked. Mom didn't know. All she knew was she felt like Oliver Twist.

As a result of this quasi-Dickensian childhood, my mother went absolutely insane when it came to birthday parties. If we hadn't stopped her, she would have gladly thrown parties for Stephen and me until we were well into our thirties. Ahab had his white whale; Mom had birthdays, but no harpoon that I know of—just an abiding sense of being cheated out of one of the great pleasures of childhood.

The thought, then, of having a Christmas baby made her nuttier than a Lady Baltimore cake. To take her mind off the impending and inconvenient delivery date, Mom had allowed herself to be dragged off to an estate sale. Now, my mother was not a woman who was given to flights of fancy, or estate sales, so what she bought that day can only be attributed to excessive hormones and overwhelming worry.

There was snow the day it came. A big red truck appeared and two men lugged an enormous wooden crate to our door. I watched with a gnawing fascination because crates did not usually arrive at our door. Groceries, yes. Laundry, yes. Jehovah's Witnesses, yes. But no crates that I ever remembered.

I decided there was only one thing it could be: a pony. I had wanted a pony ever since sitting on one at Mary Beth Hammond's third-birthday party, some eight years before. I had begged and begged for one every year afterward, but no matter how hard I tried to explain to my parents that a pony was an essential accouterment to the cowboy I yearned to be, my parents could not be swayed.

Until this year, I thought wildly. It was almost Christmas; maybe the pony was being delivered early.

"Sign here, lady," one of the delivery men said, holding out a clipboard.

I was so certain that my pony was in that crate that I piped up with a heartfelt, "Thanks, mister. Thanks a lot."

He looked at me strangely and shrugged.

Maybe he delivered ponies all day long, I thought, and it was no big deal for him. But I had hoped for a bit more enthusiasm.

"He can sleep in my room. It's snowing outside and he'd catch his death in this weather," I said, sounding remarkably like my grandmother.

"What are you talking about?" my mother asked when the men were gone. "Go get the hammer."

I ran to fetch the tack hammer, which, along with the screwdriver, constituted our entire home-repair center. Other kids' fathers had giant workshops filled with exotic-looking power tools, but my father had difficulty changing lightbulbs because he was unable or unwilling to remember if they screwed in clockwise or counterclockwise. I am proud to say that I inherited his skills, but when there was a pony involved, I made Bob Vila look like a klutz.

I ripped into the crate with abandon, worried that the pony might not have enough air. A dead pony would have presented certain difficulties when it came time to ride him.

"Slow down," my mother said. "You'll scratch it."

I didn't want to scratch "Old Paint," as I now thought of him, so I pried out the nails with more care.

"Can I ride right away?" I asked my mother excitedly.

"Ride?" she said vaguely. "Of course not. It's for the baby."

The baby! Here I had been pleading for a pony for eight years—eight years!—and when my parents finally got around to getting one, they gave it to the baby—a baby who wasn't even born yet. It was so unfair I couldn't speak. I threw the hammer down and stomped away.

"John, where are you going?" my mother called after me. "You've got to help me with the carriage."

A carriage? The pony came with a carriage! Was there no end to this outrage?

"Keep it," I yelled back. "Just keep it."

I sulked in my room for a few minutes, contemplating the injustice of life; then curiosity drove me to at least *look* at the pony. Maybe I could ride him until the baby was born. That was better than nothing.

I peered at my mother struggling with the crate, but I didn't offer any assistance. *Let the baby help her,* I thought savagely.

When she finally removed the top of the crate, my mother stood back and admired its contents. She must have seen me lurking in the doorway, because she called me to come and look at what had been delivered.

One thing was for certain: It wasn't a pony.

"What the hell is that?" I asked.

"John!"

"Sorry." I knew all the good words, but unlike my father, I wasn't allowed to use them in the house. "But what is it?"

"Why, it's a baby carriage," my mother said. "What did you think it was?"

"Nothing," I mumbled, schadenfreude rearing its ugly head. If I couldn't have a pony, I was glad the baby couldn't have one either.

The contraption in the crate was not of this Earth. To my eyes it was an alien artifact suddenly translated into my world. I knew, however, that I had seen its like somewhere before, but I couldn't quite remember where.

How to describe it? First off, it was big. I mean really big—at least five and a half feet tall with the hood in its full upright and locked position. It towered over me and my mother. We had to look up at it in awe. And it was black—not just your ordinary black, but a deep, lacquered black that was burnished to a mirrorlike finish. Thin gold pinstriping covered the sides, ending in an intricate floral filigree at each corner. The handle was solid steel and had two rubber grips, to help you hold on when the carriage reached sixty miles an hour in the straightaway.

I knocked down the sides of the crate to reveal the machine in all its otherworldly glory. The inside of the carriage—which was commodious enough to hold the Dionne quints and still have room for them each to swing a dead cat (a Canadian custom, I believe)—was fitted with a two-foot-thick mattress far superior to the one on my bed. The mattress had more positions than the Kama Sutra, and it came equipped with a built-in satin pillow about the size of Wyoming. Better still, it had enormous spoked wheels—with whitewalls—classier than those on our new Chevy wagon. And, oh, it had a curb weight of about thirty-five-hundred pounds.

My mother seemed staggered by her purchase and sat down for a moment.

"It's . . . royal," she said in awe.

She was right. This was the kind of carriage that should have been propelled by two gray-uniformed nannies, proudly airing the heir on the grounds of Buckingham Palace. In fact, what we were looking at was not a carriage at all. It was a perambulator, and it said so on a silver plaque embedded near the front of the carriage.

While my mother and I were appraising it uneasily, Stephen came careering around a corner, took one look, and stopped dead in his tracks. Without a word, he slowly backed out of the room as if he had just stumbled on a flying saucer and didn't wish to disturb its occupants. I could understand his anxiety, for the perambulator was a scary object. Just looking at it made me anxious, and it also made me rack my brain, trying to remember where I had seen it before. Then, suddenly I knew.

I raced off to my room and tore into my stack of comic books, searching for an old one I had read at least a dozen times. Finding it quickly, I thumbed through the pages frantically until I found what I was looking for. There it was. The bad guys were threatening to blow up the world with a sleek black torpedo called, appropriately, the Black Torpedo of Doom.

"Look, Mom!" I shouted, shoving the comic book under her nose. "We've got the Black Torpedo of Doom."

"Well, they do look similar," she had to admit. "But this is just a baby carriage, albeit an enormous one. Funny, it didn't look this big sitting in that old mansion at the estate sale. I guess it's because we don't have twenty-four-foot ceilings and rooms the size of parking lots."

The Black Torpedo of Doom might have been the Rolls-Royce of baby carriages, but it was also a hulking, sinister object that exuded an air of menace. I didn't even like going near it because I was afraid it might explode and take me and the rest of the world with it.

"What on Earth will your father say?" my mother wondered idly.

"He'll laugh like hell," I said.

"John!"

"Sorry," I said. "But he will."

And he did.

Chapter 4

ANTICIPATION. John (left) and Stephen on the day before Susie's arrival. Note the Christmas tree, prior to tinseling, is loaded with decorations at about Stephen's eye level and bald on top.

The Slip Inn

They hauled Mom off to the hospital on the seventeenth of December and she gave birth to a baby girl the next day. At seven pounds and change, the baby was fat and healthy; my mother was tired, but in good shape.

In those days, having a baby was a much more civilized affair than it is today. The expectant mother was given a general anesthetic; when she awoke, a nurse presented her with a scrubbed, powdered, diapered, and fed baby—no muss, no fuss, no fathers, no children, and no video cameras.

It is my opinion that the declining birth rate in the West is in direct proportion to the number of men dragged into the "birthing room" to witness or—heaven help us—assist in the gruesome task of delivering a baby. It is a sight no man should ever witness, let alone film. Once a man gets a load of what actually goes on in the delivery room—the screams, the blood, the recriminations—his tenuous desire to have more children evaporates. Thus, zero population growth.

Unfortunately, modern women have been taught to equate excruciating pain with "natural" childbirth. Sadistic doctors—the same guys who deny drugs to terminal cancer patients, fearing some ninety-year-old lady might become a crazed junkie and knock over convenience stores to feed her habit—make expectant mothers suffer for forty-eight hours before they perform the inevitable cesarean section—for fear of lawsuits. The vaunted Lamaze method quickly degenerates into the Le Mans method, a brutal test of endurance that would make male race car drivers faint dead away.

Women go along with this torture because they think they are doing the right thing for the baby. Would they have open-heart surgery without anesthetic? Of course not. Don't they care about their hearts? But when babies come into the world, reason flies out the window. It wasn't always so.

Consider my mother's editor friend Gloria Anderson. When Mom went down the hall to visit her, Gloria was propped up in her bed wearing a frilly new bed jacket. Her hair and nails had been done only a few hours after she had delivered a son. Gloria's husband appeared a few minutes later, carrying a bottle of champagne and a bit of pâté de foie gras. The three of them toasted their new babies, nibbled the pâté, and had a fine time. Gloria's husband fired up a congratulatory cigar, while his wife and Mom smoked Lucky Strikes and pondered the future.

Horrible, wasn't it? Can you imagine? Smoking! Drinking! Fatty foods! How much better, and oh, so much more natural, it is to scream in pain for hours. Of course, no one these days acts the way they did back then. And perhaps we will all live longer—or maybe it will just seem that way.

While Mom was gone, Stephen and I were agog with excitement. Not because of the baby—we were too young to be allowed in the hospital—but because it was almost Christmas. For months we had been stalking the elusive Christmas gifts, looking in every known hiding place for those brightly wrapped, tantalizingly shaped boxes that held—what? It was always our goal to find each and every one of our presents and identify it at least a week before Christmas. Many years we succeeded admirably, but we came a cropper in 1955.

"Maybe we don't got presents this year," Stephen said.

"Of course we got presents," I said. "They just hid them better this year."

"But we are getting a dog, aren't we?"

"No, stupid," I said. "We're getting a baby."

"A puppy?"

"No, dummy, a brother or sister," I said.

"Are you sure there's no Santa Claus?" Stephen asked. "Because if there is one, he won't be here until Christmas Eve, and that's why we don't got presents yet."

"Oh, grow up," I said. But, as always, he got me worried, too.

"This is all the baby's fault, isn't it?" he said, reading my mind. I had the horrible thought that maybe our parents were so caught up with the new baby, they had forgotten about us.

"The hell with it," I said.

"You said 'hell,'" Stephen said, admonishing me.

"So did you," I taunted back. "Just now, and I'm going to tell Mom."

"She won't care. All she cares about is the baby," Stephen said.

I hoped he was wrong, but I feared he was right.

Our gloomy spirits were considerably revived, however, when we bundled into the Chevy wagon to find a Christmas tree. Now, there were several places in the area to buy a tree. A local church, an adoption agency, and a hospital all had acres of pine to peddle for charity. But while these institutions were worthy of our patronage, my father traveled to the tune of a different drummer boy. That year, we drove many miles north to the hamlet of Westmont, the suburb that time forgot—if, indeed, time had ever remembered that dreary little burg.

Because it was not on the main commuter line, Westmont was enjoying its two-hundredth consecutive year of economic and psychological depression. Abandoned cars decorated the streets, bums lounged about the town square, and wild dogs fed on the ubiquitous garbage. Compared to our village, this was Poverty Row, Tobacco Road, and the Bowery all rolled into one. It was not a nice place to live or even to visit. Today, I suppose, Westmont has been yuppified and boasts eight-million-dollar houses for sale, but back then it was, as my father said, a real dumpola.

"Daddy, why is that dog sleeping in the road?" Stephen asked as we cautiously drove into town.

"He's very tired," my father said.

"And very flat," I said.

I had seen doornails with more life.

Although my father was fastidious to a fault, he had a curious affinity for crummy towns and low-life characters. The sight of an abandoned gas station or a burned-out house made his eyes blaze with pleasure. Later in life I thought he might have been looking for cheap real estate, but his total lack of entrepreneurial spirit made that unlikely. Maybe he just enjoyed slumming—I don't know—but whatever his reasons, he was as happy as I had ever seen him that gray winter's day.

He parked the wagon in a trash-festooned alley that was awash with live rats and dead-to-the-world vagrants, and led Stephen and me to a smallish door, which had originally been painted green—probably in 1793. Dad tried the door, but it was locked. Then he knocked three times, paused, and knocked twice more. We waited in suspense.

The door, which had last been oiled the same year it had been painted, creaked back on its rusty hinges; then it was flung wide open. A small man wearing a dirty undershirt peered at us in the dim light of the alley.

"Professore!" he said, smiling broadly to reveal the two or three teeth he had in his mouth.

My father smiled, too, and let the little man have a burst of some foreign language I didn't understand. I knew it wasn't French, because I heard that spoken all the time; this was a lingo that eluded me completely.

The two of them rattled on for what seemed like an hour, while Stephen and I shuffled from one foot to the other, wondering what was going on. Finally, Stephen asked the sensible question: "Where's the trees?"

The little man, whose name was either Geo or Vonny, I thought, patted Stephen on the head and said, "Good boy," as if talking to his pet cat. Stephen frowned dramatically and I moved out of head-patting range because the man smelled like new wine and old clothes. I didn't see any trees either.

Inside the building, we walked through a beaded curtain and into another world. The room we entered was at least forty feet long and nearly as wide, about the size of our gym at school. At one end was a scarred mahogany bar with red leather stools. Dozens of tables, covered with blue-and-white tablecloths, were scattered about in random order. Two or three old men sat at the bar, while four other men played dominoes in the corner. Every so often, an old lady dressed entirely in black floated around the room like some exotic bird of prey; then she disappeared into what I assumed was the kitchen.

The walls were hung with hundreds of fading photographs of men and women in some foreign country. They all looked grim and worn.

Mounted above the bar was a giant sailfish that looked even grimmer and more worn than the people in the pictures.

"Where are we?" I asked in wonder.

"The Slip Inn," my father said. "Don't tell your mother."

I doubt I had the descriptive powers to rat him out, but I knew instantly that this was not a place my mother would have sanctioned. That was a safe bet, because my mother disapproved of most of the cool places my father went without her.

As I was trying to imagine her reaction to the Slip Inn, my father gave me four dimes and told Stephen and me to go play the bowling machine, which was next to the pool table. Then he walked to the bar, deep in conversation with Geo or Vonny.

"There's dirt on the floor," Stephen whispered.

"That's not dirt—it's sawdust," I said, pushing a pile of it around with the toe of my shoe. I had been to the circus; I knew about these things. Besides, the place had a certain barnlike fragrance.

"They might have animals here," I continued. "Lions and tigers and elephants and camels like sawdust."

"Really?" Stephen said, his eyes wide.

"See that door over there?" I said, pointing to the kitchen. "I bet that's where the cages are."

"Can we go see them?" he asked.

"Let's play bowling first," I said. "We'll see 'em later."

I plugged a dime into the bowling machine, setting off a terrific commotion as the lights came on and bells clanged. The men playing dominoes looked up, and all four reached for the inside pockets of their suit coats; then they relaxed and went back to their game. They were probably checking their wallets, I thought.

"I'll whip you at this," I said to Stephen.

I was an old hand at the game, having played it in amusement parks, arcades, and the occasional sleazy bar my father insisted we visit. The object was to send a metal counter sliding down the table. If you hit the sweet spot, all ten plastic pins would flip up and you had a strike. The best strategy was to study the table, try to find the worn places, and aim there. I scored a strike immediately; Stephen only managed to get six pins. He was an enthusiastic, if unskilled opponent, and I beat him two hundred twenty to one hundred sixty in the first game. I let him win the second game to keep him interested, then destroyed him in the remaining two games.

"Go ask Dad for more money," I told him when we were done.

"Okay," he said and ran off in search of gold.

He returned with four more dimes and two 7UPs—in the bottle! That was a real treat for us because my mother thought that drinking out of the bottle—any bottle—was uncivilized. She was probably right, but Stephen and I were a barbaric lot and quite enjoyed slurping soda sans glass, sans ice.

Thus armed with cold cash and even colder green bottles of 7UP, we were content to while away the next half hour arguing over whose turn it was to bowl. All the time, my father was engaged in his secret negotiations in that mysterious foreign language. His conversation was punctuated with great belly laughs, exaggerated hand movements, and many refills of a clearish liquid, which I assumed was not 7UP.

Finally, my father stood up, bowed formally, and shook Geo or Vonny's hand, and we prepared to leave the Slip Inn.

"Daddy, can we see the elephants now?" Stephen asked.

My father looked puzzled and turned to me for help.

I shrugged.

"The elephants are asleep," my father said.

"Like the dog on the road?" Stephen asked.

"Exactly," my father said.

Out in the grimy alley, we found that someone had stashed a nine-foot Christmas tree in the back of the gold-and-white Chevy wagon. I was amazed, but we drove home in silence, mission accomplished.

The problem with buying a Christmas tree is that you have to set it up, and at our house that was a procedure that was as intricate as it was boring.

"Get the tools," my father commanded, once we were home.

Dutifully, I liberated the tack hammer and the screwdriver from their home in a kitchen drawer. My father assessed the situation and discovered that the base of the tree was much too large for our modest stand.

"Knife," my father ordered with surgeonlike authority.

I ran back to the kitchen and procured our sharpest blade, a rather dull, stainless-steel carving knife.

With a shower of needles, my father hoisted the tree onto his knee and began to whittle away at the eight-inch trunk, hoping to reduce it by half. Stephen and I watched listlessly as the long minutes dragged on and on. When he was finally done, my father shoved it into the base and frowned. For the next half hour, he adjusted the tree seven or eight hundred times, never quite satisfied with his work. At last, he gave up and secured the tree with picture-frame wire.

"It's crooked, Daddy," Stephen said.

I could have killed him.

"By God, you're right," my father said, breaking down the setup and beginning anew.

I practically passed out from a galloping case of ennui, but hours later we were ready to decorate.

"I'll put the lights on," my father said. "It won't take a minute."

His prediction was correct. It didn't take a minute—it took about two hours. The problem was the old-fashioned strings of lights: If one bulb burned out, it took the other twenty-three with it. Then, like Sherlock Holmes, you had to deduce which one was the dud and replace it. The only way you could do that was to be psychic or to test each and every one of them. Regrettably, my father was not a mind reader, but he was methodical to the core. The hours dragged by, night descended upon us, and not one shiny Christmas ornament or gilded angel had been taken from the giant cardboard box labeled XMAS.

Stephen had fallen asleep on the floor and I had nodded off by the time the lights came on in a rainbow of color.

"I'm going to make a drink," my father said. "You boys start decorating the tree—carefully."

I kicked Stephen in the stomach, my way of waking him gently, and we began. Unfortunately, we weren't very tall, so we put the ornaments—all sixty dozen of them—on the lower third of the tree. It bulged like the fat lady at a carnival, but we thought it looked beautiful.

"Ah," my father said, returning with a pitcher of Manhattans. "I see your *tannen* looks a bit *baum*-ed."

We took that to mean we had done a good job and beamed at our accomplishment.

"And now it's time for the tinsel," my father said, rubbing his hands together diabolically.

Stephen's face fell. We knew what was coming. My father insisted that the shiny aluminum tinsel be placed on the tree piece by piece to achieve the desired effect. Stephen and I preferred to fling handfuls of the stuff with abandon. That was fun; doing it Dad's way was just tedious. Knowing this was a war I could not win, I declared my brother and myself noncombatants.

"That's okay, Dad," I said. "You do it. We're tired."

"I'm not tired," Stephen said, yawning.

"Yes, you are," I said menacingly.

My father smiled gratefully, and I knew then I had given him the greatest Christmas present I ever could. He loved to string tinsel and he didn't need any bumbling kids messing it up for him.

Lying in bed that night, waiting for my father to come in and say good night, I was still puzzled about the mystifying appearance of the Christmas tree.

"But how did it get there?" I asked my father when he came in to say good night. "In the car, I mean."

"Elves," my father said.

I didn't believe the elf story for a minute, but there was something strange about the whole episode. We had slipped into the Slip Inn and slipped out with a tree, yet as far as I knew no money had changed hands. What had gone on there?

Looking back on it, I think it was awfully decent of my father to ignore the church people, stiff the orphans, and dismiss the ill in order to throw his tree business to the Mafia. Nobody does nice things for organized crime anymore—not even at Christmastime.

Chapter 5

REAL MEN DON'T WEAR PLAID. Frank carrying his brand-new daughter and sporting his brand-new plaid shirt.

A Christmas Wish

Although I remained skeptical about the elves, I had to admit that my father was the Titian of tinsel. When I woke up the next morning, the tree was magnificent. He must have spent half the night working on it because the tinsel, like snow on a dung heap, had covered all the decorating sins Stephen and I had committed. The tree positively shimmered with radiating, undulating colors, turning blue, silver, green, red, or gold depending on the light streaming in from the windows. He hadn't touched our eccentric decorative arrangements, but he had added a glorious star to the top of this cascading waterfall of color—a star that somehow made you forget that two-thirds of the tree was bereft of ornaments.

My father had transformed the tree beyond all recognition. But there was another, more profound transformation waiting to hit Stephen and me as we were gulping down our Wheaties that morning.

"Your mother and the baby are coming home from the hospital today," my father said.

"And the dog is coming, too," Stephen said confidently.

"With the elephants," my father said, assuming his younger son was joking.

Stephen, however, was deadly serious as usual.

"I thought they weren't coming till Christmas," I said.

That had been the plan. My mother, an old hand at the baby business, had originally decided that she would let the nurses do all the work for a week or so; then she would arrive home triumphantly on Christmas Day. No diapers, no formula, no crying babies, just a week of rest and relaxation. This was possible, of course, because no one had yet invented the HMO. In 1955, the average hospital stay for a new mother was seven to ten days, depending on the whim of her doctor.

Dr. Alexander had delivered Stephen some six years earlier, so he had been enlisted to attend the birth of my sister. Back then, unless there was something seriously wrong with the baby or the mother, the family doctor, like the postal service of today, delivered for you. No specialists were required. No midwives or dolphins were deemed necessary.

The day we acquired the tree, Dr. Alexander had visited my mother on his rounds at the hospital. He found her a blubbering, emotional wreck—distinctly un-Mom-like behavior.

"Good Lord," Dr. Alexander said. "Whatever is the matter?"

"I'm so happy," my mother said, the tears streaming down her face.

"No, you're not," he said, diagnosing her condition instantly. "Go home."

My mother cried harder.

"Now what's the matter?" he asked.

"I'm even happier," my mother bawled.

"I, for one, cannot stand any more of your happiness," Dr. Alexander said. "Go along. We need the bed."

So my mother, suffering from a mild case of postpartum depression, departed the hospital posthaste. Five minutes after her eviction, she was miraculously cured, even without the long journey to Lourdes. What he lacked in bedside manner with Mom, Dr. Alexander more than made up for in common sense. Even though it cut short her anticipated vacation, Mom needed to be home.

Stephen and I were ecstatic to see Mom and practically knocked her over when she walked through the door. We had worked hard while she was away to keep the house—and ourselves—in good order. But now that she was home, we quickly reverted to our slovenly ways. After all, Mom was back, so why bother to pick up our socks or make our beds? Mom was also invaluable in the lost-and-found department. Toys, books, and articles of clothing that had been readily available during her absence mysteriously disappeared once she was home. There was no point in keeping track of things when we had Mom to monitor all our possessions. Stephen took the opportunity to show her the present he had made for her in school, but first he made her promise to forget by Christmas morning. Not surprisingly, Mom was a genius at forgetting and acting surprised.

The baby, however, was an entirely different kind of surprise: a strange kettle of sights, sounds, and smells. My brother and I didn't quite know what to make of her.

Some people like to prattle on about how perfectly beautiful babies are, but in truth newborns are perfectly ugly. The phrase "a face only a mother could love" was invented especially for them.

"Is she supposed to look like that?" Stephen asked me. I could hear the distaste in his voice.

"I guess," I said,

I didn't know, but I sure wasn't going to admit that to my brother.

"She's all . . . blotched," he said.

He was right. Her face was purple, and it bore a remarkable resemblance to a clenched fist when she cried, which seemed to be most of the time. Worse, she had been born with long fingernails that she had used to scratch her face enthusiastically. She looked to me as if Zorro had taken a strong dislike to her. For weeks afterward, she had to wear little silk mittens on her hands to prevent further damage.

"And her head's funny," Stephen said, continuing his critique.

He was right about that, too. She had an elongated head like the pate of an Inca king, but instead of long, luxurious hair, she was mostly bald.

We were thankful that she didn't make much noise even when she attempted to wail. A two-year-old can shatter glass with his cries and bring down tall buildings with a single scream. Newborns have an insistent, irritating whine that sounds like the drill of an angry dentist. A very angry dentist.

"She stinks," Stephen observed.

Whether he was referring to the baby in general or to the malodorous emanations that occasionally wafted from her crib, I don't know. I do know that neither one of us was dazzled by the tiny creature who had entered our lives.

"She doesn't look like a blessed 'vent to me," Stephen said, stalking out of her room.

I was more willing than Stephen to give the baby a chance, but I had the nagging suspicion that my father had not brought home the top of the line. Like the station wagon, this baby was a stripped-down model who could have used more options. For one thing, she didn't come equipped with a penis. That was a stunning discovery. Neither did she possess a decent set of choppers. Perhaps, I thought, those extras could be purchased later on, like mag wheels and a tachometer for a car. I hoped Dad had the money to pay for them—the teeth and penis, too.

When I had finished my inspection of our new resident, I asked my mother what her name was. It never occurred to me that babies needed to be named. At the prices hospitals charged, according to my father, I figured they took care of all the details. But I was wrong.

"There are two names I like," my mother said. "Anne and Susan."

"There are no Annes or Susans in *my* family," my father said indignantly.

"Fancy that," my mother said with mock surprise. "Which name do you like, John?"

"Susan," I said immediately.

I knew a girl named Anne, and I hated her because she had tripped me in the schoolyard—on purpose. I was going to clobber her, but my teachers frowned on that sort of thing. I felt, however, that I owed her one and I wasn't going to do anything to perpetuate her name.

My father agreed with me, my mother was leaning toward Anne, and Stephen, who was still under the impression that we were getting a dog, held out for Sparkles. After a brief discussion, Stephen's vote was deemed invalid, and the baby was duly named Susan by a two-to-one vote with one abstention. I'm sure that later in life she regretted not being called Tiffany, Taylor, or Tatiana, but at least she wasn't stuck with Sparkles.

However, she was stuck with being the center of attention during the Christmas season. That meant she had to endure the sudden onslaught of well-wishers who arrived at all hours of the day and night. The visitors came early and stayed late: Some because they were polite; most because they became incapacitated by my father's heavy hand with the drinks. At one point he was the proud host to the mayor of the town, the superintendent of schools, the minister from our church, a gaggle of neighbors, Dr. Alexander, Geo or Vonny from the Slip Inn, and Hank, the delivery guy from our local grocery store. Hank had dropped off an order at nine in the morning and was still there at noon, sampling Manhattans and discussing medical theory with Dr. Alexander.

"What a damned cute baby," the mayor exclaimed for the twelfth time. Mayors are like that.

"I'll drink to that," Hank agreed. "Let's go look at her again."

"Good idea," my father said, leaping to his feet.

"Frank, she's finally asleep," my mother said.

"Nonsense," my father snorted. "One little peek won't wake her."

The whole group then trooped into Susie's room to ogle her, which, of course, set her off on another crying jag. When the noise got unbearable, my father and the tourists adjourned to the bar to field the increasingly hysterical phone calls from Hank's employers and the occasional emergency page for Dr. Alexander.

That day the people in our town were without medical care, government services, religious guidance, food, or education. Even the Slip Inn was closed for the day—devastating news for bowling and domino addicts everywhere.

Mercifully, the flow of visitors had dried up by Christmas morning. Stephen and I were both up for the five a.m. feeding, not because we wanted to help, but because it was Christmas. Christmas! Although there were no canines or equines awaiting us under the tree, we were relieved to find a mountainous pile of presents, and that took some of the sting out of having to endure a squalling new baby—for me at least. Stephen was still dubious at best, downright cantankerous at worst.

"I made a present for her," he told me. "But I'm not going to give it to her."

"Why not?" I asked.

"I don't like her," he said, closing the subject.

I was surprised that he didn't get a lump or two of coal in his stocking. But my brother's less than sunny countenance did nothing to dint my joy in Christmas . . . greed. I received a neat cap pistol with removable bullets, a holster with real rawhide ties, a basketball, a new Rawlings baseball mitt, a bell for my bicycle, and a battery-powered robot that walked, talked, and shot sparks out of its eyes.

In her continuing, but losing, battle to loosen up my father's strict sartorial conservatism, Mom had bought him a plaid shirt from Rogers

Peet. He smiled wanly when he opened the box, even tried it on, but he never wore the shirt outside the house. For him, if it wasn't white, starched, and from Brooks Brothers, it wasn't really a shirt. Rather it was some sort of costume that embarrassed him to wear. He held out until 1974, when he finally bought a *blue* Brooks Brothers shirt. But he didn't like it. He thought it made him look a clown, and every time he wore it, he would start humming calliope music as if the circus were in town.

Among the presents he gave Mom that year was a hot item from Bloomingdale's—a black velveteen clutch coat, nationally advertised at $22.95, but on sale that Christmas for only $14.90. The coat had the feel of a plush stuffed animal and my mother liked it except for one thing—the size. It must have been made for the fat lady at the opera because there was enough room inside for the whole family. Mom put it on and was immediately engulfed in its soft folds. She looked like a little kid playing dress-up.

"I know I gained some weight," my mother said. "But this is ridiculous."

"A tad large," my father observed cannily. "Perhaps I overestimated."

Whether he was being mean, funny, or absentminded, I still don't know, but my mother glared at him.

"If you don't want it, can I have it?" Stephen asked.

"Whatever for?"

"A teepee," Stephen said.

"Certainly not," my mother said.

"But what are you going to do with it?" he asked, his voice almost a whine.

"I'll just return it to Bloomingdale's and get a different size," she said, looking at my father. "*My* size."

"Can you do that?" Stephen asked.

"Of course. That's the nice thing about department stores," my mother explained patiently. "If you don't like something, or it is the wrong size, you can just take it back to Bloomingdale's or Bamberger's or Lord & Taylor or wherever you bought it. No questions asked."

That was a new concept for Stephen, and while he was mulling over the implications, Mom went to check on the turkey. Despite looking a bit gray in the face and tired around the eyes, she gave her all to provide us with a "normal" Christmas dinner.

Normal, of course, means different things to different families. My mother was to cooking what Julia Child is to aircraft maintenance—she didn't know much about it and she didn't want to learn. Mom was an enthusiastic supporter of the Swanson Corporation's newly invented TV dinners and she spent an inordinate amount of time trying to convince us that the frozen lumps of food on the tin plate were delicious.

However, for some reason she had become adept at cranking out a traditional Thanksgiving or Christmas turkey dinner. The rest of the year we ate out, fasted, or defrosted.

"We'll be ready at about two o'clock," my mother said. "I think I'll lie down for a few minutes before I start the rest of the meal."

"I'll take care of it," my father said with a burst of ill-conceived enthusiasm. "The boys and I will do the cooking. You relax."

Stephen and I stared at our father. We had certainly never cooked a meal, and except for the odd sandwich, brain, or egg, neither had he. Yet there he was, a modern-day Don Quixote, offering to accomplish the impossible. Worse, he had drafted me and my brother as his Sancho Panzas. Frankly, the three of us were eminently more suited to tilting at windmills than to producing a palatable meal.

Even my mother, who usually would have jumped at any excuse to avoid cooking, had qualms about this enterprise. But she was very, very tired.

"Really?" was all she could say.

Then, with her eyelids drooping, she retired to her bed for a short winter's nap.

"John, go get the baby," my father directed. "I think she'd like to watch this."

"Mom says she needs quiet to sleep," I said.

"Nonsense," my father said. "You forget. I know a thing or two about babies. And one thing I know is that they like to be included in exciting activities—like cooking."

How he knew that escaped me, but I couldn't help thinking that Mom was right about this one.

I lugged the protesting baby into the kitchen and placed her on the linoleum floor; then I retrieved two small pillows from her room and looked around to see where I could set her up. There didn't seem to be any place where she could see what was going on, yet be out of the way. That was when I spotted a gigantic pot my father had unearthed while poking around in the depths of the kitchen. I had never seen it before, but I shoved the two pillows into it, added one medium baby, and I was done. Susie looked like an oversize, if underdone, leg of lamb sticking out of the enormous pot.

"Neatly done," my father said. "Who needs expensive baby furniture? But we must be careful not to cook her instead of the turkey. *Une flambée de bébé* would upset your mother."

I could understand that.

"Now let's see," my father said rubbing his chin. "I believe we should create a variety of adscititious dishes."

I couldn't understand that.

"Ah, here's your mother's list," he said. "How on earth does one cream an onion, I wonder."

"Pour some cream on 'em?" I suggested.

"Perhaps, but I believe we should consult our reference material, to wit, *The Joy of Cooking*," he said.

That was a title my mother found oxymoronic, or perhaps simply moronic, but we pored through the thick cookbook while my father took notes with his fountain pen.

When he was satisfied, he said, "These recipes seem quite straightforward. Cooking is not the onerous task your mother makes it out to be."

Without further ado, we began the ordeal by cooking, a little known medieval test of insanity.

"Stephen, run ask your mother where the tools are," my father said.

"You mean like the hammer?" Stephen asked.

"No, like paring knives, turkey basters, long wooden spoons—I believe long wooden spoons are essential—potato peelers, that sort of thing," he said. "Although it is a poor carpenter who blames his tools, we must begin somewhere."

Stephen took off like a shot.

"Isn't this fun, Susie?" my father said to the baby.

She yawned and spit up.

"I see," he said, laughing.

"What are we going to make?" I asked.

"Mashed potatoes," he said. "Now where are the potatoes?"

"I don't know, Daddy," I said truthfully.

"Go ask your mother where they are," he said.

I met Stephen rushing back in the other direction, reciting the hiding places of the kitchen utensils. We passed each other like ships in the night.

When I received the vital spud information, I hurried back to the kitchen and dug up the potatoes from their cleverly concealed hiding place—next to the stove.

"Where did my long wooden spoon get to?" my father asked no one in particular.

"*She's* sucking on it," my brother said. "Ick."

"Ah," my father said, taking the spoon away from Susie and wiping the baby spit on the front of his plaid shirt.

"John, would you say this is a four-quart pot?" he asked me.

"I don't know," I said.

"Perhaps we could measure out four quarts of water to see if this is the correct size," he said. "Or better yet, take it to your mother and ask her."

"Okay, Daddy," I said, grabbing the pot.

"And here, take these others, too, and ask her what they are," he said, loading me down with six or seven pieces of kitchen equipment. I dropped most of them on the way, making such a clatter that my mother leaped out of bed to see what was the matter.

"Are you sure you don't want me to help?" she asked me.

"Nonsense," I said, trying to sound like my father. "Daddy and I find that cooking is not the odorous task you make it out to be."

"Well, you've got a point," my mother said. "I can't smell anything cooking, but I sure can hear it."

For what seemed like several hours, we made inspired guesses about the length of time to cook peas, the desirability of leaving the skin on the onions, the location of the can opener, and the proper way to baste the turkey. My father put so much energy into mashing the potatoes that he broke the masher right off at the handle. The pot crashed to the floor.

"Cheap, goddamned son-of-a—" he began, waving the useless wooden handle in his hand; then he noticed that I was paying rapt attention, getting ready to memorize a new profusion of profanities. So he stopped in midcurse and picked up the potatoes without another word. But his face was red and he had the crazed look of a man caught in a world he couldn't comprehend.

Susie, who had been asleep in her pot for almost ten minutes, woke with a start and began to wail when the potatoes hit the floor.

"John, take her in the other room," my father said, wiping the sweat from his forehead. "I believe she's had quite enough excitement for one day."

We all had, and tempers were beginning to fray.

Having been disturbed at least thirty-nine times by our tiny inquiring minds, my mother grudgingly bowed to reality and got up. She peeked into the kitchen to see what was going on. I could hear her gasp as she recoiled in horror. Stephen and I were well-coated with grease, oil, and flour; my father was scarlet and sweating; odd smells perfumed the house; and every inch of counter space was covered with a phantasmagoria of food, plates, utensils, pots, colanders, Dutch ovens, frying pans, cookie sheets, bowls, long wooden spoons, steak knives, carving knives, whetstones, and the broken potato masher. I hadn't known my mother had collected all this equipment—certainly, I had never seen her use any of it.

"Everything's under control," my father said grimly. "Just go into the living room and take it easy."

Seeing the mad look in his eye, my mother wisely retreated to the relative safety of the living room, glad to be out of range.

For the next two hours we would shout out important cooking questions for Mom to answer, but she never dared venture back into the kitchen. I can still see her cringing on the couch, baby in her arms, wondering what that particular crash meant or what specifically my father's curses referred to. They must have been the longest hours of her life.

With the turkey nearing completion, we redoubled our efforts to complete the adscititious dishes, attempting to finish cooking everything at the same time—or within an hour or so. To ensure this happy outcome, my father set about making calculations on the fly leaf of *The Joy of Cooking*. He used numbers and letters, so I guess he was making algebraic equations to determine the exact moment the turkey would be at its peak of perfection.

"What time is it, John?" he asked me.

"Two-fourteen."

" 'If it were done when 'tis done, then 'twere well it were done quickly,' " he quoted from *Macbeth*.

"What?" I said.

"Time to take the damn turkey out of the oven," he translated.

"Oh."

"All right, John, put on one of these oven mitts and I'll take the other. Stephen, stay out of the way. Now let's move this bird. We'll go on three," he said opening the oven door.

I put my mitted mitt on the scorching-hot turkey pan.

"Ready? One, two, hup!" he said.

His side of the pan came up and out of the oven, but I stood there dumbly, waiting in vain for the *three* that never came. All I got was a *hup*—and the full force of a fourteen-pound turkey hitting me square in the chest. I staggered backward, the juices spattering me, but not doing any harm.

The turkey hit the freshly waxed floor and skidded in Stephen's direction, leaving a trail of brown liquid. My brother succeeded in executing a standing broad jump to escape the runaway bird, and the wild turkey finally came to rest against the refrigerator.

Once he was assured that I was uninjured, my father let out a string of invectives, not caring if I heard this time. Or, indeed, if the neighbors for miles around were privy to his outrage. To my delight, I noted a tremendously evil new word that was well worth trying out on the playground.

"Are you sure everything is okay in there?" my mother called apprehensively from the living room.

"Fine, fine," my father called back. Then he muttered, "Damn thing. We'd better clean it up."

He walked carefully around the slime trail, bent down, and attempted to lift the turkey by its legs. He darn near succeeded, but the left leg came off in his hand and the bird settled back to its resting place by the refrigerator. He stared at the disembodied leg with amazement.

"Slippery son of a bitch," he said. "But done to a turn."

"But, Daddy—"

"Don't tell your mother. It would just upset her," he said. "Get me a towel and the soap."

Using a dishtowel, he wrapped the bird up like a baby and placed it on top of the junk-strewn counter, sending a shower of pots and pans smashing to the floor. Then he poured Lux dishwashing soap on one end of the towel and swabbed away at the bird. When he was done, he washed the entire turkey with hot water.

"There," he said. "That's better."

It wasn't, but I didn't say anything.

"Now what to do about the leg?" he asked, holding the offending limb like a cigar.

"Maybe we can staple it back on," I suggested. "Or use string."

"No," he said. "We shall simply present the turkey as an unfortunate victim of a premature amputation."

"A Long John Silver turkey?" I asked.

"Exactly."

We gathered up all the other dishes and were preparing to bring them to the table when my father noticed the long skid marks left by our out-of-control turkey.

"John," he said, "go get the paper."

"The *Times* or the *Herald Tribune*?" I asked.

"The *Times,* most definitely," he said. "After all, we've amputated the left wing."

I ran into the living room, waved to my mother, who was looking paler than ever, and returned with the first section of the Saturday *New York Times*.

With the precision of a professional wallpaper, my father neatly put pages of the *Times* over the stains. When he was done, he said, "There, that will prevent anyone from slipping. Ninety percent of all accidents occur in the home."

He was precise in his statistics, but the biggest accident we suffered that day was the Christmas dinner. After a brief delay in the proceedings, while Stephen and I bathed and changed our clothes, the festivities began.

Luckily, my mother had surreptitiously set the table. We had been so obsessed with cooking that we had forgotten about the china, linen, and silver. I suppose we would have been content to dine with plastic forks on bare wood.

Then there was the food. Ah, the food. The peas were like BBs, only a bit bigger and harder; the creamed onions looked like golf balls embedded in concrete; the cranberry sauce had melted into a semiviscous purple goo; the mashed potatoes contained lumps the size of Cleveland, due to the broken masher; and Long John, the one-legged turkey, had the distinct odor of Lux soap and floor wax. But Mom never said a word, except to praise the chefs. My father and I basked in the glow of her compliments, proud of ourselves beyond all measure—or reason.

"That was delicious," my mother said at the end of the disastrous meal.

She was as good at acting polite as she was at acting surprised.

"Shall I help you clean up?" she asked.

"No, no," my father said gallantly. "The boys and I will take care of all that. Won't we?"

"You're #$%&!* right," I said happily.

Silence fell over the room like a shroud. I could see the dazed expressions on my parents' faces. Even Stephen was openmouthed—I could tell because I could see a hunk of apple pie hiding out in there.

"What did you say?" my father asked slowly, enunciating each word.

"That you're right?" I said, suspecting immediately that I had underestimated the power of the new word I had learned from my father.

"Frank," my mother said. "You've got to stop swearing around the children."

"Don't ever say that word again," my father said.

"Why not? You said it."

"It's inappropriate for a child," he said. "But I'll tell you what. You can use that word on your sixteenth birthday, but not before."

"Okay," I said.

Less than seven years to go, I thought, but I vowed to wow 'em on the playground as soon as I returned to school. That was one damn fine word.

So we cleaned up. That meant we put all the dirty dishes, pots, and pans in the sink for my mother to wash at her leisure. The *Times* was doing a fine job absorbing the turkey juices and preventing home accidents; therefore we left it in situ. For weeks afterward, my brother and I would get down on all fours and read the headlines—"France Minimizes New Troop Moves in Algeria Crisis," "President Feels He Cannot Take Rest Trip South," and "Floods Rise in California"—which defied all efforts to get them out of the linoleum.

Cleaning done, we retired to the living room, my father to collapse in a chair, Stephen and I to play with our presents.

"Let's all be quiet so Susie will go to sleep," my mother said.

We waited tensely for the baby to stop crying; then my mother breathed a sigh of relief and uncrossed her legs. The sound of her stockings rubbing together woke Susie instantly and the yowling began anew. How the baby had heard such a slight noise all the way across the house puzzles me still, but it was obvious that kid had one good set of ears.

We waited a few more minutes until the crying stopped again; then Stephen asked me if he could play with my walking, talking, spark-shooting robot.

"Sure," I said because I was engrossed with polishing my new cap gun to a brilliant sheen.

He put the robot on the floor, but before he could activate it, my mother stopped him. "Oh, Stephen, don't play with that thing now," she said. "You'll wake the baby."

"Then can I watch TV?" he asked.

"No, it makes too much noise."

"How about listening to records?"

"No."

"I can't do anything around here, and it's all *her* fault," he raged, the sound of his voice waking the baby again. "It's not fair!"

"Fair or foul, we must accommodate the new baby," my father said. "Why don't you go outside and play?"

"I'm going outside, all right," Stephen said. "And I'm going to stay there all night."

"John, go with him," my father said.

"Why? What did I do?" I whined.

"Go."

We went.

There was the smell of snow in the air that dark, gloomy Christmas afternoon and the icy dampness knifed through my jacket. But as cold as it was, Stephen's heart was colder.

"I think she's 'tarded," he told me confidentially.

"You mean retarded?"

"Yes. She can't talk. She can't walk. She can't even sit up or roll over or shake hands or play dead," he said.

"Or bark," I said, knowing where he was heading.

"Right. Billy Easton's dog can do a lot more tricks. All *she* does is sleep and poop," Stephen said, resting his case.

"You're just mad because you're not the baby of the family anymore," I said.

"I'm not a baby!" Stephen yelled.

"Then why are you acting like one? Waa, waa, baby!" I taunted.

Then, in a moment that would have stabbed Charles Dickens through the heart with a stake of holly, choked Truman Capote on his homemade fruitcake, and reduced the entire Walton clan to tears, Stephen made a fervent Christmas wish.

"Why don't they just return her to Bloomingberger's?" he said. "No questions asked."

Chapter 6

BON VOYAGE. An unsuspecting Susie gets her first look at the Black Torpedo of Doom. Mary wanted a memorial picture—in case we never returned.

Moby Torpedo

As it turned out, my mother did return her coat to Bloomingdale's, but we kept the baby, despite Stephen's protests.

For the first three months of her life, Susie got bigger and louder, but she didn't progress significantly in her walking, talking, or bowel-control skills. Stephen avoided her as much as possible, but I found her intriguing and set about to learn all I could about *Infantus americanus,* the American baby.

I took as my bible *Baby and Child Care* by Dr. Benjamin Spock, and while my mother was actively engaged in taking care of the baby, I read to her from the book.

"'He will need daily oiling,'" I informed my mother, like a monk reading to his confreres in the refectory. "'And he will need cotton swabs and a soft brush for his hair.'"

I put the book aside. Obviously, there was a problem here, and I knew what it was.

"I hate to tell you this, Mom," I said. "But you bought the wrong book. This one is for boy babies, not girl babies. You'd better return it, no questions asked."

In those days, issues of grammar trumped gender issues, but once I got the pronouns sorted out, I read with interest about how babies grew. The eccentric Dr. S. was pretty much right about what babies did when, but my mother was oblivious to his professional advice. She had been through this twice before and no guy in a long white coat was going to tell her what to do. Fortunately, she put up with my know-it-all behavior because she was totally relaxed with this baby.

When I had been born, both my parents had been hopeless novices who were terrified they might break me. By the time Susie came along, however, child-rearing was old fedora. I cringed, though, when I saw my father toss her around with a great air of incaution. I knew from Dr. Spock that failure to support a baby's head correctly would cause irreparable damage, and I had visions of Susie's head popping off at the shoulders. That made me much more cautious than my parents at first. A headless baby, like a headless horseman, was not something I wanted to see. I quickly discovered, however, that babies, like the Timex watches advertised on television, could take a lickin' and keep on tickin'. And soon I was able to care for her with almost the same speed and efficiency that my mother displayed.

My interest in baby wrangling, however, embroiled me in a hair-raising adventure that required all my nautical know-how to survive.

For a week or so, my mother had been making noises about taking Susie for an airing in the Black Torpedo of Doom. I think Mom was afraid to go it alone, so she enlisted my help to keep the Torpedo running straight and true.

On a cold Saturday in January, Susie was wrapped like a mummy against the icy chill; then she was swaddled in blankets, comforters, and quilts. Amazingly, despite pounds of apparel, she was difficult to spot within the vast confines of the perambulator.

"It sure is big," my mother said, getting at the business end of the machine. "Are you ready?"

"I guess," I said.

Susie let out a tentative *waaa* to let us know she was prepared for this risky venture, and with the final application of a pink knit hat to her head, we were off on the maiden voyage of the Black Torpedo of Doom.

"You guide the front end down the steps and I'll hang on behind," Captain Mom directed, trying to get us out of safe harbor and onto the high seas.

I scurried around to the front of the carriage and put my back into its cold black steel. As it bore down on me, I had visions of a cartoon character being squashed pancake-flat by a rogue steamroller, a recurring theme of my favorite TV shows. Cartoon steamrollers, however, weighed considerably less than the Black Torpedo.

With much grunting and effort, we managed to navigate the carriage to the brink of the steep hill upon which we lived. There, we paused to gather our courage.

"Steep, isn't it?" my mother said.

"We need Queequeg," I said.

I had been plowing through a child's abridged edition of *Moby-Dick*. I thought Melville's story was okay, but not as good as *Treasure Island,* which I was sure was the best book ever written. However, in our current situation, the giant harpooner would be of more use than a one-legged ship's cook.

"Hoist the mainsail," I said.

"What?"

"Let's go," I said. "It's cold."

Mom released the brake and the carriage sprinted ahead, glad to be free from the surly bonds of our house. The large spoked wheels and whitewall tires spun faster and faster.

"John, hold it back," my mother cried as she was being dragged down the hill.

I ran to the front of the malevolent machine and tried to stop its increasing momentum.

"Hit the brakes, Mom!" I yelled. "Hit the brakes!"

She fumbled around, looking for the brake handle, while the Torpedo continued its quest to run me over.

"I can't find the brake," my mother said, her voice near panic.

There was only one thing to do. I let go of the front end of the carriage, and when it rocketed past me, I leaped for the handle. With every ounce of strength I possessed, I pulled back on the freezing metal and dug my Buster Browns into the concrete sidewalk. Between us, Mom and I couldn't stop the carriage, but we slowed it down sufficiently for me to find and apply the brake. We stood halfway down the hill, at a forty-five-degree angle, reappraising the wisdom of this expedition.

"Heavy, isn't it?" my mother said.

Her breath looked like smoke signals in the frosty air.

When we had gained sufficient confidence, I joined my mother at the back of the carriage and played brakeman as we lurched down the hill in fits and starts. The baby rocketed around in the Torpedo like a lone BB in an empty tin can.

Once we reached level ground, we encountered a second navigational problem. The carriage was more than five and a half feet high with the hood up. My mother was five-two and I wasn't even that tall. For the first few yards of our journey we sailed ahead blindly, sending old ladies leaping for the bushes that lined our route. We left them lying prostrate in our wake, arms and shopping bags akimbo, as we sailed blithely on. But after almost knocking down an elderly and outraged gentleman, who shook his cane at us, Mom sent me ahead as an outrigger to clear a course for us.

"Wide load!" I shouted happily, running ahead of the carriage. "Wide load coming through!"

That wasn't exactly what Mom had been thinking, and she told me to be more circumspect. Not knowing what circumspect meant, but figuring it was akin to circumnavigate, I switched to the nautical jargon I loved so well.

"Hard a-starboard, Mom! Avast, thar she blows!"

Many a plump housewife probably took umbrage at my words, but if I hadn't been familiar with *Moby-Dick,* we would have surely wrecked the Torpedo on the rocks of our own incompetence.

We made several ports of call that day, careening into a cardboard display filled with Snickers bars at the drugstore, plowing into a pyramid of canned peas at the grocery, and cracking a glass counter at the bakery. When all the reparations were paid, the operating cost of the Black Torpedo of Doom zoomed to about sixty-five dollars an hour. However, the carriage proved to be a useful conveyance at the cleaners. We were able to squeeze in four or five tons of laundry without disturbing the snoozing Susie.

Then, our maiden voyage almost completed, we shoved off for home. Like a remora guiding a shark, I managed to get us back to the bottom of the hill without serious mishap. We paused for a moment to look up at the vertical incline and wonder how we had made it down alive.

"Steep, isn't it?" my mother said.

Gamely, Mom put her shoulder into the carriage, but the Black Torpedo of Doom wasn't ready to go home yet. It stalled at the base of the hill and refused to go any farther. No amount of pushing would make it move.

"Is this a quandary, Mom?" I asked, using a new word I had learned at school.

"I daresay it is," my mother answered, brushing a stray lock of hair from her eye. I noted that her permanent had been rendered temporary by all the pushing.

"Why don't we dump the ballast?" I suggested.

"The baby or the laundry?" my mother asked wearily.

"The laundry," I said practically. "It weighs more."

"We can't just—" my mother began.

"Is there a problem here?" a deep baritone voice interrupted our quandary.

The voice belonged to Officer Lindemann, all six-foot-six, two hundred and fifty pounds of him. He was, as ususal, riding his tiny three-wheeled motorcycle. Imagine a pro-football lineman on a child's tricycle and that was how ludicrous he looked on his diminutive trike. Even little kids like me made fun of him behind his back. But I suppose the three-wheeler was perfect for his job—giving out parking tickets. He would ride through the village, holding a stick with a piece of blue chalk attached to the end. His task was to mark the tires of parked cars; then he would ride back an hour later and ticket any cars with blue-marked tires. Employing such a huge man for such a minuscule chore always seemed ridiculous to me. He should have been beating up bad guys, not playing with chalk, in my opinion.

"Oh, Officer Lindemann," my mother said. "Yes, we seem to be having difficulty pushing the carriage up the hill."

"Nice carriage," Officer Lindemann said, probably because it was bigger than his tricycle.

"Thank you," my mother said. "Do you think you could help us?"

Officer Lindemann, confronted for perhaps the first time in his career with a non-traffic-related problem, thought about the situation deeply, searching for an answer. After some minutes, it came to him.

"You know, you could have your laundry delivered," he said, slashing through our Gordian knot.

"I do, usually," my mother said, growing impatient. "But I wanted to air the baby."

"Baby? What baby?" Officer Lindemann said, leaning off his trike and peering into the Torpedo.

"Oh, there she is," he said. "What's her name?"

"Susan," my mother said tersely.

"I have a niece named Susan," Officer Lindemann said. "We call her Sue."

"How unconventional," my mother said. "You must be very proud."

"I am," he said, beaming. "Do you want to see her picture?"

"Not right now," my mother said, a definite edge in her voice. "Do you think you could help us? I can't see over the top of the carriage and I'm afraid I'll hit someone."

Officer Lindemann knew all about hit-and-run accidents and he was delighted to display his expertise.

"Have you thought about putting the top down?" he asked.

"Yes, I have thought of it," my mother said tensely. "But it seems to be stuck."

"Aha," Officer Lindemann said.

"Then you'll help us?" my mother asked.

"Of course," Officer Lindemann said. "You push and I'll clear the way for you."

That was not what my mother had in mind, and she was simmering mad by now. What she didn't know was that Officer Lindemann was surgically attached to his trike and no one had ever seen him dismount from it while on duty.

"Nincompoop," my mother said under her breath.

I was shocked. I thought the policeman was my friend—or at least that's what they told us in school.

"Come on, John," she said. "Let's go."

Then she said something about "lard" and a three-letter word I wasn't allowed to use in public.

"Mom!"

"Well, it's true," she said. "He could push this thing up the hill in about ten seconds. But we won't give him the satisfaction."

Like sailors straining at the capstan, Mom and I urged the Torpedo uphill. Slowly at first, then with speed born of anger, we overcame inertia, and the lumbering carriage began to fly. Officer Lindemann rode alongside us shouting through his bullhorn to clear the pedestrians from our path. A knot of people gathered on the other side of the road to watch our progress, no doubt astounded by the spectacle.

Red-faced and exhausted, we made it to our door without running anyone down, but my mother was mortified.

"Thank you for *all* your help," she said. "We couldn't have made it without you—or your bull . . . horn."

Officer Lindemann smiled.

"All in a day's work, ma'am," he said, cheerily saluting.

I suppose my mother's words, though not meant that way, were as close as he ever came to receiving a compliment. Nobody likes the purveyor of parking tickets.

When we got inside, my mother took to her bed for a nap, while I took a moment to stare at the Black Torpedo. It seemed to glare back at me, wishing me ill, and cursing itself for not doing more damage. I kicked one whitewall tire, but it didn't respond, except to sway slightly like a cobra preparing to strike. I fled.

Whenever I find myself growing grim about the mouth, whenever it is a damp, drizzly November in my soul, I don't think about going to sea. I think, instead, about the first voyage of the Black Torpedo of Doom, that jinxed ship of my childhood, and how I mistrusted its motives and manners. The metallic monster needed a police escort just to get it home, but like Susie, for good or for ill, the Torpedo had become a permanent part of our household.

Chapter 7

EGGS-TRAORDINARY BABY. Stephen eventually learned
to accept the new baby and later became her biggest
fan. But it took Susie's uncanny abilities as an
Easter egg finder to convince him.

Beep, Beep, Beep

If my dislike for the Torpedo was disturbing, Stephen's continuing antagonism toward the new baby was becoming intolerable. His aloof attitude wasn't actively hostile, but he ignored poor Susie, pretending she didn't exist. My parents talked to him, argued with him, and yelled at him, but nothing would shake his studied indifference. He was a rock, unyielding and dogged in his determination to dismiss her undeniable reality.

One of the ways my mother devised to bring him around was "quality time." I know that sounds like a modern concept developed in the 1980s to assuage the guilt of working parents, but in 1955, Mom had found a story about Q-T in a women's magazine. And because she wrote for women's magazines, she tended to believe everything she read in them.

"You are going to have 'quality time' with Susie from six-forty-five to seven every evening," my mother announced one evening. "While I'm making dinner, the three of you will play with her and make her feel like a part of the family."

That was inconvenient for me because I always watched Bill Stern with the sports news on WABC-TV at that hour. I protested feebly, mostly for show, but I could tell by my mother's tone of voice that "quality time" was an order, not a suggestion. My father glared at me with his "don't rile her up" look, so I caved in quickly.

Stephen had a different opinion.

"No," he said.

"Yes," Mom said.

"No," Stephen repeated.

"Go to your room," my mother said.

"No."

"Stephen!" my father thundered.

He went, but he wasn't happy about it.

That incident was the opening shot of an all-out war between Stephen and my parents—a very short war that lasted all of two days. Stephen finally surrendered to superior size and strength, but his recalcitrant attitude remained intact.

The first night of "quality time" he said, "I'd rather eat dog doo."

"Sit down, shut up, and have fun," my father said grimly. "If I have to participate in this nonsense, so do you."

We had placed a blanket in the middle of the living room floor and planted the baby on it. She looked at us warily, wondering what would happen next. So did we.

"Go ahead and play with her," my father said to me.

"Play what?" I asked. "Checkers? Monopoly?"

"Wise guy," my father said. "Gitchy-goo her or something."

"Ick," Stephen said.

"I don't hear the sounds of a happy family out there," my mother called from the kitchen.

"We're working on it, dear," my father called back. Then he muttered something about lady magazine writers.

With a sigh, he reached out a tentative hand and tickled Susie's foot. She squealed with delight.

"That's better," my mother called from the kitchen.

For the next fourteen minutes we gave Susie a lifetime of attention. We tickled her, tossed her in the air, threw forward passes with her, bounced her on our knees, jostled her, shook her, shuffled her back and forth like a medicine ball, turned her upside down, and spun her around like a top. Noting that she was dribbling like a faucet, I suggested we employ her as a basketball. But my father nixed that idea. Much to my disappointment, I discovered that a "bouncing baby girl" was just an expression.

At the stroke of seven, we got up and went our separate ways, leaving a shaking, purple-faced, near psychotic baby writhing on her blanket. Her legs were rigid, as if she had been seized by rigor mortis; her eyes were wild with terror. She had had so much quality time, she emptied a quantity of bodily fluids on the floor.

"What have you done to her?" my mother wailed, coming to the rescue. "My poor baby."

After that, my mother was forced to find other means to reconcile Susie with her brother. One of the ploys she attempted was to get Stephen to help her care for the baby. She made a point of showing him how to wash her, feed her with a bottle, and change her, figuring that he might become as interested in baby tending as I.

"What's the first thing you do when you change a baby's diaper?" my mother asked him one day.

"Hold your nose and go pee-yew," Stephen said, wandering away from the infant hygiene lesson with his usual sangfroid.

My parents had tried reason, threats, treats, and punishment, but nothing had worked. They had consulted Drs. Spock and Alexander, relatives, friends, and lady magazine writers—all to no avail. They were well on the way to sending Stephen to military school, when a miracle occurred, appropriately enough, at Easter.

Although we weren't much of a churchgoing family, we religiously observed the pagan aspects of Christian holidays—Christmas trees and gifts, Easter-egg hunting, and Halloween trick-or-treating. I considered Easter to rank third on the holiday kid-meter, but I did enjoy dyeing eggs the night before and eating forty or fifty pounds of chocolate the next morning.

That year I informed my mother that I was too old to go a-hunting, but I graciously consented to coloring the eggs. We boiled up the water, added the dye pellets and vinegar, and set to work. Stephen favored pastels, but I liked deep, rich colors—blue, red, green, and purple. I also made two special eggs each Easter: One I soaked long and hard in all the primary colors until it turned a revolting brown-gray-green shade that looked as if someone had thrown up on it. The vomit-colored egg appalled my mother anew each year, but it made Stephen laugh, so it became an accepted, if nauseating, tradition.

The other special egg was designed to fool my Uncle John, who, when he came to Easter dinner, would always crack eggs on his forehead to amuse Stephen and me. We thought it would be neat if we substituted a raw egg for a hard-boiled one, so I secretly sneaked in an extra egg for that purpose. Mom never knew, but Stephen couldn't stop giggling, thinking about Uncle John with egg on his face.

Every year my father took great pains to hide the eggs the night before Easter—such great pains that he forgot where he had hidden them by the next morning. Stephen and I would generally find all but one or two; then we would have to wait for a few weeks until the missing eggs got good and rotten before we could sniff them out.

In 1956, we held true to form. Stephen found ten of the dozen eggs, including the dark green one that was uncooked, and I, sitting in lordly splendor on the couch, directed his attention to one more. The twelfth egg, however, was a goner.

"I think 'Esther' is missing," I said, taking inventory. That was what my brother had written with a wax pencil on a pale blue egg—"Esther," as in "Happy Esther." In his defense, he was just learning to write.

"Frank, you really must remember where you hide the eggs," my mother said, resigning herself to a house that would soon be filled with the same sulfuric atmosphere found on the planet Venus.

"Don't blame me," he said. "Blame the Easter Bunny."

"I blame a shaker or two of Manhattans," my mother grumbled.

"What a terrific idea," my father said, retreating to the bar, scratching his head, and wondering just where he had stashed that last egg.

It was almost noon and Uncle John and Aunt Eliza were due at any minute. The canned ham and the yams out of the can were cooking away nicely, and Stephen and I were looking forward to seeing Uncle John perform. He not only cracked eggs on his head, he cracked jokes, and he could also crack his nose. The nose routine entertained us for years. Uncle John would put both hands to the sides of his nose; then, unbeknownst to us, he would hook his thumbnail under a front tooth and snap it, making it sound as if his nose were breaking. He would repeat this trick over and over, first to the left, then to the right, much to our amazement. The groans that accompanied the cracking added to the fun. I was eighteen years old before he revealed his closely guarded secret to me. But unless Stephen reads this, he still doesn't know.

I was also glad to see Uncle John that year because I had a surprise for him—in addition to the raw egg. I wanted to tell him the first dirty joke I had ever heard. Brian Thompson had told it to me in school and I thought it was the funniest joke on record. Repeating it to my parents was out of the question. They would have only censured me, but I knew that Uncle John had the cerebral and sophisticated sense of humor it took to appreciate such a cerebral, sophisticated, and ribald joke.

After a bout of nose-cracking, I took my uncle aside and told him I wanted to see him. Bemused, he followed me into my room and I shut the door. This joke was not for the likes of Stephen or the womenfolk.

"Do you want to hear a dirty joke?" I asked him.

His eyes widened in surprise.

"I guess," he said noncommittally.

"Okay," I said, gathering steam. "Did you hear about the man who didn't swear, smoke, or drink?"

"I don't believe I have," Uncle John said with an air of caution.

"Do you know what he said?" I blurted out, racing for the punch line.

"No."

"Goddamn it! I left my pipe at the bar!" I said gleefully and laughed uproariously.

After the stunned expression wore off his face, Uncle John smiled. "Good one," he said, no doubt trying to suppress his laughter at me, not the joke.

I felt vindicated that I had found the right audience for that joke and begged him not to tell my parents about it. He swore he would remain silent, and he kept his promise—in a way.

Easter dinner got off to its usual rousing start with Uncle John offering to crack eggs on his forehead.

"Oh, John, must you do that?" Aunt Eliza said. She was a very nice lady, but she didn't do any tricks.

"Of course I must," Uncle John said. "What would my public think?"

He pointed to Stephen, who was wiggling in his chair, trying to stifle his giggles.

"Now, let's see," he said. "I believe I'll start with this dubiously hued beauty."

He picked up my vomit-colored egg and smacked it into his head. It made a satisfying sound that sent Stephen into a full-blown paroxysm of laughter.

"One for you," he said, handing me the egg.

I thanked him and suggested that the forest green egg—the raw one—should be next.

"This one?" he asked, picking it up and hefting it suspiciously. Then he spun the egg on the table.

"Mmmmmm," he mused, putting it back into the straw basket lined with green excelsior.

I sighed. He had escaped for the fourth year in a row, but like the Dodgers losing the World Series, there was always next year.

Uncle John cracked two more eggs, but all the fun had gone out of his performance. Then he made a fatal error. He returned to the green egg and again spun it on the table.

"This one seems to be a bit different from the rest," he said. "But I suppose an egg is an egg."

My heart was racing. Was he really going to do it?

Uncle John tossed the egg about a foot into the air and caught it.

My stomach lurched.

"Aerodynamically speaking, this egg is something special," he said. "Here, Frank, catch."

He tossed the egg down the table to my father, who fielded it neatly and fired it back.

"Cut it out," my mother said. Mom didn't do tricks either.

Uncle John rolled the suspect egg in his hand like Captain Queeg; then with a slow, deliberate swing, he smashed the raw egg into his forehead. Shell and yoke exploded in every direction—cascading down his face, spattering the tablecloth, and slowly oozing down his tie and suit coat.

I about wet my pants, but Stephen did me one better. He laughed so hard, he toppled out of his chair and crashed to the floor, holding his stomach.

While the adults looked at him with uncomprehending horror, Uncle John did a slow burn—a burn almost fierce enough to fry the egg.

"Goddamn it!" he said in a voice that instantly silenced my unrestrained laughter.

"Goddamn it!" he repeated, a smile barely visible beneath the egg mask. "I believe I left my pipe at the bar."

That set me off again and I knew he had known about the egg all the time. What I didn't know then was that you can tell if an egg is cooked or not by the way it spins. I was spun off to my room, while my mother rushed around with a damp cloth soaked with soda water, trying to save her tablecloth and Uncle John's suit. My father had to leave the table so he wouldn't collapse with laughter and join Stephen, who was still on the floor gasping for breath.

Mom and Aunt Eliza were not amused, and I was sentenced to a week without television. But that was a fair enough price to pay for cracking up the entire table, as it were. And that memorable Easter dinner proved beyond a doubt that Uncle John was a good egg, always ready to entertain us kids, even if it meant sacrificing his jacket, tie, and dignity.

That evening, after our guests had left, my father had a sudden revelation. He gathered the family in the living room and announced he had a plan to find Esther, the missing Easter egg. We swallowed the bait.

"The problem: methodology," he said. "The solution: science."

That sounded reasonable.

"What we must have," he continued, "is a direction finder capable of homing in on the target. Then, by means of triangulation, we can locate the egg."

That still sounded reasonable, although my mother rolled her eyes.

"I have such a device," my father said triumphantly. "And I shall unveil it for you now."

He left the room like a magician exiting stage left and reappeared moments later holding a sleeping Susie in his arms.

"What's *she* doing here?" Stephen asked contemptuously.

"She is going to find that egg for us," Dad said.

That didn't sound reasonable at all, and even Stephen knew it.

"*She* can't do that," he said. "*She* can't do anything."

"Of course she can," my father said. "Do you know what the letters in her name stand for?"

We shook our heads.

"Susie—Search out Unidentified Sites Involving Easter eggs," he said. "Susie is just an acronym—very big in army and navy circles."

My mother laughed, but Stephen stared, not quite sure to make of this pronouncement.

"No, it doesn't," he said, tentatively.

"Watch and learn," my father said.

He was holding a snoozing Susie in the crook of his arm.

"First we extend the antenna," he said.

He picked up Susie's arm and held it out straight like a pointer; then he spun around three times as if he were trying to get his bearings.

"Beep, beep," he said softly. "She's on the trail."

Waving the sleeping baby's arm, he moved to his left, and whispered, "Beep, beep."

"She's getting colder," I said, getting into the spirit.

My father went to his right and the beeping got louder.

"Hotter," Stephen said, despite his misgivings.

Dad slowly covered every inch of the living room with radar baby beeping away, sometimes louder, sometimes softer. Finally, he vectored in on a bookcase and made the baby's arm spin like a windmill.

"Beep! Beep! Beep!" he shouted.

"She's found it!" Stephen cried. He was sitting on the edge of his chair, the suspense making him squirm.

"Why, I believe she has," my father said solemnly, reaching behind a quaint and curious volume of forgotten lore, and producing the pastel blue egg named Esther.

"I didn't know she could do that," Stephen said in a shocked voice.

"There are many things about your little sister you don't know," my father said. "Mysterious things. Wonderful things."

"Really?" Stephen asked, still dumbfounded at Susie's magical egg-finding prowess.

"Really. And once you get to know her, you'll find that she is not only talented, but awfully cute, too," my father said, placing the sleeping baby in Stephen's arms.

"Can she do anything else?" Stephen asked.

"Not tonight," my father said. "She's eggs-hausted."

My mother and I groaned.

"I bet not every baby can find Easter eggs," Stephen said, rocking Susie to and fro, a new respect and pride in his voice.

"She's a very special baby," my father said. "But she needs two big brothers to help her grow up—not just one."

"You mean me?" Stephen asked.

"I most certainly mean you," Dad said.

"Well, I guess she's not so bad," Stephen admitted. "For a baby."

After that eventful Easter, Stephen completely reversed his attitude toward the baby and became her advocate, protector, and pal. He took such an avid interest in Susie that he made my own involvement with her seem positively petty—much to my mother's amazement.

"How could this have happened so quickly?" my mother wondered later. "Almost overnight he goes from angry to angelic. I did what I was supposed to do with him, but I failed."

"Well," my father said with an insufferable air of superiority, "I suppose lady magazine writers don't know everything about children, now, do they?"

"You can't possibly think that your silly egg-finding routine changed Stephen, can you?" Mom said.

"Beep, beep, beep," my father said enigmatically.

PART TWO

QUARANTINE

Stunned by Dr. Alexander's diagnosis, we fell silent for a moment. Then my father exploded: "Scarlet fever! How the hell could she get scarlet fever? Is there some epidemic around that I don't know about?"

"There hasn't been a case in the county since about 1890," Dr. Alexander said.

"This makes no sense at all," my father said, sinking back into the couch.

My mother had the defiant look of a person who had accepted the bad news and intended to fight. Her face was taut; her hands were clenched. She looked as if she were about to growl.

"What do we have to do?" she asked, her voice grim but steady.

"Bed rest, antibiotics, and lots of liquids," Dr. Alexander said.

In those days, that was the treatment for everything from cancer to carbuncles. Come to think of it, not much has changed.

"And you must keep the other children away from her," Dr. Alexander continued. "Scarlet fever is highly contagious. So contagious, in fact, that I am obligated to notify the county board of health."

"Notify anyone you want," my father said. "I have to get to work."

"Not so fast," Dr. Alexander said.

"What do you mean?"

"I mean you're quarantined," Dr. Alexander said. "The whole family."

While we were trying to absorb that bit of dire news, Dr. Alexander phoned the pharmacy with his prescriptions; then he got into his green Caddy and left in a cloud of exhaust fumes.

"This is just great," my father said after the doctor had gone. "The next thing you know, we'll be required to wear yellow robes and carry clappers to warn the populace that the lepers are coming."

"We will just have to make the best of it," my mother said.

"That's like making chicken salad out of chicken sh—"

"Frank!"

And so the ordeal began. Five people trapped in a house that grew smaller and smaller every day. I spent most of the time hiding in my room, wishing I were somewhere else—the moon, Philadelphia, hell—it didn't matter. To pass the time, I struggled through *A Journal of the Plague Year* by Daniel Defoe, which my father, with his mordant sense of humor, had given me to read. London, overwhelmed by the bubonic plague in 1665, was about the same as our house, give or take a bubo or two.

Every afternoon after school, Brian Thompson would bring my homework and set it down by the front door. Then we would talk through a closed window and make exciting plans to do exciting things that we would never do once I was uncaged. Our fantasy lives were much better than our real lives. Brian's visit was the highlight of my day. But things were so boring that, for the first and last time in my life, I actually looked forward to doing my homework. I swore, as God was my witness, I would never be that bored again.

But while I was complaining about my travails, poor little Susie was the one who was really suffering. Her temperature shot up to 105 degrees before the antibiotics finally kicked in. She had a sore, pus-filled throat, a headache, a tongue the color and texture of a strawberry, and the most remarkable complexion I had ever seen. Her face was, well, scarlet, except around the mouth. The contrast of the deep red face and the pale lips made her look like an old-time minstrel. I kept expecting her to break out into a chorus of "Camptown Races" at any moment.

What was most amazing, however, was not her condition, but her toleration of it. Susie's stoicism was incredible. Once she had gotten over the initial shock to her system, she just accepted what was happening to her as if it were normal. That was something I could never have managed. If I had contracted scarlet fever, or any lesser disease, or even a hangnail, I would have complained bitterly from morning to night, making a royal pain of myself and enjoying every moment of feeling sorry for myself.

Susie suffered in silence—mostly. The hardest part of her illness was the isolation. No one but my mother was allowed in her room and Susie was not allowed out of it. She missed playing with Stephen and me, but what upset her most was that she couldn't see her daddy. Susie missed him desperately and would call out his name piteously.

"Daaa-dy,"she would cry. "Pway wif me, Daaa-dy."

"This is making me crazy," my father said to my mother. "I can't stand it any longer. I'll be haunted for the rest of my life by that little voice."

"You can't go in there, Frank," my mother said. "For an adult, scarlet fever can be fatal."

He let out a rapid-fire string of invectives that turned my mother's face as red as Susie's.

"Why don't you sit in the doorway and read to her?" my mother suggested. "I think she'd like *Heidi*. I know I loved that story when I was little."

"Not *Heidi*," my father said. "That's the most insipid book ever written. You read it to John when he was four and he remarked, quite rightly, 'Too many girls, not enough goats.' How about *Huckleberry Finn* or *Treasure Island* or something with ghosts in it?"

"Just read *Heidi*," my mother said. "I don't want you to scare her with pirates, murders, hauntings, swordplay, or ferocious, man-eating animals."

"You take all the fun out of reading to children," my father said.

Resigned, but not happy about it, my father placed a rocking chair just outside Susie's room and opened the book. I was listening in the hall.

"Once upon a time," he began, "there was a little girl named Heidi."

"How old was she?" Susie asked. She always liked to know how old everybody was.

"As luck would have it, she was five years old, just your age," my father said. "But unlike you, she had a wen on the side of her nose."

"What's a wen?"

"It's like a mole or a wart, and it wasn't very attractive," he said. "Anyway, Heidi hated that wen."

"What was the wen's name, Daddy?" Susie asked.

"Uh, Wendolyn," my father said, thinking fast. He was a master of making up stories as he went along. "Yes, Wendolyn was about the ugliest thing alive and Heidi wanted to get rid of her in the worst way. And after you hear this story, you'll know she certainly chose the worst way."

"What did she do?" Susie asked.

"She called Dr. Alexander."

"*My* Dr. Alexander?"

"The very same. He was just a young man in 1807, so he wasn't the pride of the AMA as he is today. But he recommended that Heidi visit her grandfather in the Swiss Alps. The snow, he reasoned, would make Wendolyn so cold she would jump off Heidi's nose in short order. So Heidi hopped on a train and sped north to the Alps, where her grandfather met her at the station."

"What was her grandfather's name?" Susie asked.

"Grandfather."

"Oh."

"Grandfather was an old geezer with long white whiskers like Santa Claus, but instead of a red suit, he wore a Tyrolean hat and lederhosen."

"Leder what?"

"Short pants—to emphasize his knobby knees and varicose veins," my father said. "Not a very practical garment in all the ice and snow, but that's what they wore in them days. It says so right here," my father said, consulting the book in his lap for the first time.

"'Howdy, Grandfather,' Heidi said. 'Will you help me rid myself of this dreadful wen?'"

"'Certainly, my dear,' Grandfather said. 'But first we must milk the goats.'"

"You milk cows, not goats," Susie informed him.

"Right. But you can milk sheep, goats, and coconuts, too," my father said. "When they had finished milking the goats, they made cheese—chèvre it's called—and it was deee-licious."

"Can I have some?" Susie asked.

"Of course," my father said. "How about a grilled chèvre sandwich?"

"Okay."

My father relayed the order to my mother and continued on with the increasingly mad story that would have made the unfortunate author of *Heidi,* Johanna Spyri, wish she had stuck to goatherding.

"Now let's see, where were we?" my father said, settling back into his rocking chair.

"Cheese," Susie said.

"Oh, yes. Cheese," my father said. He had lost track of the plot line, but that didn't stop him.

"Suddenly, there was a high-pitched scream that made Heidi and her grandfather practically jump out of their lederhosen."

"Who was it?" Susie asked.

"It was Ben Gunn and he said, 'Cheese, cheese, my kingdom for some cheese.'"

"'What are you doing here, Ben?' Grandfather asked. 'I thought you were marooned on Treasure Island.'"

"'I was,' Ben said. 'But I escaped and now I want some cheese. A hogshead of cheese, please.'"

"'We have some lovely chèvre,' Heidi said."

"'Pshaw!' Ben said. 'I didn't come all the way to the Alps for chèvre, I want *Swiss* cheese! And the hole-ier the better.'"

"'Sorry, we're fresh out,' Heidi said."

"'Drat!' Ben yelled. 'Double drat!' And with that he skied down the Alp and out of the story. However, he had brought young Jim Hawkins with him and Jim stayed to help tend the goats."

"How old was Jim?" Susie inquired.

"Eleven and fifteen-sixteenths," my father said. He recognized the importance of detail in making a story seem believable.

"Heidi loved to go up to the high meadow and smell the wildflowers and pet the goats," he continued. "She and Jim Hawkins became fast friends. And do you know what their favorite game was?"

"What?"

"Why, Heidi-and-go-seek, of course," my father deadpanned.

"Daddy!" Even Susie wasn't buying that one.

"Well, it *was* their favorite game," he insisted with mock defensiveness. "And one day while they were playing, Wendolyn the wen began to grow.

"'Oh, my,' Heidi said. 'Wendolyn is as big as a watermelon. I can hardly hold my head up.'"

The story was interrupted by mother delivering the grilled chèvre sandwich. It wasn't chèvre, of course. It was Kraft American, but Susie didn't seem to notice. Caught up in the story, she munched the sandwich absentmindedly.

"Then what happened, Daddy?" she mumbled, her mouth full.

"That's when Huckleberry Finn arrived," my father said.

"Who's he?"

"A fugitive from another story," he said. "But since this tale is set in a French-speaking canton of Switzerland, he was known locally as Framboise Finn. That's because they didn't have any huckleberries there, only raspberries.

"Framboise Finn said, 'I don't believe I've ever seen a bigger or uglier wen in all my life.'

"'I know,' Heidi said. 'Isn't it awful?'

"'Do you want to get rid of it?' Framboise asked.

"'Oh, yes, please,' Heidi said. 'But how?'

"'We have to go to the cemetery at midnight and swing a dead goat over our heads three times and say the magic words: abra cadaver,'" my father said.

"How did the goat die?" Susie asked in a worried voice.

"He choked on his goat-tee," my father said. "But he was an old goat, so it was no loss."

"Poor goat," Susie said, tears welling up in her eyes.

Realizing that he had gone too far, my father hurriedly backtracked. Blood and gore and death and destruction had been fine for Stephen and me when we were her age, but Susie had a tender heart, especially for animals.

"Oh, wait," my father said, flipping through the pages of the book, as if he were looking for clarification. "My mistake. The goat wasn't dead after all. He was simply afflicted with narcolepsy."

"What?"

"He liked to sleep a lot."

"Oh."

"So Framboise Finn, Jim Hawkins, and Heidi decide to visit Indien Josef's cave in the Swiss Alps, hoping to find a cure for the still-growing wen."

"He was an Indian?" Susie asked. "I thought Indians were in the West."

"This was West Switzerland, home of the Geneva Bureaucrats, a fearsome tribe who will Sioux you at the drop of a Tyrolean hat," my father said.

"Frank, stop ruining a nice story," my mother said interrupting him. She had been listening in the hall with me.

"You tell it then," my father said.

"All right, I will," my mother said. "Give me the book."

"No, I want Daddy to read to me," Susie said, getting out of bed and crawling into his lap.

"You're supposed to be in bed," my mother said. "You don't want Daddy to get sick, do you?"

"I want Daddy to read me stories," Susie said, snuggling in. "He makes me feel gooder."

My mother shook her head, but she didn't have the heart to separate a sick little girl from her father—hygiene be damned.

My father kissed Susie on the top of her head and shrugged. He didn't care if he contracted scarlet fever or sprouted a wen on the side of his nose. He knew he was comforting her, and that was all that mattered. No amount of penicillin could work such wonders.

The lunatic story continued for a few minutes, while Susie nodded sleepily in her father's lap. She could barely keep her eyes open and stopped asking questions about plot holes, obscure words, and character names and ages. That was a good thing, too, because the finale would have frightened small children and literary critics. I listened avidly.

Heidi and the boys were lost in the cave and Indien Josef, the Geneva Bureaucrat, was coming after them. After a series of intricate and miraculous escapes, Heidi was in imminent danger of being caught and served with a writ.

"She didn't want to go to trial," my father intoned, "but there was no place for her to Heidi and she was gone with the wen. The end."

My mother winced at the punch line and plucked the sleeping child from my father's lap and put her back in bed.

"Framboise Finn, indeed," she whispered. "Why can't you just read from the book?"

"That's no fun," my father said.

"None of this is any fun," my mother replied somberly.

Story time was over for the day, but that evening I heard something that chilled me much more than the adventures of Heidi in the cave of the Geneva Bureaucrat. Stephen, who had worked himself up with worry about Susie's condition, asked my mother what was going to happen.

"Susie will be fine in a week or two," my mother said airily.

The words were reassuring, but the tone of my mother's voice was false.

I could recognize a lie when I heard one.

Chapter 8

SUSIE X, MONSTER FROM MARS. John makes a thorough study of the mysterious alien creature in preparation for his first novel. Although Susie was small, she had many dangerous talents.

A Novel Idea

When I was ten, lying interested me a great deal more than babies. It seemed to me that there was no percentage in telling the truth when a lie might save me from punishment. I had come to that conclusion in kindergarten when I had taken a bright red crayon and proudly written my name in foot-high letters on my bedroom wall. When confronted by my less than enthusiastic mother, I told her I didn't do it. No, a big giant gorilla had come into my room and done the deed.

I wasn't stupid enough to think my mother would actually believe such a wild tale, but what choice did I have? If I admitted to writing on the wall, punishment was one hundred percent certain. But if—somehow—she believed the gorilla story, I would get off scot-free. Even if the chances were a million to one, I figured, lying was the only way to go.

So it was with that lesson in mind that I decided to write a novel. I had only recently learned what the word *novel* meant—basically, a pack of lies—and I saw no reason why I shouldn't try my hand at writing one.

I approached my father one evening and told him about my plan. As usual, he had sound advice to offer.

"Why don't you read a few novels before you write one?" he suggested, finding me a copy of *The Adventures of Tom Sawyer.* The book was long, but at least it had pictures and the type wasn't densely packed. Size mattered, even then.

Dutifully, I read every word and drew my own conclusions: If you run away from home (a prospect that thrilled me), make sure everyone thinks you're dead; then if you turn up alive, they'll forgive you anything. Also, rafts were cool and so were caves, although I didn't see much hope in finding either one within biking distance.

Having absorbed the lessons learned by Tom and Huck, I plotted out my own effort with skill and care until I was ready to present the idea to the public.

"Okay, I've read it," I told my father, handing him *Tom Sawyer*. "And I'm ready to start my novel."

"Fair enough," he said. "What are you going to call your tome?"

"My first choice was *Roy Rogers and Superman Fight Bad Guys*," I said. "But I used the thesaurium and changed it to *Roy Rogers and Superman Fight Footpads*." I thought that had a nice ring to it. "Footpads is like bad guys."

"Perhaps a tad too sophisticated for the mass market," my father said. "Besides, your title characters are copyrighted and trademarked. If you use them, you might go to jail."

Jail! I had heard that the pen was mightier than the sword, but this writing business was a lot more dangerous than I had thought.

"What should I do?" I asked.

"Why don't you try reading another novel? It might give you some ideas," he said, producing a copy of *Adventures of Huckleberry Finn*.

"Not another one," I moaned. Reading a novel was a lot harder than just writing one.

Like many amateur writers, I had the unshakable belief that anyone who could pick up a pencil could write a book. Why beginners think this way is a mystery to me. People who pick up pencils don't usually expect to draw like Rembrandt, but they all think they can write like Henry James, or at least like Stephen King or Danielle Steel. I, too, was sure that Mark Twain was nothing special, even a little dull in places, and when the world got a look at my book, Tom, Huck, and all the rest would soon be forgotten.

Teeth gritted, I plowed through *Adventures of Huckleberry Finn* with grim determination. It took me a week to finish the book, but at the end of the ordeal, I decided that rafts were, indeed, cool, but I was skeptical about the king and the duke. They just didn't seem like royalty to me. Certainly, King Arthur would never have seated them at the Round Table.

"There," I said, slamming the book down on the dining room table. "I finished it."

"Fine," said my father. "How did you enjoy Twain's use of irony?"

"There wasn't any iron in it," I said.

"How ironic," my father said. "But what have you decided to write about?"

"Susie," I said.

"A wonderful choice," he said, beaming.

"It's called *Susie X Invades Earth from Mars and Kills Stephen*," I said. "She's this wrinkled red creature with tentacles who gets into her flying saucer and invades Earth and kills Stephen." Hence the descriptive title.

My father's smile faded, and he was probably considering sending me to a psychiatrist, but all he said was, "Derivative, but intriguing."

I scratched my head. I realize now that the only reason I ever went to college was to figure out just what the hell my father was talking about. But his bemused look seemed to indicate approval, so I began my first book.

Not surprisingly, I hit a snag immediately.

Just how do you write a novel, anyway? The real answer, based on thirty years in the publishing business, is: Keep churning out the pages until you have four stacks of paper, each about three feet high. Then you're done. I know that sounds facile, but if you have the fortitude to crank out so much paper, you might find a novel in there somewhere—or at least that's what Jack Kerouac thought. But at the age of ten, I was having a desperately difficult time getting started.

"You'll need the proper tools," my father told me. "Paper, pencils, pens, ink, blotters, erasers, rubber bands, glue, carbon paper, and, of course, a typewriter."

"But I can't type," I said. Writing was not only dangerous—it was complicated.

"Then you'd better learn," he said. "Unless you are Balzac, all manuscript pages must be typed."

There was only one solution to this problem.

"Mom!"

My mother looked up from her book.

"Will you type my novel for me, please?" I begged, making the word *please* sound as if it had seven syllables.

"Of course, dear," she said. "Give it to me in hundred-page increments."

I didn't know what an increment was, but it sounded like a lot.

"Just how long do novels gotta be?" I asked. Surely not as long as Mark Twain's. I wanted my readers to get through my book in one sitting so they could go outside to play baseball and not be stuck in the house reading, as I had been for the past week.

"A novel should be only as long as it needs to be," my father said mysteriously.

I took that to mean short. Interpreting my father's comments was akin to reading Nostradamus: The words had any meaning you cared to find in them.

"I would suggest, however, that you study your subject thoroughly," he continued. "Verisimilitude is all."

"How true," I said. I had no idea what he was talking about, but that was what my mother said when she was being sympathetic and understanding. So I stole the line. Lying and stealing are a novelist's stock-in-trade.

Every writer is to some extent dependent on his life experiences for material, so my being only ten was a distinct handicap. I really hadn't had much of a life that could be translated to the page. That was a problem I solved by purloining other writers' plots and passing them off as my own, a practice, I believe, that still goes on today. But with all the authors in the world, which ones should I choose?

I'd like to say that the two most profound influences on my writing were Proust and Goethe. I'd like to say that, but it's not true. Actually, my early writing was affected by two movies I saw in 1955. Both of them scared the bejesus out of me and made me a lifelong admirer of schlock, pulp, and smut. It all had happened the summer before.

The temperature was in the nineties and there was no air. Worse, there was no air-conditioning. The bulky old Westinghouse had burped, coughed, and blown out its condenser in a shower of sparks.

"It's a bit warm in here, don't you think?" my father said, wiping the perspiration from his face. "Why don't you get the machine fixed?"

"Why don't you take the boys to a movie or something?" my mother said, brushing a damp strand of hair from her brow.

"Movies!" I shouted. Movies were even better than comic books because all you had to do was sit there and be entertained. No reading was involved, and movies were always better than television, which, except for Superman and Roy Rogers, seemed to be dominated by Tennessee Ernie Ford, Arthur Godfrey, and Art Linkletter.

"What's playing at the local theater?" my mother asked.

"I don't know," my father said. "Something about ants."

"That sounds educational," my mother said, perhaps expecting the young Edward O. Wilson to be doing the narration.

What neither of them knew was that the film, *Them!*, was about ants all right—giant twenty-foot ants that lusted after human blood and devoured starlets for breakfast.

Innocently, my father found us seats, and bought us popcorn, candy, and Cokes; then he settled down for a long summer's nap in the arctic chill of the theater. The lights went down and so did my father, out like the lights. Movies, and in later years the New York Mets, had a soporific effect on my father.

The movie began innocuously enough with a blank-eyed little girl clutching a doll and wandering down a deserted highway. Stephen and I wolfed down our popcorn and slurped our Cokes, saving the Raisinets and Goobers, our favorites, for later.

"Where's the ants?" Stephen asked.

Before I could tell him to shut up, out popped a giant, antennae-waving, saliva-slobbering insect that wrapped its mandibles around the first victim and tore the poor woman to shreds. That was enough for Stephen. He let out a cry and slid to the floor. There, amid the chewed bubble gum, squashed Jujubes, melted Hershey bars, and grayish popcorn, he stayed, wrapped in a fetal position, his hands clasped to his ears. I dropped my popcorn on his head because I needed both hands to cover my eyes.

For the next hour, I watched in terror through my fingers as the ants invaded Los Angeles and dispatched countless victims, mostly military men and ladies with big bosoms. When the action got too intense, my fingers would snap shut like the shutter of a camera, blocking out the horror. Thus blinded, all I could hear were the ululating cries from the screen and the occasional whimper from Stephen. My father's snores were completely drowned out by the shrieks of the human ant chow awaiting a chewy, gooey death.

During the climactic scene, while the soldiers were racing to find the queen ant before she could lay two million eggs, my father abruptly woke up. Appalled to find Stephen cowering on the floor and me sitting rigidly in my seat, hands over my eyes, he picked up his younger son, dusted him off, and took us home. We rode in silence, except for the occasional slurping sound, remarkably antlike, of Stephen picking Milk Duds and Jujyfruits off his shirt and eating them. Such recycling wasn't really necessary, however, because we both had uneaten boxes of candy clutched in our clammy hands.

Stephen had nightmares for a week, and every night my mother would get up to put a stop to his screams, while muttering dark imprecations about my father's sanity. I spent that summer killing as many ants as I could find, seeking vengeance for the human race.

I never did see the end of *Them!*, so I don't know for sure if the ants lost. All I know is that every time I visit Los Angeles, I'm wary. As far as I know, those pesky creatures are still there, hiding in the storm drains. Waiting.

If *Them!* gave me ants in my pants, another movie I saw that summer profoundly affected me. No, it wasn't *Citizen Kane*, as you might expect, it was *Invaders from Mars*. Here's the story: A boy wakes up in the middle of the night to see a flying saucer whizzing past his bedroom window. It lands in a wooded area behind his house. He and his father go to investigate and the father disappears into what looks like a sand trap on a golf course. The boy runs home, sure his father is dead. But the old man returns alive—except he has a glazed look in his eye and a mechanical quality to his voice, rather like my own father early in the morning.

Pretty soon the entire town is infested with these zombies, who have had devices drilled into their necks by the Martians from the saucer. The kid is frantic because everyone from the friendly local policeman to his friendly elementary schoolteacher is under alien control—and they want him to join their hivelike society, which is led by a severed golden head in a glass jar.

No socialist, the boy thwarts the Martians and their slaves at every turn. Of course, the Mars men were a pretty slow-moving bunch, impeded perhaps by their monster suits, which were ill-fitting. You could actually see where the suits zipped up the back, but the movie was convincing enough for me. When I was not squashing ants, I spent a considerable amount of time surreptitiously peering at people's necks, hoping to find and expose some Martian spies. But other than a boil or two, I never did discover anything definitive.

At the conclusion of the movie—and here comes the good part— the army defeats the Martians and sends them scurrying back to their hellish planet. The end, right? Wrong. The kid wakes up—it was all a dream. He's a bit shaky, but his parents calm him down and he goes back to bed. Then, just as he's about to drift off, a flying saucer goes whizzing past his window! Is it happening for real this time or is the kid only having a new dream? I was astounded by the brilliance of this conceit and used it freely for years. I inserted dream sequences into everything I wrote, including book reports and one-page essays about famous Americans—much to the distress of my teachers.

Here's a sample that has survived. I've cleaned it up to make it intelligible to the general reader.

Last night I woke up and saw some wood teeth on my pillow. They belonged to George Washington. But the tooth fairy said she wasn't going to pay any money on them because they were false and I couldn't wear them anyway because they were too big and had splinters in them. But they were okay for our First President who didn't have any real ones to wear. He said, "I cannot tell a lie." And I can't either. I didn't really find his wood teeth on my pillow. It was all a dream. Ha, ha. Or was it?

What a clever kid I was—a master of the surprise ending at the age of ten. Take that, Ambrose Bierce. Stuff a sock in it, O. Henry. With writing like that, was it any wonder I thought I could knock out a novel in record time? By combining the story lines of my two favorite movies, I was confident I could produce a masterpiece over the weekend. First, however, I had to thoroughly investigate my bloodthirsty protagonist.

Armed with my trusty Midland Insurance Company ballpoint pen and a lined notepad from Woolworth's, I stalked my quarry. Tentacled creatures from Mars are notoriously touchy, apt to burst out crying at odd moments, so I tiptoed into Susie's room, bent on observing the beast in her natural habitat.

The lair of the monster was hideous—creepy yellow walls covered with nursery-rhyme characters who cavorted about in what could only be described as a dance of death. Grotesque stuffed animals haunted every corner of the room and stared at me menacingly with cold, beady eyes. Worse, over Susie's cage was a massive energy cannon cleverly disguised as a mobile of ducks, sheep, and cows. The cage itself was a flimsy affair. The wooden bars of the crib (as the cage was called) were insubstantial and could hardly be counted on to contain the fierce creature within. There had to be a force field at work somewhere to keep her immobilized.

The creature herself was smaller than a breadbox. She was encased in a kind of jumpsuit, one with built in feet, just like the space guys wore. The embroidered pink bunnies on her space suit were, I was sure, Mars men in rabbit clothing, waiting to be activated by their mistress.

The monster's head was particularly revolting because there was a soft spot right in the middle of it. That was the port where she hooked in her communications device. The device itself was a white crocheted cap with chin straps to prevent it from flying away during Martian hurricanes and to keep her hair in place. Not that she had much hair. But what she did have was pale and frizzy, much like the tufts of hair found on a mammoth. (We had been studying mammoths in school.)

Her eyes were dangerously blue—all the better to hypnotize you with, my dear. You had to be careful of those eyes, because they could almost make you think the creature was harmless and lead you to utter such nonsense as "Awww, isn't she cute." I had seen it happen before— many times.

The monster's mouth was lined with sharp, retractable teeth. Oh, the casual observer might see only smooth pink gums, but those of us who studied these things knew that any time she wanted, she could produce hollow fangs; and like Dracula, she could drink your blood.

The creature stirred.

"Gleep," she squeaked.

Uh-oh, it was waking up.

"Waaaa."

Then it did what I had been dreading. With a fearsome burp, it disgorged a white, milky fluid—all that was left of her last victim.

In addition to mammoths, we had been studying birds in school. I knew that owls, when they digested a mouse, cast a pellet that contained the inedible parts of the mouse, such as the bones and fur. This monster did the same thing. Gross.

"What are you doing?" Stephen asked me as I was making notes.

"Saying good-bye to Aunt Eliza," I said.

"Is she here?" he asked.

"Yes, in a way," I said mournfully and with great reverence.

"Where?" he asked.

"Right here," I said, pointing to the pool of spit up in the crib. "Poor Aunt Eliza. That's all that's left of her."

"Mom!" Stephen yelled, running out of the room, his eyes wide.

That was the great thing about Stephen in those days: He believed everything I said—a trait, by the way, that has not carried over into adulthood.

Susie X, the Monster from Mars, looked up at me with her dangerous China-blue eyes, intent on hypnotizing me, and then she smiled. I ran from the room before she could shoot out her fangs and drink my blood. But it was a narrow escape.

As a creature from another planet, Susie fulfilled every expectation, but as a literary character, she presented some monstrous problems. The first problem was language. If I had been Anthony Burgess, I could have created an entirely new vocabulary and included a dictionary at the back of the book as he did in *A Clockwork Orange*. I settled, however, for a narrator who translated her remarks. That was much easier.

The second problem was one of authenticity. Not many people viewed Susie with such pretend fear and loathing. I had to convince my readers just how horrible Susie X was—not an easy task when my entire audience consisted of her doting parents. However, when in doubt, I have always relied on spurting blood and fearsome teeth, a formula that has proven effective over the years.

The work was arduous, but I had a supreme confidence born of supreme ignorance that saw me through (most) of the task. So here it is. I left in some of the more obvious mistakes to give you the flavor of this epic—and to titillate the copy editors who will think they have stumbled upon an erroneous zone.

It was a very red day on the Red Planet. Not a creture was stirring not even a mouse except Susie X a horribel monster from Mars. Her tentikles itched with hungar and she had to get to earth to eat food so she wouldn't be hungry any more. There was no food on Mars.

"How do I get to earth?" she wondered to herself. She was so hungry she spit up and wet her spacesuit. "I know, I will get in my flying sawcer and fly to earth."

She used her slimy tentikles to fly the flying sawcer to earth. "Boy am I hungary," she said. But no one could understand her because she talked Martian.

She put on the breaks and yelled at the other drivers like Dad does and stopped. Using her anti gravety devise she flyed through the sky looking for a victem. She found her first one. He was a boy named Stephen and he was eating a ham sandwich.

"Waaaa," she said.

That meant she was going to kill him and drink his blood like a Marteeny. A Martian Marteeny, which she liked with an olive.

"Oh pleeezeee don't eat me," cryed Stephen.

"Waaaa."

That meant something bad which I'm not allowed to write.

"How about eating my ham sandwich instead of me? It's got mustard," articulated Stephen. [The *thesaurium* at work.]

"Waaaa."

In Martian that is "Fee fi fo fum, I smell the blood of an Stephenmun."

She was 10 feet high and mad. Real mad and real hungary and in no mood for ham sandwiches even with mustard. She wanted blood.

I'll spare you the sanguine details, but be assured that the diabolical Susie X eats her way through most of the United States—until the army blows her up into "a thousand million pieces."

Then—and here comes the good part—Stephen wakes up. Surprise! It was all a dream. Relieved, he tries to go back to sleep, but he finds, to his horror, that he has changed into a giant spider. (O, Kafka, where is thy sting?)

I was going to have Stephen/Spider travel to Mars on a long piece of spiderweb to kill Susie X, but I ran out of steam on page twelve and abandoned the project. But who knows? Maybe I can punch it up and sell it one day. *Susie X Invades Earth from Mars and Kills Stephen* features evil aliens, plucky kids, and a shocking surprise ending. Further, the story has been crafted entirely from stolen plot lines and is filled with outrageous lies—important requisites for the modern screenplay.

Wait a minute, is that Steven Spielberg calling?

No, I lied.

I probably just dreamed the whole thing.

Chapter 9

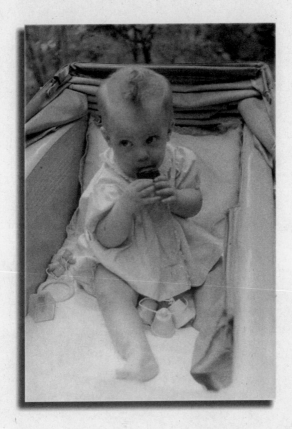

TEN CENTS A RIDE. Settled comfortably in the spacious
Torpedo, Susie awaits the next inning of The Game
with cleverly concealed enthusiasm.

The Game

In June of 1952, three years before Susie was born, we moved to a new neighborhood and I left all my friends behind. I believed then that I would live the rest of my life in solitude, never seeing anyone my own age again. That was a depressing thought for a six-year-old, especially one who had to endure an endless summer before school started in the fall. I was miserable and not shy about taking it out on anyone close at hand. Stephen, who was three, took the brunt of my unhappiness.

"Stop moping around," my mother told me countless times. "And stop using your brother as a punching bag."

But what else could I do? Moping around and beating up on Stephen were the only ways I could express my anger at being ripped away from everything that was familiar. Luckily, I wasn't allowed to play with matches, or the alternative might have been arson. Looking back, I think my mother should have been grateful for my nonincendiary behavior.

"Why don't you go to the playground?" she would ask me every day.

"Too far," I'd say.

Of course, it wasn't too far at all, but I needed an excuse to maintain my maudlin moping and to keep up my pugilistic predations.

In secret I had skulked around the perimeter of the playground, which was bound on three sides by a wire fence; along the other side was a stone wall and, above the wall, a row of attached houses. There was a parking lot to the right of the dusty field and, beyond that, a warehouse with a low roof that even the clumsiest of climbers could scale. As I watched from behind a parked car one day, I saw that most of the children were busily engaged in playing what I came to know as kick baseball or simply The Game. I had run away quickly because I was afraid that someone might talk to me or, worse, might not talk to me at all.

Fortunately, Job had a lot more patience than my mother, and she soon grew weary of my nonsense.

"Come on," she said with grim determination. "I'll take you to the playground myself and introduce you to all the children."

The sheer horror of that thought propelled me out the door in a flash. I walked the last mile as slowly as I could, a practice, I believe, that was invented by prisoners facing imminent execution. My plan was to waste a few minutes watching The Game, then return home and tell my mother that no one would play with me. But like most plans I have made in my life, this one didn't work out either.

Fearfully, I stood outside the fence, looking in with envy as the kids played with utter concentration and intensity. In one corner of the playground there was a large sandbox filled with babies, toddlers, pails, shovels, dolls, dogs, and even some sand. As I discovered later, the sandbox was a kind of jail for little kids who were too young to play The Game.

I was just about to leave when I heard a voice call out, "Hey, kid."

I looked over my shoulder like the Three Stooges did when addressed as "gentlemen." But there was no one behind me. So I pointed to myself and looked puzzled. The speaker was a big kid, maybe eleven or twelve. He was wearing a blue baseball cap, a white T-shirt, and red shorts—very patriotic.

"Yeah, you," the big kid said. "You wanna play?"

Did I! But I just shrugged.

"Go out to right field, up there on the hill. Try to catch the ball on the fly. If you catch the ball on the bounce, throw it in to me," he said.

I could do that!

I hustled out to where I had been directed, took up my position, and stared anxiously at the playground. The big kid was pitching (actually rolling a soccer-size red rubber ball) on the ground for the batter. The object of the game was to kick the ball and run the bases. Each side got three outs, which could be made by catching the ball on the fly or by tagging the base ahead of the runner or by hitting the base runner with the ball.

There was no second base, I noted, and the rules were fluid, changing with the makeup of the teams, the weather, and the whims of the players. You had to pay attention—what was foul one inning might be fair the next.

Games were nine innings long; then adjustments were made if the previous game had been a laugher of, say, eighty-nine to fourteen. The teams stayed the same after a squeaker of thirty-two to twenty-eight— unless, of course, somebody had to go home for lunch or visit his grandmother or leave for some equally bogus reason.

As I stood in right field that day, I prayed that nobody would kick the ball to me, but I soon realized, not for the first time, that the power of prayer was definitely a hit-or-miss proposition. The very next player powered a line drive in my direction. Instinct took over and I raced for the ball, determined to grab it before it hit the ground. I took a flying lunge at the last moment and managed to catch the ball on the tips of my fingers—just before I smashed head-first into a large elm tree. Stunned, I fell flat on my face, seeing explosions of light, but the red rubber ball was clasped to my chest. No one was going to take that ball away unless they pried it from my cold, dead fingers.

"Good catch," the big kid called out to me, as I struggled to my feet. "Watch out for trees."

However sage, his advice was a bit late. I could feel the sticky blood trickling down my left eyebrow and into my eye. I wiped the blood away with a grimy hand, willing myself not to cry, and threw the ball back to the pitcher. My head was throbbing, my vision was blurry, and the blood kept oozing out of a gash in my forehead. But it didn't matter. I was a player, a part of The Game. It was the best day of my short life.

For the next few years, kick baseball *was* summer. I played The Game from sunup until well after sundown, with only a few time-outs for water, bathroom, and TV breaks. I was impervious to heat and fatigue and I would have played all day and all night if that had been possible. The problem was the damn sun. It kept setting just when The Game got interesting. We didn't have any lights, and playing in the dark was hazardous. Once we attempted to illuminate the field with massed flashlights, but that ploy met with little success. In desperation we even tried crushing fireflies and smearing their glowing parts on the ball. That didn't work too well, either, but it proved that our obsession with The Game was total. Nothing on Earth was more interesting than kick baseball, unless it was cramps.

I was fascinated by cramps. I didn't quite know what they were, but my mother had told me that if I drank too much cold water, too quickly, I would get cramps. I drank gallons of ice water every summer, trying to get them, but I never succeeded. After years of trying, I had to conclude that I had been the victim of a tale from an old wife.

Although I was dedicated to The Game, I would quit playing every weekday afternoon and run home to watch *Superman* on our giant, twenty-one-inch, black-and-white Muntz TV. I would sit for a half hour and gulp down ice water, hoping for cramps, totally enthralled as the Man of Steel outwitted some pretty dumb enemies. I mean, here was a guy who could change the course of mighty rivers beating up on petty criminals who had robbed a country store run by someone called "Pops."

Kryptonite, however, was almost as interesting as cramps, and I spent an inordinate amount of time trying to acquire some. If I were able to corner the market, I thought, the bad guys couldn't use it to threaten Superman. I had a miscellaneous collection of rocks stashed in an old cigar box under my bed. Although I couldn't tell feldspar from Fels Naphtha, I was positive that one greenish stone was indeed kryptonite. I knew this because, when I held it, I really felt faint. But that was probably just the ice water.

At five-thirty-three I would return to The Game and we would play until dark—and sometimes beyond, depending on how long the firefly guts held out. The day ended when it was time to go home and go to bed. Then I would dream about kick baseball until it was time to go out and play again.

My endless fascination with The Game was based on its mutability. Each day—no, each inning—brought rule changes or even player swaps. The idea was to field two roughly equal teams, a difficult task when each side had between four and ten players, ranging in age from five to twelve. The big kids made the arrangements, sorting out the bad players and the good, trying for balance. If someone were having a particularly good day, he might find himself traded to the losing side, just to even things up. The closer the score, the better we liked it. That led to some odd configurations. A team might consist of two ten-year-olds, two nine-year-olds, two eight-year-olds, and a kindergartner. The opposition might be two twelve-year-olds and an eleven-year-old (the big guns), and six bumbling first-graders, who were pretty much useless in the field or at bat. But if they could kick at all, they could play.

This was a kid-run game and that was the point. Adults had no part in it. Nobody over the age of twelve was around to cheer or boo or create confusion. No one needed to drive us anywhere or to provide us with any equipment—have legs, will kick. Today, such a game would send icy chills into the hearts of Little League officials everywhere.

On occasion, of course, we descended to a *Lord of the* (Fire)*Flies* level, but we worked out our problems quickly, using fists or insults, and we did not require adult referees to make us behave or conform. Kick baseball was truly democratic, run by and for the kids. No parents even knew or cared about what we did on the playground—as long as it kept us occupied fourteen hours a day and it didn't involve playing in traffic or with matches.

Then one lazy July morning all the good times almost came to an end.

"Remember, I want you back here at ten o'clock to take care of your sister," my mother told me that morning. "Stephen has a doctor's appointment."

"Do I got to?" I whined

"Yes, you have to," my mother said in her "you're doomed anyway, so you might as well do it" voice.

"But The Game," I double-whined. I looked down at my bowl of Kellogg's Sugar Frosted Flakes and pouted. All of a sudden they didn't taste so *gr-r-reat!*

"Take Susie with you," my mother said. "She'd love to watch you play."

Now that was the dumbest thing I had ever heard. At seven months, Susie still didn't do many tricks. She could sit up, gurgle, and poop pretty good, but that was about it. Didn't my mother understand? I had The Game to play and I couldn't be distracted by a baby. Besides, I was Keeper of the Ball that week, a position of awesome responsibility. The Keeper was trusted with making sure that the volleyball (which we now used, since the red rubber ball had burst several years before) was inflated to the proper pressure and to see that it was more or less clean. But the most important function of that important functionary was to be the first on the field every morning. Slackers, slugabeds, and layabouts were severely chastised and banned from ever holding office again. Tears, recriminations, oaths of fealty, and saying "pretty please with sugar on top" were of no use. A disgraced Keeper was a Keeper no more.

It was almost seven-fifteen and I had to run.

"Don't forget," my mother called after me as I slammed out the door, the volleyball under my arm. "Ten o'clock sharp."

The Game began promptly at seven-thirty with three-man pickup teams playing halfheartedly until we had a quorum of eight players. Then we got down to business—or at least they did. I was so distracted that I missed two easy catches.

"What's wrong with you?" my friend Brian Thompson asked me.

"Nothin'."

"You're playing like an old lady," he said.

"Shut up," I said, always the master of the witty riposte.

We went back to playing, but my mind was busy sorting out options. I could just not turn up at ten o'clock sharp. But then my mother would come looking for me and yell at me in front of the other kids. I could run away to Texas and become a cowboy. That was appealing, but I couldn't be sure that Texas cowboys played kick baseball. I could take Susie to the lake and we could feed the ducks. But that would take hours while The Game went on without me. The more I thought about my predicament, the fewer choices I seemed to have.

A ball sailed past my head, almost decapitating me. I hadn't even noticed.

"Let's trade him," Brian said about me. "We'll take any first grader."

"Thanks a lot, boogernose," I said, appalled at the thought of being traded for a gap-toothed seven-year-old.

"Then pay attention," Brian said.

"I gotta go," I said.

"Good riddance," Brian said.

"But I'll be back," I said.

"Thanks for the warning."

I ran home close to tears. My day—no, my life—was in ruins. By making me take my sister to the playground, my mother had destroyed me. I thought it couldn't get any worse, but when I slunk home, I found waiting for me a horror that was more chilling than any I could have imagined. Even Superman would have been struck dumb with terror. I know I was, for there waiting for me were my mother, my sister, and the Black Torpedo of Doom.

"Doesn't she look adorable?" my mother said.

Adorable? That was not a word in the vocabulary of a ten-year-old boy. In fact, it was a restricted word like *cute, vegetables,* or *bath*—a word uttered at one's peril.

Poor Susie was decked out in a little pink dress with puffy sleeves. White lace and blue bows ran riot over the silky fabric. Worse, she was wearing a matching pink bonnet that kept sliding off her head and covering her face, much to her distress. She began to wail with the intensity of a dentist's drill.

I eyed her critically and instantly knew two things. First, I would be laughed off the playground. My days of playing The Game were over. And second, I had been right about her being from Mars.

"She's crying," I said, as if that might spare me.

"That's because she can't wait to see you play kickball," my mother said, fixing Susie's bonnet and tying it under her chubby chin with a pink ribbon.

"Kick baseball," I corrected, but I wasn't buying any of it. "Do I have to take her?"

"John," my mother said in her patented warning voice.

"Do I have to take the Torpedo?" I moaned. "Couldn't I just carry her under my arm like a football? She's not that heavy."

"John Smith!"

Oh God, now she's using my middle name, I thought. *I'm lost.*

Under duress, I hoisted Susie into the Black Torpedo of Doom and propped her up against the back of the commodious carriage. She gave me a gummy smile and said something in Martian.

"Here's a spare diaper," my mother said, "in case you have to change her."

Yeah, right, Mom.

"Have fun," my mother said cheerily.

She really didn't get it at all.

"Come on, Mars girl," I said, wheeling the baby out of the house.

I paused at the top of the hill to work up my courage. The Black Torpedo of Doom weighed about as much as a small car and probably could have hit a hundred miles an hour if unchecked. Fortunately, it had good brakes and I used them liberally on the way down the hill, filling the air with the smell of burning rubber.

When we reached level ground alive, which was always gratifying, I took a moment to catch my breath and appraise my little sister. Something had to be done about her sissy clothes. The first thing I did was to remove the ridiculous bonnet, which made her look like a pint-size wagon-train lady. That was better. Then I took off the frilly pink dress, wondering just what my mother had been thinking. In all my years as a playground rat, I had never seen a kid dressed like Susie. She looked totally unsuitable for wallowing in the dirty sandbox.

I shoved the dress and bonnet under the carriage mattress. Susie was now wearing a pink check diaper, little white shoes, and pink scalloped socks. The shoes might have been suitable for playing kick baseball because they had sturdy square toes, but they were only about three inches long, and anyway, Susie couldn't kick unless she was lying on her back. Then she looked like a hapless turtle. Hell, she couldn't even stand up by herself. The shoes and socks joined the dress and bonnet.

I was now down to basic baby, but there was still something wrong. I took off my favorite red baseball cap and put it on her head. I turned up the brim so she could see; then I stood back to inspect my work. Better, I thought. Not great, but at least I hoped I wouldn't be tossed out of The Game for arriving unannounced with a frilly pink alien.

Pushing the monstrous carriage to the playground, I parked Susie under the shade of the cherry trees, where she could see the little kids in the sandbox.

"Do anything you want," I told her sternly. "Just don't cry and make spectacles of yourself."

She gurgled and drooled in response.

Suddenly, there was silence in the playground—the players stopped The Game, the babies stopped squalling, the dogs stopped barking, and even the birds stopped singing. Had the earth opened up and swallowed me, I wouldn't have been surprised.

I took a deep breath. The moment I had been dreading had arrived. Several of the players came over and surrounded the carriage.

"What's that?" Brian asked.

"That's my sister," I growled, my fists balled, ready to fight. "What of it?"

"No," Brian said. "That thing she's in."

I relaxed.

"That's the Black Torpedo of Doom. And you'd better not mess with it," I said with all the menace I could muster, "unless I give you permission."

"Whadda you mean?" he asked.

"What I mean is: If you give me a quarter, I'll let you push it."

"How about a dime?" he said. "That's all I got."

"Sold," I said, releasing the brake.

For the next hour, The Game came to a halt as kid after kid paid his money and pushed the Black Torpedo of Doom and its passenger up and down the field, usually at breakneck speed. Susie loved it. I could tell because she wet her diaper in appreciation. Several times.

When everybody had had his turn, I parked the gargantuan vehicle under the cherry trees again and Susie promptly fell asleep. She and the Torpedo were both a bit tired and dusty, but a little water would quickly revive them both.

So it turned out I hadn't slogged through Mark Twain for nothing. Tom Sawyer had his whitewash, I had the Black Torpedo.

That day I made a buck twenty and The Game continued.

PART THREE

COMPLICATIONS

"Come on, gang. My father has a theater in the backyard. Let's put on a show!" my mother said, doing her best to sound like the young Judy Garland.

"Good Lord," my father said, not sounding at all like Mickey Rooney. "The strain has finally snapped your mother's shower cap."

"It will be fun," she said with as much exuberance as she could muster.

"No, it won't. Can't I just get out of this house?" Stephen whined. "I want to live somewhere else."

We were entering our second week of quarantine and everybody, including the patient, was heartily sick of the isolation and mind-numbing boredom. So far, none of the rest of us had shown any sign of catching Susie's scarlet fever, but the poor little girl was getting sicker each day.

"Let's do it for Susie," my mother said. "She'll love it."

"Why not?" I said. "If I have to watch one more minute of Arthur Godfrey on TV, I'm going to jump off the roof."

Afternoon television in those days was appalling and appallingly awful—rather like it is today. Even a stupid idea like putting on a show for Susie sounded preferable. So that's how our tribute to the late, great Jules Verne began.

My father selected *Around the World in Eighty Days* because his original concept was to perform the play entirely in French. But after carefully considering the caliber of his cast and crew, he wisely switched back to English.

To prepare us for this extravaganza, my father read us the novel, chose four scenes to dramatize, and coached us in our parts. Stephen and I were put to work on the scenery with paint and crayon; Mom whipped up a few costumes; and Dad wrote the script. Susie lay in bed, unaware that her suffering was about to increase severalfold. Our effort would have caused M. Verne not only to spin in his grave, but to pop out of it and come looking for us, murder on his deceased mind.

Because we were still supposed to avoid contact with her, our stage was a narrow hallway just outside Susie's bedroom. That gave the production a certain claustrophobic feel that might have been considered brilliant if Alfred Hitchcock had thought of it, but for us, it was just crowded.

The scenes my father chose were: Phileas Fogg at his London club, betting that he could travel around the world in eighty days; Fogg and his faithful servant, Passepartout, in Spain; the rescue of Mrs. Aouda from certain death; and Fogg's triumphant moment, collecting the wager. Curiously, after his initial horror of the project, my father threw himself into the play with a certain monomaniacal brio seen mostly in the works of early twentieth-century German directors. For a while, it even seemed as if he had developed a slight Teutonic accent to accompany his dictatorial manner. My mother told him that if he took to wearing jodhpurs and carrying a whip, she would go on strike.

"Actresses," my father muttered. *"Mein Gott!"*

Of the four scenes my father had chosen, the most dramatic was the rescue of Mrs. Aouda from the suttee. For those who haven't read the book, or seen the 1956 movie starring David Niven and Shirley MacLaine, here's what's going on:

Phileas Fogg, a rich and mysterious British gentleman, bets his whist partners at the Reform Club of London that he can circumnavigate the globe in just eighty days. His friends wager twenty thousand pounds he can't do it. But bursting with confidence—some would say arrogance—Fogg takes his new servant, Passepartout (roughly "passkey" in French), and leaves England that very night. After many adventures, Fogg finds himself in India, racing for the coast. Well, not exactly racing, for the train line ends suddenly in the middle of a jungle (roughly "rain forest" in modern English), fifty miles from his destination. Stranded, he is forced to purchase an elephant named Kiouni at a ruinously expensive price. When Fogg and his companions stop for the night, they witness a strange procession of Brahmins on their way to perform a suttee—the ritual burning of a dead maharaja's very much alive widow. The ceremony was supposed to be voluntary, but Mrs. Aouda is not a willing victim. Fogg, outraged at such a heathen custom, vows to rescue the unfortunate damsel in distress from the bloodthirsty fakirs, and make the world safe for British fair play and good manners.

The cast of our production was as follows:

Phileas Fogg, British gentleman extraordinaire, world traveler, and David Niven look-alike: Frank Littell.
Mrs. Aouda, beautiful widow, condemned to die on a funeral pyre: Mary Littell.
Sabu, evil, bloodthirsty fakir: John Littell
Kiouni, ruinously expensive elephant: Stephen Littell
Captive Audience: Susie
Key Grip: I never did know what that was.

Our costumes, by the way, matched our acting abilities. My father wore his tuxedo, which he maintained was the proper attire for a British gentleman in the jungle—or at least he thought David Niven would approve. Mom found a multicolored scarf that served as a sorry sari. I had a bath-towel turban, shorts, and a plastic sword. Stephen, who won the coveted role of Kiouni because of his excellent elephant impression, was decked out in huge ears made of paper plates. He used his arm as a trunk, and to make it more convincing, he wore a gray sock on his hand to simulate the correct color.

The scene took place at night, so we turned out the lights in the hall. That made it difficult to see our scenery, but that was probably just as well. Our flats were pretty flat, although I thought I did a good job portraying the pagoda where the action took place. Here's how it went:

SCENE: Exterior: Night. Near the Pagoda of Death.
FOGG: I say, this is a bit of a sticky wicket, what?
KIOUNI: (ear-shattering elephant sounds)
FOGG: Quiet, Kiouni, you'll alert the natives.
SABU: Halt, who goes there?
KIOUNI: It is I, Kiouni. [My father was a stickler for good grammar.]

SABU: Okay, then. It's only an elephant. I thought it might be a wandering and debonaire Englishman come to rescue Mrs. Aouda.

CAPTIVE AUDIENCE: Hi, Mommy.

MRS. AOUDA: Shhh.

KIOUNI: Shut up, Susie.

FOGG: Will both of you cheeky beggars put a lid on it please?

CAPTIVE AUDIENCE: Okay, Daddy.

MRS. AOUDA: Oh, will no one save me from these bloodthirsty fakirs?

SABU: (twirling mustache, applied with burnt cork) Ah ha, ha, ha! You're in for a hot time on the old town tonight, Mrs. Aouda!

FOGG: Not if I can help it, old man.

SABU: (incredulously) Phileas Fogg!

FOGG: It is I and I have come to rescue the fair, uh, the dusky Mrs. Aouda from certain death and spicy Indian food.

SABU: I'll run you through like a shish kebab.

FOGG: Don't try to *curry* favor with me, Sabu. Take one step, old boy, and I will instruct my ruinously expensive elephant to trample you.

SABU: Elephant? Elephant? I don't need no stinkin' elephant.

KIOUNI: (charging) Stinking? I'll get you!

SABU: (lying on ground, trampled to death) Arrghh!

CAPTIVE AUDIENCE: Don't hurt Mommy, Kiouni.

MRS. AOUDA: Oh, thank you, brave Phileas Fogg, for saving me from the bloodthirsty fakirs. Will you marry me?

FOGG:

MRS. AOUDA: Frank!

FOGG: What? Oh, whatever you say, my dear.

SABU: (still dead) Arrghh!

Around the World in Eighty Days was published in 1873, but never in its long history had it ever been so damaged. At the triumphal moment when Phileas Fogg realizes that he has won the bet because crossing the international dateline has given him an extra day, Susie drifted off into a restless sleep. She looked a lot sicker at the end of the show than she had at the beginning. And who could blame her? But Mom, still dressed in her ridiculous scarf, quickly shed her character, and phoned Dr. Alexander. Although it was a Sunday afternoon, he came right away.

The news was not good. In fact, it was disastrous. Susie's scarlet fever had turned into rheumatic fever, a much more virulent disease that can lead to valve damage and other heart disorders. My parents were crushed by the diagnosis. I looked in on Susie a little later and found her clutching her stomach in pain and crying softly. As I stood there, her nose began to bleed. I got a tissue and mopped her up as best I could, but I realized that all the king's horses and all the king's men—even a ruinously expensive elephant—might not be able to put poor Susie back together again.

Chapter 10

NO DAY AT THE BEACH. Taking a break before
going to collect Susie's prize—the fateful
and highly incendiary pizza.

Gwill Go Boom

In the summer of 1957, my father rented a house on the beach in Westhampton, Long Island. That sounds ruinously expensive, but in those days Westhampton was not the tony community it is to-day. It was more Petticoat Junction than Rodeo Drive. Dune Road, where we lived, was a deserted rural street that meandered through long stretches of howling wilderness.

The house itself was a rambling, ramshackle . . . shack set behind an enormous sand dune that towered ominously over the roof. We had a dazzling view of the asphalt road and trackless acres of scrubby brush. On cloudy days the place exuded such gloom that my father compared it to living behind a slag heap in a Welsh mining town.

"And I'm paying three hundred dollars a month to live like this?" he complained, his valley not green at all.

What I remember most about the house was the smell of oilcloth. In small doses, that is not an unpleasant odor, but in our place it was overpowering. The walls were covered with oilcloth, the curtains were made of it, the counters in the kitchen were plastered with it, and even the floors, which were linoleum, were cleverly designed to look like oilcloth. The house, naturally, smelled like oilcloth and, unnaturally, of Bain de Soleil, then a new suntan lotion on the market. My mother, proud that she could pronounce the name correctly (ban de solay), bought it by the carload and smeared it on Stephen, Susie, and me at every opportunity. The problem with suntan lotion, of course, is that once you slather it on and lie in the sand, you end up looking like a veal cutlet.

Yet despite its drawbacks, we loved Westhampton. These days an address on Dune Road is considered a sign of success and celebrity. But back then it was an indication that you were too poor or too poorly connected socially to join your betters in East Hampton or Southampton, farther out on the Island. The closest house to us belonged to the stage manager of *The Ed Sullivan Show,* but neither Ed nor any of his headliners ever ventured our way until many years later. Topo Gigio was much too snooty for Westhampton, I guess.

But the great advantage to being penniless and déclassé was freedom. Had we taken a house in East Hampton, my mother would have felt it necessary to dress us up and take us out to concerts, plays, and fancy house parties. We would have had to behave and be polite all summer. As it was, we ran wild for a month, descending into a kind of primitive state that, fortunately, precluded jackets, ties, and manners.

Stephen and I lived in our bathing suits, an inconvenience Susie never really took to. She preferred to go au naturel most of the time. I got tired of finding her shed suit and stuffing her back into it, so I just let her run naked and free. Who cared? The beach was practically deserted. Looking to the left, as far as I could see, there was a solitary person on a blanket, maybe half a mile away. To the right, again in the distance, a lone dog was charging the surf and retreating with the waves. That was it. We had miles of beach to ourselves.

At first I was dubious about taking Susie to the beach. I was afraid that she would be a pain in the neck, but she proved to be pretty self-sufficient. When she got restless, I would stop our games, grab her by an arm and a leg, and toss her high into the air. She would land in the water, gasping and giggling, and demand another ride through space. Stephen also kept a watchful eye on her, running down the beach to retrieve her if she wandered too far away. He would admonish her to stay put and she usually obeyed. When I yelled at her, Susie just laughed at me. Stephen's threats were a lot more believable than mine. Susie knew a sucker when she saw one and I never got an even break.

What occupied us that summer, among other things, was engineering. Abetted by the kids next door, we built elaborate sand castles near the ocean and provided them with sluice ways to drain off the incoming surf. The idea was to make a castle that could stand up to the sea for as long as possible. We graded ourselves on how well our creations fared.

When castle building became boring, we would body surf, play chicken, or toss a ball around. Susie, who was eighteen months old, watched us splash through the waves, and was usually content to dig up pailfuls of sand, then empty her bucket and begin again. She especially liked the tiny sand crabs she uncovered in her excavations, and she named them all.

"Sally, come back," she would cry when one of the startled creatures escaped her clutches and dove back into the sand for protection.

And those little crabs needed protection or they would have wound up as guests at a mad tea party given by their tormentor. Susie would place the crabs in a circle on her overturned pail, and talk to them. She offered them tea, but not sympathy.

"Dwink tea," she would exhort them. "Dwink. Bad Patty, bad Judy."

As far as I could tell, all the sand crabs had girls' names, but male or female, they had a universal desire to escape. Lewis Carroll should have gone to the beach once in a while if he really wanted to know about demented tea parties.

Every morning we would escape the house at dawn, and by eleven o'clock, we were starving. Lunch was easy. Most mornings my mother would pack us a plastic bag containing a dull knife, lemon wedges, Cokes, little blue containers of Morton's salt, and a peanut butter and jelly sandwich for Susie. We put the Cokes in the water to keep them cool; then when we were hungry, we went clamming. In a couple of minutes we would uncover dozens of Little Neck and Cherrystone clams, open them, salt them, lemon them, and eat them while they were still kicking. I don't believe shellfish can get much fresher than that. Today, I suppose you would die of diphtheria or some other dread disease if you ate raw seafood from Westhampton beach.

Susie was not a clam aficionado like we were, hence the PB&J. She did try to eat a sand crab once, but it nipped her nose and she went back to serving them tea.

After lunch, we would wait an hour before going back into the water. Why we thought we would cramp up and die if we went swimming fifty-nine minutes after eating escapes me. But everybody's mother knew it to be true, and they imparted their misinformation to us in the form of stern lectures.

So, we would lie on the beach and watch the sun progress across the high blue sky and attempt to guess what time it was. Nobody had a watch or felt the need for one. The days stretched out endlessly before us—days filled with hot sun and cool green water, scorched sand and succulent clams. I couldn't imagine it would ever end.

During those long afternoon siestas we were often visited by Skippy the Dog. Not plain, old Skippy, but Skippy the Dog, like Smokey the Bear. We used all three names to distinguish him from Skippy the Boy, who lived next door, and it was an important distinction when it came to passing out the blame.

"I didn't break it. Skippy did," could lead to all kinds of confusion and false accusations.

"Skippy the Boy threw up on the porch," however, left no doubt as to who the culprit was.

Unfortunately, Skippy the Dog was not a friendly beagle, but a cold-blooded mercenary. He wouldn't play with us unless a luncheon was provided. So we would bribe him with the remains of Susie's peanut butter and jelly sandwich to buy a few minutes of his valuable time. Then he would take off on his rounds, ignoring us until the larder was restocked.

Around one p.m. my mother would make a foray to the beach to work on her tan. We were always glad to see her because she was invariably accompanied by Oreo cookies, and when she retreated to the house, she took Susie with her. Then the games could really begin.

We held swimming races that took us perilously close to the shores of Europe, which we knew were out there somewhere to the east. And we had monster games of Frisbee, then newly invented. My favorite sport was making flying leaps for the silvery Frisbee and smashing into the waves. After a score of body-pounding crashes, I would be the pitcher and fling the thing just over the other kids' heads so they had to jump into the air for it, then crash into the boiling surf.

We ran full tilt until the sun went down, around eight-thirty or nine at night. Then, reluctantly, we would trudge home, grab a bite to eat, and hit the hay. There was no point in staying up any later because the house lacked a television, and quite frankly, we were exhausted. That whole month, I don't believe I spent more than a few waking hours in the company of adults and that was fine with me. My father, who came out on weekends, would put on his bathing suit Saturday morning and swim out about a mile toward Europe, then return quickly to the beach. His Australian crawl was sharp and powerful, betraying a misspent youth at the shore. After he dried off, he would disappear from the beach until the next week. That meant, he never tired of telling us, he paid seventy-five dollars a swim. But the rest of us got more than our money's worth from Westhampton—except in the culinary department.

My mother's legendary ineptitude in the kitchen became increasingly obvious that summer. Two incidents, especially, did not bode well for her election to the prestigious Cooking Hall of Fame. Twice, in fact, she almost killed us.

The first episode began innocently enough. One rainy morning we decided to forsake the soggy beach for the wonders of a traveling carnival that had set up camp nearby. Despite the rain, we had a lot of fun riding the rides and playing the games, while stuffing ourselves with popcorn, peanuts, cotton candy, and hot dogs of dubious origin. On a whim we stayed around to see if we had won a door prize, and damned if we didn't. Susie held the winning ticket stub for tenth prize—a free pizza.

Oddly, from the time she was eighteen months old, Susie won more prizes in a couple of years than I've won in my entire life. She colored in a picture on the back of a cereal box and won a TV; she sent a postcard to a television show and won a trip to Los Angeles; and she won a bicycle from a candy company.

The pizza, however, was her first and, as it turned out, most inflammatory prize.

"I won, I won," she shouted with glee—and promptly wet her pants.

I don't believe pizza has that effect on children today, so ubiquitous a food item has it become, but for us pizza was as exotic as the calves' brains in cream sauce my father occasionally ate for breakfast. There just weren't any pizza parlors near us and frozen pizzas hadn't yet made it to the supermarkets. So it was with a sense of adventure that we crowded into Cosmo's, some of us soggier than others, to claim our prize.

"Congratulations," Cosmo said. "Whadda ya want on it?"

"What do you have?" my mother asked, perplexed.

I suppose my mother knew what pizza was, but I don't believe she had ever ordered a whole one.

"We got everything," Cosmo said.

"I see," my mother said.

I don't think she did.

"Does it come plain?" she asked, taking the safe way out.

"Sure. One plain coming up," Cosmo said, yelling to the guy in the back.

We waited tensely to see what would come out of the kitchen, none of us quite sure what to expect. A few minutes later, Cosmo handed Mom a gigantic cardboard box and urged her to take as many napkins and straws as she desired.

Struggling with the box, Mom bumped into the side of the door and caromed back into the shop.

"Tilt it, tilt it," Cosmo said.

Mom nodded and upended the pizza box, so that it was vertical.

"No, hold it flat, hold it flat," Cosmo yelled in a panic.

"I can't do both," my mother said indignantly, but she righted the box and managed to get it out of the store and stash it away in the back of the Chevy wagon. By the time we got it home, however, the pizza was stone cold.

"I don't think you're supposed to eat it cold," my mother said, not anticipating the generations of college students who regularly breakfast on cold pizza. "I believe we should heat it up."

That was an inspired guess, but how to do it?

My mother scratched her head; then the obvious solution presented itself.

"Look," she said. "It says right here: 'Sizzling Hot Pac—Guaranteed Hot and Crispy.'"

"Didn't work so far," I noted.

"We'll just put it in the oven and heat it up in its own insulated Hot Pac," she said.

She lugged the enormous box to the electric oven, opened the door, and shoved it inside. The door, of course, wouldn't close.

"Oh, I suppose it will be all right," my mother said, setting the dial to high. "It's not as if we're *really* cooking. We're just reheating."

"I won!" Susie said, doing a little dance in the kitchen.

"Come on, let's get you changed," my mother said. "Then we'll all enjoy a nice piece of hot pizza."

"I won!" Susie repeated, looking as if she might lose control of her bladder again.

I sat on the living room floor and occupied myself updating my baseball-card collection. My cards were housed in five shoe boxes, two for the American League, two for the National League, and one for extinct teams, like the St. Louis Browns. Each box was divided into teams; each team divided into positions. Never before or after in my life had I ever been so organized and neat. I lavished a monstrous amount of time on my cards and was furious when my mother pitched them out—about five minutes after I left for college.

In later years, however, I got even with her. I would read in the paper that a Mickey Mantle rookie card had fetched several thousand dollars and I would say, "Too bad you threw out my baseball cards. They would be worth $25,000 by now." That was an exaggeration, but not much of one. I had four pristine Mickey Mantles, my favorite player, plus a bunch of real oldies that kept escalating in price. I could almost reduce Mom to tears with that ploy.

I bring this up not because I was an expert collector, but because I spent much of my childhood playing with cardboard. I knew what it looked like, what it felt like, and what it smelled like when it burned. And the aroma wafting from the kitchen was definitely burning cardboard.

Reluctantly, I filed away a spare Enos Slaughter and went into the kitchen to investigate. Flames were shooting out of the open oven door, as the pizza box burned merrily.

"Mom!" I shouted, "Come quick!"

Then I grabbed an oven mitt and opened the door all the way. Beneath the charred cardboard the blackened pizza looked like molten lava bubbling away furiously.

I turned off the heat, hauled the burning box out of the oven, and threw it on the floor. Then I stamped out the flames with my sneakers. By the time my mother arrived on the scene, the fire was out, the smoke was dissipating, and the ruined pizza had melded with my sneakers and become an integral part of the linoleum.

"I won?" Susie said tentatively, looking at the gooey mess. "Where pizza?"

I pointed to the floor, and Susie burst into spontaneous . . . tears, not combustion, as you might imagine.

"What a disaster," my mother said. "I'm going to write the manufacturer. Sizzling Hot Pac, ha!"

Through some miracle of nature, the pizza bonded with the linoleum, forming a star-burst shadow that defied the most caustic of cleaners. My father claimed he could make out Abraham Lincoln's face there, but I think he was kidding. It was definitely Mickey Mantle at bat. Anyone could see that.

After our disastrous experience with the pizza, you would have thought that we would have stuck to raw clams and peanut butter sandwiches. You would have thought that, but you would have been wrong. Although my mother had a difficult time with conventional food preparation, she maintained a belief that one day she would find a technique she could master. Obviously, reheating prepared foods was out of the question, but Mom decided that it would be fun to have a barbecue on the beach.

"How hard can that be?" she asked me. "Barbecuing doesn't require a stove or anything."

I was skeptical about this enterprise, but Mom's enthusiastic attitude won me over, and we acquired a large bag of charcoal briquettes, a bottle of fire starter, and a tiny portable grill from the local hardware store. Then we went to Cibulski's Meat Market for the hamburgers themselves.

Cibulski's was a dark, odd-smelling general store occupying the ground floor of a weathered old house—a house that leaned precariously to the right. My mother had discovered this emporium our first week at the beach and had pronounced it "quaint." But that was just an excuse. She didn't want to drive twenty miles to the nearest supermarket.

The wooden floors of the shop rolled and creaked alarmingly when we entered, protesting the appearance of actual customers, no doubt. Old Man Cibulski was behind the counter, glowering. That was apparently what he did all day—glower.

"Good afternoon," my mother said cheerily. She always adopted a fake bonhomie when dealing with shopkeepers. "I would like a pound of ground chuck, please."

"Take the sirloin," Mr. Cibulski warned.

"No, thank you. I prefer the chuck," my mother said. In her experience, the ground chuck was more flavorful than the expensive sirloin.

"Your stomach," Mr. Cibulski grunted, wiping a dirty hand on his dirty apron.

We walked away with some grayish-looking meat, insecurely wrapped in greasy brown paper.

"It smells funny," I said.

"Oh, it will be fine once we barbecue it," my mother said.

That evening I assembled the little grill, screwing the three legs into the bowl. Then I stacked the charcoal in a pyramidal pattern.

"Just the way Craig Thompson does it," my mother said approvingly, referring to Brian's father, who was an enthusiastic barbecuer.

I squirted a quart and a half of kerosene on the briquettes, and when the match hit them, they exploded into a towering inferno. You could almost hear James Cagney screaming, "Top of the world, Ma! Top of the world!"

"Goodness," my mother said, wondering what had happened to her eyebrows. Maybelline must have enjoyed record sales that year, with the eyebrow pencil division leading the way.

"It's a conflagration," I said, exercising a new vocabulary word.

"Boom!" Susie said, finding a better word and clapping her hands in delight.

"Put the hamburgers on before the fire goes out," Stephen said. He knew as much about barbecuing as Mom.

My mother reached into the round Scotch cooler, pulled out the four quarter-pounders, and threw them at the grill. What happened next will forever be the subject of wild speculation and endless controversy.

When the meat hit the heat, a remarkable chemical transformation took place. In the ghastly flickering light of the roaring fire, the hamburgers turned a bright fluorescent green and gave off the odor of burning hair. They bubbled and squeaked for a moment; then they began to melt like Judy Garland's nemesis in *The Wizard of Oz*.

"They're melting. They're melting," Stephen cried on cue.

Mom had forgotten to pack a spatula or knife or fork, so we stood by watching helplessly as, one by one, the burgers gurgled and died, oozing through the grate and hitting the red-hot coals. Vast, billowing clouds of noxious smoke arose, blanketing us in an eye-watering shroud of fumes. The fire roared on, fueled by the meat, until we heard the hard cracking of tortured metal.

Suddenly, one of the screws holding a leg wrenched free and shot five feet in the air, barely missing an inquisitive Stephen.

"Stand back," my mother said a bit late.

I was already on the run, Susie under my arm, headed for high ground. I was not about to be grill-killed or the victim of hibachi homicide.

From a safe distance, I heard another popping sound, as a second screw made a bid for freedom. The grill, deprived of support, collapsed gracefully into the sand, spewing hot coals and a meatlike substance onto the beach.

"Gwill go boom!" Susie trilled.

Stunned, we sat on the sand, looking at the remains of our barbecue. While we were wondering what to do, Skippy the Dog, drawn by the smoke, ambled over to the fallen grill. He sniffed the charburgers, wrinkled his nose, and lifted his leg. For a long time, he watered the steaming coals.

My mother, observing the scene, pursed her lips and sighed.

"Well, I guess that about sums it up," she said.

That night we grilled, all right: We grilled cheese sandwiches on the stove.

"Gwill go boom!" Susie kept reminding us. "Skippy the Dog go potty! Gwill go boom!"

She kept it up until Mom sent her to bed.

Chapter 11

SUMMER OF DISCONTENT. Prisoners Stephen, Susie, and John contemplating a breakout from the repressive Hazel regime. Fortunately, Stephen, who possessed the mind of a trial lawyer and the soul of a hit man, found a solution to the problem.

Witch Hazel

Although our town was graced with many successful and even celebrated residents, I found them to be quite ordinary. They must have saved their passion and talent for the stage, the screen, the boardroom, or the atelier, because they seemed like regular people to me. They smiled and waved and said hello just like everyone else did. If I hadn't seen them on TV or in the newspapers, I would never have known they were famous.

Much more interesting to me were the people who toiled anonymously for the rich and famous. There was an entire subculture of unheralded entrepreneurs who had somehow made themselves indispensable. A former pianist, for example, had drunk himself out of the concert hall and pursued a life of dissolution. Pixilated from dawn to dusk, he nevertheless tuned every piano in town, which allowed him to pursue his dyspeptic dream. He wasn't cheap, he wasn't sober, but he did have perfect pitch.

Then there was the odd story of a Chinese immigrant who had stumbled into town around 1910. He was broke, hungry, and unable to speak English. Forty years later, he owned a dozen laundries all over the county and lived in a mansion staffed by fifteen servants. Every time I had a shirt laundered I liked to think that the money provided a tip for the butler. But of all these characters, four ladies made the biggest impression on me. They summed up, I think, the spirit and ingenuity that made these people so extraordinary.

Arthel Posey was a black lady of a certain age, though just what age no one was quite certain. She might have been fifty-five or a hundred and five or somewhere in between. Nobody knew and no one had the courage to ask. But when it came to parties, Arthel made Pearl Mesta look like an amateur. She didn't actually cater parties and dinners herself, heaven forfend; she was the liaison between the hostess and the caterers. In her role as go-between, Arthel made sure that every party went off without a hitch: that the food was good, hot, and on time; that the waiters waited properly; and that the bartenders could mix a dry martini with alacrity, or gin if you preferred. She was highly regarded in town and any resident wishing to make a social statement could not do without her. Oh, some tried to cut out the middle lady, but they found, to their horror, that the canapés collapsed and the crown rib of beef tasted more like an actual crown than beef. Whether Arthel had anything to do with the sudden incompetence of the catering people or not, I don't know. I do know that hiring Arthel was like taking out disaster insurance for your party. You needed her, even if you thought you didn't.

The O'Leary sisters, who had immigrated from Ireland, were almost as famous as Arthel. They had worked as maids in some of the finest houses in New York City, but decided to set up their own business in the late twenties. A house was not really clean unless the O'Leary sisters attacked it with the ferocity of twin grizzly bears. These ladies put the White Tornado to shame and they were in such great demand that they eventually hired other ladies to help them.

The O'Leary sisters died within a few weeks of each other some years ago. They had worked hard, well into their eighties, rarely taking a day off. When their wills were read, the people in town were amazed to discover that the sisters had left an estate of more than fifteen million dollars. How did these women amass such a fortune? Simple. They always made sure they cleaned the houses of the richest, most successful people in town. Then, while chasing away the cobwebs, they might take a peek at what the owner of the house was buying in the stock market. If they saw a statement from Merrill Lynch, Pierce, Fenner, and Beane indicating the purchase of a thousand shares of General Motors, the O'Leary sisters would buy ten shares. Five thousand shares of IBM? The sisters bought twenty-five. They weathered the Depression quite nicely, while many of their clients went broke, and they wound up with a staggering net worth, giving a new meaning to cleaning house.

And then there was Hazel, the picture of a stout English lady. She wore long tweed skirts, tweed jackets, and sensible brogans. Hazel also affected a cape to finish off the look. Her business was taking care of children, but she never let her profession interfere with her true vocation—meddling.

In an image business like child care, Hazel's personal shortcomings were insignificant. What was important was her reputation as a no-nonsense, highly professional, extremely competent baby-sitter. Parents lined up around the block, hoping to entice her into their employ. My parents, in an amazing stroke of luck, managed to engage Hazel for ten days that summer—a summer that will live in infamy.

Now, if my parents had wanted to throw a party, they could not have afforded both food and Arthel at the same time. Similarly, if they had really wanted a clean house, they would have failed the O'Leary sisters' credit check. How they inveigled Hazel into caring for us still remains a mystery. Our usual baby-sitters were high school girls who ignored us kids while they talked on the phone with their boyfriends. They were absolutely no threat to our usual dangerous pursuits and obnoxious behavior.

Hazel was a different species of trouble all together. The deal must have been struck months before, because she was in more demand than a skilled plumber. Engaging Hazel's services was considered quite a coup because she had a certain cachet: Hiring Hazel was affirming your own good taste and refinement. She was the right sort of person for the right sort of person to employ.

Fortunately, I was ignorant of this impending disaster and had returned from the beach tanned, fit, and ready to kick. I was on the field before I had shaken the sand out of my Keds. There were six more weeks of summer—more time than I could imagine—and I knew this was going to be the happiest summer of my life. What I didn't know was that admitting to myself that everything was going well would inevitably lead to disaster. Happiness, like psoriasis, should be kept a secret.

"Your father and I are going to St. Louis," my mother informed us one evening.

Not interesting.

"I've got a woman coming in to look after you children," she said.

Still not interesting.

"Her name is Hazel."

Now that was interesting—in the way a bloody car crash was interesting. Everyone had heard of Hazel. Of course we had heard about the boogeyman and Dracula, too. Generations of children had been frightened into good behavior when threatened with Hazel.

"Oh, I'm sure you'll like her very much," my mother said when I voiced my fears. "She comes highly recommended."

"By who?" I asked. "Lex Luthor?"

"Who?"

"Some bald guy," I said, knowing this was a lost cause.

Hazel appeared at our door in her tweeds and a man's felt hat that fateful morning looking as big as the mountain in the Paramount Pictures logo. Nearly six feet tall, she was an impressive woman, with short brown hair and smooth, smooth skin that had battled the elements for forty years and won.

My mother, who believed that all domestic help was a little dim, had typed up a five-page, single-spaced report on how to run the household and deal with the children. Hazel took one look at the sheaf of papers and deposited them in her trunk-size handbag. Then she threw off her cape, rubbed her hands together, and said, "Have a nice trip."

Stephen, Susie, and I were lined up in a row, watching wide-eyed as Hazel almost bodily threw my parents out the door. When they were gone, she made an inspection of the house, poking around into closets, and running her large sausagelike fingers under tables and on top of doors. She was not impressed. In fact, she was downright disturbed.

"Remarkably dusty," she muttered.

Even her muttering was loud, but as much as she looked like Margaret Rutherford on a jolly tramp through the Cotswolds, Hazel's voice betrayed the flat tones of the American Midwest.

"I'm going out to play," I said.

It had taken me the better part of an hour to work up the courage to say anything at all to her.

"Oh, no, you're not," Hazel said. "Not until the house is clean."

I looked around. The house seemed pretty clean to me.

"What do you mean?" I asked.

"I mean that you will scrub the bathtubs and toilets until they shine," she said, producing a can of Babbo from her purse. "Now get to work."

Most baby-sitters brought toys and games; Hazel brought cleaning supplies.

"You there!" she boomed.

Stephen jumped.

"Get a rag and clean every inch of the furniture from top to bottom," she said. "And you, the little one. Take off those disgusting shoes."

Susie looked up at her with big blue eyes.

"Now!"

Susie sat down where she had stood and took off her shoes, which were tiny, leather, and gray. Hazel produced a bottle of white polish from her bottomless purse and immediately set to work on them. When she was done, the shoes gleamed like new. But Hazel wasn't satisfied. She whipped off the laces and put them in a bowl. Then, under the sink, she found a bottle of Clorox and splashed the contents into a bowl. She let the laces marinate until they were white as snow. I knew then that Hazel was no ordinary clean freak—she was a maniac.

"How could you get so dirty?" she said to Susie.

Susie burst into tears. Hazel beamed, thinking that Susie was shedding tears of joy at finally having clean foot gear.

So on a glorious morning in July, with the temperature hovering in the eighties, under a clear sky, with the birds singing and the insects buzzing, the three of us spent hours cleaning the house. Somewhere out there, The Game was going on without me.

When we had finished with our labors, had our work inspected, criticized, and redone, it was time to go shopping. My mother had bought a copious amount of food and had even devised menus for Hazel to follow. But that was like telling George Patton how to fight a tank battle. Hazel would have none of it. She marched us to the A & P and resupplied the house with all the nutritional horrors she could imagine.

Like most fat people, Hazel was as much consumed with the *idea* of food as she was with the actual consumption of it. Our trip up and down the aisles of the supermarket seemed to take hours, while we listened to Hazel considering the merits of corn, beans, and peas. When we had exhausted the supplies at the A & P, we moved on to a specialty vegetable store nearby to partake of the spiritual qualities of kohlrabi, chicory, and highfalutin aubergine—no humble eggplant for Hazel.

I had just resigned myself to ten days of deprivation, when we ducked into the bakery. Now that was my kind of place. It smelled of cookies and cake and fresh bread. To my surprise and delight, Hazel bought not one, but two chocolate cakes. I guess she didn't tip the scales at two hundred pounds because of all the kale she consumed.

When we returned home, Hazel put Susie down for a nap and, wonder of wonders, sprung me to play kick baseball. But I had to be home at five or playground privileges would be suspended. So, munching an alfalfa sandwich on gluten bread, I shot out the door.

An obedient child, I returned home at five o'clock, was fed some kind of disgusting vegetable stew, and was ready to go back out to play.

"I'll be home by dark," I told Hazel on my way out.

"You certainly will," she said, "because you'll be in bed."

"But it's only five-thirty," I said.

"All right, you can stay up to six o'clock," she said. "Then I want all you children in bed."

I had fought for years against my parent's odd egalitarian leanings when it came to bedtime. As far as they were concerned, Susie, Stephen, and I should all retire at the same hour and leave them alone. However, being the oldest, I demanded a bedtime later than Stephen's, and he demanded one later than Susie's. It was a matter of honor. Even if I could hardly keep my eyes open, I would not go to bed until Stephen had been in his room for at least half an hour.

The thought of losing three hours of playtime, combined with the ignominy of being sent to bed at the same time as Susie and Stephen, left me in a sputtering rage. Stephen reacted with cold fury, and Susie cried for no particular reason. But Hazel was unswayed, and at six p.m. I found myself in bed, listening to the kids playing outside—little kids, allowed to stay up later than I!

What do you do when you are abused and wronged and not even allowed to read in bed? Why, think thoughts of revenge, of course. I spent a good two hours planning Hazel's murder or imagining Superman flying to my rescue. The Man of Steel would have needed all his mettle to combat an archenemy like Hazel. Before I drifted off to sleep, I was determined to fix her little red wagon. The only problem was, I didn't know how.

Stephen provided the answer the next morning. A much more devious thinker than I ever was, he had come up with a plan to bring Hazel down a notch. Even though he was only eight years old at the time, he had the mind of a trial lawyer and the soul of a Mafia hit man.

"I hate that woman," he told me that morning. "She's a witch and I'm going to get her."

I assured him that I was available for any sort of foul crime and most anxious to participate in murder, mayhem, or mischief against Witch Hazel.

"I've got an idea," he said, a wicked grin on his face.

But before he could tell me, Hazel decided that we should help her rearrange the furniture in the living room.

"We'll move the couch over there against that wall to hide the faded paint," she said.

We lugged the heavy couch to the desired location.

"No, that won't do at all," she said. "Perhaps over there."

Straining and struggling, we inched the sofa into position.

"That's better," Hazel said. "Except that now the drapes look shabby."

"Tough noogies," Stephen said under his breath.

I giggled.

"What's that?" Hazel demanded.

"Nothin'," I said, recovering brilliantly.

"Well, I think we'll go shopping for new drapes," Hazel said.

"But I've got a game," I said.

"You can play anytime," she said. "This is an emergency. I cannot live with these drapes for one more moment."

"I like the drapes," I lied defiantly. I hadn't ever noticed them before.

"Then it's time you learned about taste, sophistication, and color coordination," Hazel said.

So instead of spending the day on the playground, Stephen, Susie, and I went from store to store, looking for proper drapes. Hazel poked and pored over the samples, inquiring and demanding explanations about every single one. At the end of the day I was more exhausted than if I had spent the entire afternoon on the playground, and I was almost glad to go to bed at six o'clock. Unfortunately, I was still color uncoordinated, and remain so to this day.

While Hazel was putting Susie to bed that evening, Stephen motioned for me to join him in the living room. He produced a box of gentle, chocolated Ex-Lax from under his shirt. It was empty.

"I melted it down and poured it under the icing of her chocolate cake," he said, grinning broadly. "Don't eat any."

I laughed. "You didn't!"

"I sure did," he said. "She'll poop herself to death."

Hazel strode briskly into the room and told Stephen and me it was time for us to go to bed. But to give her credit, she offered us both a piece of chocolate cake before we retired. We declined and ran off to bed before we burst into laughter.

The next morning we watched Hazel like hungry buzzards, but we failed to detect any changes: no groaning, no moaning, no sudden trips to the bathroom.

"You didn't really," I said to Stephen.

"I did, too," he said. "The whole box. I don't know what's wrong."

Deprived of our revenge, we quickly settled down to Hazel's hateful regime. We cleaned, we shopped, and we moved furniture most of the day before we received short furloughs to do as we wished. The kids on the playground commiserated with me, but there was nothing any of us could do. After the glorious freedom of the beach, life under Hazel's tyrannical rule was truly terrible.

Then, two days after Stephen dosed the cake, Hazel made a serious mistake. She was doing a load of laundry in the basement when she stumbled upon the Black Torpedo of Doom.

"What a magnificent perambulator," she gushed. "Help me get it up the stairs."

Slowly, we pushed, step by step, inch by inch, until the malign machine crested the basement steps and rolled menacingly into the kitchen. I stood back waiting for it to lunge at me, but it just stood there . . . waiting. Hazel wiped off a thin coating of dust and the Torpedo gleamed anew.

"It's beautiful," Hazel said in awe.

No, it's not, I thought. *It's evil.*

She ran a meaty hand over the glowing black sides of the Torpedo, and I swear it quivered with excitement. I expected a feline purr to erupt from it at any moment because, finally, the Black Torpedo of Doom had met a worthy opponent—Hazel. A titanic clash of wills was about to begin, and there could be only one winner.

That afternoon I was summoned from the playing field and instructed to take my second bath of the day in preparation for a trip to pick up the new drapes that Hazel had ordered. Like tuxedos and brown shoes, eleven-year-old boys and water do not mix. One bath a day was a hardship; two a day was water torture. I would have been perfectly content never to have bathed at all. I liked the smell of grass, dirt, sweat, and yesterday's lunch. But I did as I was told because I wanted a front row seat at the fight of the century.

Round One went to Hazel. Somehow, she managed to get Susie into the Torpedo.

"No carriage!" Susie screamed. "Stroller!"

Even at a young age, Susie could recognize evil when she had to ride in it. Actually, she didn't like her lightweight aluminum stroller much better. She used it like an old person uses a walker—for support. She had to be utterly exhausted before she would stop walking.

Hazel, however, wouldn't hear any objections, so she hoisted a screaming, writhing Susie with one hand and deposited her in the carriage. When she tried to crawl out, Hazel gave her a withering look that pinned her to the spot. Afraid to escape, Susie threw a fit, pounding her fists into the thick mattress and giving out bloodcurdling yells of protest.

"Behave yourself," Hazel said menacingly.

Always a practical baby, Susie recognized that her protests were useless and went to Plan B—sulking. Equally practical, Hazel was willing to exchange quiet sulking for loud fits. So, somewhat disgruntled, we set out in search of the elusive drapes. But the Black Torpedo of Doom was not finished with us.

A powerful woman, Hazel managed to get the carriage out of the house and launch it down the hill all by herself—a feat that had defeated Mom on countless occasions. Then, with competence and assurance, she navigated the carriage to the center of town, looking very much like a royal nanny with her cape flying in the wind. But just as she was gaining mastery over it, the Torpedo struck back. Hazel had halted our progress to gaze in the window of Best & Co., a now-defunct department store that had a branch in our town. As she leaned forward to get a better look at the mannequins on display, the Torpedo began to roll—right over Hazel's sensible shoes.

"Oww!" she cried as the whitewall tires caught her on the instep. From personal experience, I knew that it must have hurt like hell. Hazel jumped up and down on one foot, looking for all the world like a stout pogo stick.

"Sugar and spice!" she roared, clutching her foot in one hand. For a big woman, she had remarkable balance.

Stephen sniggered and Susie clapped her hands in time to Hazel's prance of pain. But I wasn't fooled. Round Two might have gone to the Torpedo, but the fight wasn't over.

Limping slightly, Hazel led us to the drapery store and minutely examined the custom-made curtains. When she was satisfied, she told the clerk to charge them to Littell and gave the address. That was the nice thing about our town in those days: You could charge anything to anyone's account anytime. Because no actual cash money changed hands, people like my mother and Hazel didn't worry much about such mere trifles as cost. In today's world, credit cards serve that useful function.

As we strode home, the Torpedo struck again. It stopped dead in its tracks for no apparent reason, sending Hazel flying over the handle and smashing into the leather top. Miracle of miracles, the hood, which had been frozen in place as long as I'd known it, suddenly folded in on itself. Then, with Hazel lying prone in the carriage, almost crushing Susie, the Torpedo began to roll backward. Gaining speed, it careened unchecked down the sidewalk heading toward the street. Hazel, squawking like an outraged chicken, struggled to free herself from the out-of-control machine, but she was all flailing arms and legs, hopelessly caught in the belly of the beast.

For a moment, I was too stunned to move; then I took off to the rescue. Unlike Lassie, however, I was too late. The carriage bounded over the curb and was hurtling into oncoming traffic when, as quickly as it had begun to roll, it stopped. There was nothing supernatural about the Torpedo's sudden cessation of movement. That was entirely due to

Hazel's outstretched legs slamming Officer Lindemann in the chest. Lindemann rocked for a moment on his trike, but recovered his seat like a medieval knight who had been struck with the glancing blow of a lance.

"Say now—" he said, obviously startled by the woman riding on a baby carriage, her large round legs poking him.

"This is a no parking zone," Officer Lindemann said.

"Get me out of here, you idiot," Hazel said.

"Hazel, is that you?" the policeman said.

"No, it's Mother Hubbard," Hazel hissed.

"Oh."

Struggling with all her might, Hazel finally righted herself and stood again on solid ground. The Torpedo bounced up and down on its springs, enjoying a hearty laugh. Poor Susie didn't know what had happened, so she began to cry.

"Why, Hazel, it *is* you," Officer Lindemann said.

Hazel didn't bother answering the astonished cop, but smoothed out her tweeds, straightened her cape, and tried to restore her lost dignity. Score another round for the Torpedo, I thought.

Red-faced and quivering, Hazel pushed the carriage through the large crowd of onlookers and headed for home, with Stephen and me tagging along behind, laughing silently. When we hit the base of the hill, we heard a loud rumbling noise—a noise, I fancy, similar to those preceding a volcanic eruption.

"What was that?" I asked, but one look at Hazel answered my question.

From flush to livid to light green, Hazel's face told the story. She bent over and moaned.

The Ex-Lax had kicked in at last.

"Take Susie home," she gasped and began a limping trot up the hill, never looking behind her.

Stephen laughed so hard he fell to the pavement and I wasn't far behind. We watched Hazel's retreating form lumber up the hill—double time.

When I recovered, I shook Stephen's hand and congratulated him. Together, we pushed the Torpedo back home and banished it once again to the basement. It had done its work well.

For her remaining days with us, Hazel was a changed, if not broken, woman. She no longer cared if we cleaned the house or ourselves. We stayed up as late as we wanted, while she kept to her room. She did manage to put up the new drapes, but I think they reminded her of the ordeal and she avoided the living room as much as possible.

Susie was much distressed by Hazel's sudden personality change.

"Hazy sick," she told me. "I take care of her."

"Good," I said. "Make sure she gets to bed early. I'm going to the playground while it's still light."

The meals, too, improved. No more obscure vegetables and legumes appeared on the dinner table. We got a lot of sandwiches—cheese or peanut butter—because Hazel had a sudden aversion to food of any kind.

"This is more like it," Stephen said, eating chocolate ice cream out of the carton for breakfast.

Hazel, the world's most highly recommended baby-sitter, had been reduced to the level of our usual high school girl guardians. Susie's shoes quickly got dirty again and the laces were a disgusting gray.

Our parents returned home on a Sunday evening, walked in the door, and froze.

"Good Lord," my father said. "We're in the wrong house."

All the furniture had been rearranged and the new drapes gave the room a completely different look.

"What happened here?" my mother said.

I didn't have time to answer, because upon hearing my mother's voice, Susie came rocketing out of Hazel's room and flew into her arms, screaming, "Mama! Mama!"

Stephen's reception was somewhat cooler. He looked at Mom and Dad, shrugged, and went to his room.

"Where's Hazel?" Mom asked.

"Hazy sick," Susie said happily.

"She's sick?"

"I'm perfectly well," Hazel said in the doorway of the living room. She had regained some of her former bravado under Susie's tender ministrations. "But I would like a ride home."

After my father had paid her and was driving Hazel home, my mother cornered me.

"All right," she said. "What gives?"

Unable to withstand such pressure, I told her about the Torpedo and the furniture and the drapes, but I didn't squeal on Stephen's diarrheal depredations.

"The nerve of that woman," my mother said when I had finished spilling my guts.

"The drapes are nice," I ventured.

My mother muttered something about white trash and tar paper shacks, then went to check on Stephen. When she asked him what was wrong, he said, "Hazel." It sounded like a curse word.

"What about her?" my mother asked.

"Never do that to us again," he said in as hard a voice as an eight-year-old can muster. *"Never."*

Taken aback, my mother dropped the subject faster than she dropped the new drapes into the garbage and restored the furniture to its original configuration.

Hazel was a martinet who was used to having her own way. But looking back, I realize now she never had a chance against two arch-enemies. She might have defeated the Black Torpedo of Doom, and certainly she had managed to keep Stephen in check for a while, but when the two ganged up on her, she was done for.

Although we never saw Hazel again professionally, we used to run into her in the village and wave. She would smile pallidly and wave back, but I don't think she meant it. Hazel continued her successful career in child management, constantly in demand and constantly working. The last time I saw her, she was as full of bluster as ever, but I was no longer in awe of her. Once you've seen someone rolling down the street while reclining on a baby carriage, and enjoyed watching her do the outhouse trot, intimidation quickly changes to amusement.

One curious postscript, however, remains worth relating. Throughout my childhood, there was a persistent rumor that a local resident had used Hazel as his model for the eponymous cartoon in the *Saturday Evening Post*—a cartoon that was later translated into a hit TV show, starring Shirley Booth. But the Hazel America loved—winsome, happy, devil-may-care—had nothing at all to do with the woman who had made our lives miserable. Still, it made a good story, and I repeated it for years, adding gory details whenever reality became intrusive.

I was thoroughly put in my place many years later, however, when

I was having a row with a woman I knew. What we were arguing about escapes me, but I suppose it was about something I had done—or hadn't done. She was familiar with the Hazel episode in my life and used it against me to end our quarrel.

Pained beyond all endurance at my recalcitrant behavior, she put her hands on her hips and said: "Well, what can I expect from someone who was raised by a cartoon character?"

I laughed.

What indeed?

Chapter 12

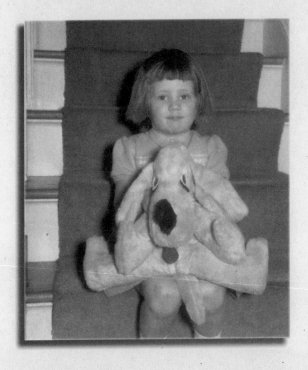

PLUSH SADLY. Both Mary and Sadly's owner took a dim
view of sleepovers, so Susie had to be content with
a Sadly substitute, one that never needed
to be walked or de-fleaed.

Susie and Sadly

Of all the great friendships in history—Damon and Pythias, Timmy and Lassie, Ken and Barbie—none can compare to that of Susie and Sadly. As the person who introduced them, I take full responsibility.

They met in the summer of 1957, when Susie was nineteen months old. At that age, she could walk, talk, and go to the toilet by herself—after a fashion. No child had ever had more desire to be mobile than my kid sister. All around her, everybody was walking and she hated to be left out. As soon as she had the strength to pull herself upright, she cruised around the house holding on to chairs, tables, and people, tripping a light fantastic on her tiptoes. When I was her age, I was such a competent crawler that I saw no need to totter about on two feet and preferred the safety of the floor. Susie crawled for about a week; then she stood up and never looked back.

So eager was she to join the conversation that she talked up a storm from the time she was eleven months old. Not all of what she said was intelligible—you needed a trained ear—but she seemed to have an opinion about everything and wasn't at all shy about expressing it. Her often confusing monologues delighted everyone—except Stephen. Always a stickler for precision, even at the age of eight, he would get furious with her.

"Talk English!" he would yell at her.

"Engrish," she'd yell back, then toddle over to him, signaling that she wanted to be picked up. Dutifully, Stephen would comply, forgetting he was mad at her. Cuteness trumps crankiness every time.

Her "Engrish" was rendered even more equivocal because she pronounced *th* as if it were an *f*.

"I fink I'm hungry," she would say.

"Well, it's lunchtime."

"I fought so," she would confirm.

My mother would get furious at me and my father for encouraging her, claiming that the child would never learn to speak properly unless we corrected her.

" 'The art of language is in the speaking,' " my father quoted pedantically.

"Who said that?" my mother asked, falling into his trap.

"William Makepeace Fackeray—or was it Henry David Foreau?"

In addition to the "f-problem," Susie had a tenuous relationship with the letter "r." Her normal mode of speech sounded like a bad rendition of Elmer Fudd. She knew a "wabbit" when she saw one and she told everyone she could "won weal" fast. Despite my mother's concerns, I found her a pretty funny little kid.

One thing that wasn't funny about her babyhood was the pile of diapers she created—diapers that were deposited in a large metal can in the bathroom. The smell would have corroded titanium. Disposable diapers were expensive and exotic in those days, so my mother hired a diaper service that came three times a week to pick up the dirty diapers and to drop off the clean ones. If the service had come three times a day, it wouldn't have been enough.

"It smells like pneumonia in there," Stephen said one day, hovering outside the bathroom door.

"Ammonia," I said. "Just hold your nose."

"I'm going to pee outside from now on," he announced.

And he did.

These days, I have to laugh when I see a four-year-old still wearing diapers and hear a lot of blather about the agony of toilet training. All a child needs is motivation—or Stephen for a brother. His withering glares, snide remarks, and the occasional fist in her face were all Susie needed to comprehend the fine art of staying dry. When she reached her first birthday, the hated, smelly diaper can was removed from our bathroom. My mother was amazed, Stephen was smug, and the diaper service was desolate: Pneumonia was cured, Air Wick was triumphant, and the yew bushes outside eventually recovered from Stephen's daily watering.

That summer The Game went on as usual—with three changes. First, for some reason, there was a dearth of babies and toddlers. I thought perhaps the ants or the Martians might have gotten them, but I could never prove it. Whatever the reason, the sandbox was empty most of the time and poor Susie had nobody to play with on the days I had to watch her. That would become a vexing problem.

Second, we had been graced with a pair of ravening eight-year-olds who threatened to destroy The Game with their barbaric behavior. Eight is probably the worst age imaginable—too little to be civilized, but big enough to cause real damage. Brad, who immediately earned the nickname "Brat," was the ringleader (if a ring can consist of only two kids). A skinny, dark-haired boy who was coiled tighter than a spring, Brat was a good enough athlete, but he had a mean streak wider than the outfield at Yankee Stadium. He liked to pick on younger kids and make them cry.

His accomplice was named Dick. And he was. A born follower, Dick wouldn't have been such a bad kid if he hadn't done everything Brat told him to do. My friend Brian Thompson and I, as the oldest kids on the playground, tried to control the dangerous duo—without much luck. Toilet training Susie had been a breeze by comparison.

The third change was a much happier one. Although the regular players were mostly boys, we did have the occasional girl who joined the action. The most memorable was Don. Well, her name was really Dawn, but she was a recent transplant from Boston and the way she pronounced her name sounded to us like "Don." So that's what we called her. She was a tall, lanky girl with short red hair and freckles, and she was one hell of a good player. She could run, kick, and field with the best of us—everybody wanted her on his side. Dressed in her trademark Bermuda shorts and Izod tennis shirt, Don was one of the boys.

My sister, Susie, however, was definitely not one of the gang, as she proved one warm morning in late June. I had consigned her to the calaboose—the sandbox—but like a Mexican jumping bean, she just wouldn't stay still.

I was on the mound, but I wasn't in top form for some reason. The first batter I pitched to knocked the ball out of the park for a home run. Bad pitch. While I was muttering to myself, Susie ran onto the field or, more accurately, toddled onto the field. Always a conscientious child, she began in the infield and worked her way around the bases, smiling, waving, and saying hello to each of the players.

I caught her between third and home, scooped her up, and deposited her in the sandbox with orders to stay put. I got the next batter to pop up; then Susie ran back onto the field to say hi to everyone. I captured her again and returned her to the sandbox. But no matter how harshly I remonstrated with her, she insisted on running out onto the field every second play. The Game could not go on like this. Something had to be done.

"Why don't we break her legs?" Brat, the ravening eight-year-old, said. "Then she'd *have* to stay in the sandbox."

I pondered that for a moment, but only for a moment.

"I'll go home and get my father's hammer," Brat said, hope in his voice.

"No," I said, trying to picture my mother's reaction to a brace of broken baby legs.

"Maybe if you gave her an at-bat, she'd leave us alone," Brian said. He could afford to be reasonable. He didn't have a kid sister.

"You want to play, Susie?" I asked her.

"Frow ball me!" she squealed. She spoke like the niece of Tarzan and the aforementioned Mr. Fudd.

I sighed, and with many pairs of disapproving eyes boring furiously into my back, I called a time-out.

"Stand over there," I told her, "and kick it."

Susie tottered over to home plate, which was a square scratched in the dirt, and looked at me expectantly.

I rolled the ball as slowly as I could.

She watched it intently; then she bent at the waist and inspected the ball as it rolled past her.

"No, no," I said. "You're supposed to kick it."

"Oh, I fought so," she said sagely, nodding her head.

Again, I sent the ball creeping toward home plate. Susie eyed it critically and waited until it came to a stop behind her; then she touched it with the toe of her red sneaker.

"Whee!" she trilled joyfully.

"You kick like your brother," Brian yelled from the outfield.

I didn't dignify his insult with a response. This was *his* idea, not mine.

"One more time," I said. "Kick the ball while it's rolling."

I eased the ball toward the plate. With agonizing slowness, it crept toward an alert Susie, who was, presumably, judging its angle and velocity and gearing up to boot it a mile. But, with an almost miraculous lack of coordination, she prematurely preformed a Rockette-style kick with her right leg; the ball rolled under her outstretched leg and hit her other leg. She went down in a perfectly executed split; then she toppled over on her side and burst into tears.

"I want her on my team," Brian yelled from the field.

Disgraced by my own sister, I ran to home plate, picked her off the ground, and dusted her off.

"You're too little to play," I told her, plunking her in the sandbox.

"No, no, no!" she cried, the tears coursing down her cheeks. "Pway ball!"

"She does a pretty good split," Brian said, coming in from the outfield. "Maybe she can be a cheerleader."

"We could nail her feet to the sandbox," Brat suggested.

"Up!" Susie said, clenching and unclenching her fingers, wanting to be picked up.

I hauled her into my arms, thinking that maybe we could nail her sneakers into the sandbox, avoiding her toes. Eleven-year-olds are much more humane than eight-year-olds.

"Naw," I said at last. "It won't work."

"We could tie her to a tree," the cretinous Dick suggested. "I got some rope at home."

"She'd only howl," I said, looking around for a solution.

"Howl," I said again, getting an idea.

"I'm marooning her to left field," I told everyone. *Maroon* was one of my favorite words and had been ever since I had read *Treasure Island*. Marooning Susie seemed like a proper punishment and a suitable way to put an end to her antics.

Left field was the home of our most ardent (and only) fan, Sadly, a brown, black, and white basset hound with floppy ears and the saddest eyes anyone had ever seen. All day long, he lay on his belly, his paws stretched out in front of him, watching The Game with great intensity. His head would move slowly, following the runners around the bases, or strain upward tracking a fly ball. Nothing escaped his attention. He seemed to be a very serious dog.

Sadly's domain was a small, fenced-in yard located in extreme left field. He sat by the gate, looking for all the world like a canine sphinx, and when a player hit a ball into his yard, he would let out a deep, phlegmy whoof that sounded more like a cough than a bark. Whoever retrieved the ball would pat Sadly on the head for good luck and lock the gate behind him. Although the rules changed constantly, a ball kicked into Sadly's territory was usually a homer.

That day Sadly was confused because I had opened the gate before a ball landed in his yard. Never a dog of lightning intellect, he swiveled his head around, looking for the ball that had escaped his notice. Then he gave me a mournful look, his drooping eyes displaying a world of hurt, and shook his head disbelievingly.

I put Susie down next to him and said by way of introduction, "Susie, this is Sadly. Sadly, Susie."

She took one look at the basset hound, threw her arms around his neck, and gave him a big, wet kiss. He slobbered on her in return. It was love at first sight and The Game could go on unimpeded.

After their first date, all I had to do was sit Susie down next to Sadly, and she would stay there quietly all day. She and the basset shared everything: maggoty bones, rubber dog toys, dolls, blankets, snacks, Cokes, and secrets. And they would talk. Susie would lift one of his pendulous ears and prattle into it for hours at a time. Doggedly (if you'll excuse the expression), Sadly endured this constant verbal assault and somehow maintained his lugubrious composure. Together, they watched the progress of The Game with an ironic condescension and an icy hauteur that was almost spooky.

"What do you think they're talking about?" Brian wondered, observing one of Susie's marathon gossip sessions.

"About what a jerk you are," I said.

"Screw you," he said.

As you can tell by that exchange, we were best friends.

And Sadly was definitely Susie's best friend. Every time a ball was kicked into the yard, Sadly would cough his approval and Susie would throw both arms up in the air, as I had taught her, and shout, "Home won!" From then on, whoever retrieved the ball would pat both of them on the head for luck.

They were as content as an old married couple. If Susie got tired, she would use Sadly as a pillow and fall fast asleep. He would lie there without moving until she awoke. While she was sleeping, we would call the yard out of bounds so we wouldn't wake her; when she regained consciousness, left field would again be in play. Sometimes, however, Sadly would tire of watching The Game and he would retreat to his wood-shingled doghouse. Susie would follow after him and crawl in to join him. They would lie next to each other, paws and arms extended in front of them, looking companionably comfortable and quite pleased with themselves.

If they got cranky, I'd give them a Tootsie Roll to share. That would keep them busy for an hour or more, chewing away with steadfast determination thanks to a lack of superior dentition. Mrs. Davis, Sadly's owner, caught me giving candy to her dog one day and told me that Tootsie Rolls were bad for him. So after that, I'd give Susie the Tootsie Roll and Sadly got a dog biscuit.

When Susie polished off her candy, without giving any to Sadly, she would attack his dog biscuit. Sadly would give her a baleful eye when she took the biscuit out of his mouth, but he never bit her hand off as any normal dog would have done. He would just stare at her, well, sadly, waiting for her to finish gnawing on it and shove it back in his mouth. It was a disgusting process to watch, but they didn't seem to mind. Besides, The Game had to go on, and revolting table manners were preferable to breaking Susie's legs or nailing her feet to the sandbox.

I have to say that Sadly was the more generous of the two. He really knew how to share. In fact, he was so generous, he even gave Susie a few fleas, which sent my mother straight to Hysterialand, a magical kingdom that Uncle Walt never dreamed of.

I didn't know it then, but that was to be my last summer playing The Game. By the next year, I would be too big and too strong to find kick baseball enjoyable or challenging. I moved on to baseball, softball, and Wiffle ball, played other places, other times. But for that one special moment, it seemed to me that The Game would go on forever; that glorious summer would never end. Cool, fog-shrouded mornings gave way to blistering-hot afternoons in a seemingly unending procession. The smell of the lilac bushes and the sour odor of the dirt, the sound of kids shouting just for the hell of it, and the feel of the sun burning my neck were all a part of that endless summer. Of course, if I had been one of those prescient children one finds in sensitive novels, I would have known that my childhood was coming to an end. But I was just a dumb eleven-year-old whose concept of the future was limited to thinking about the next pitch.

Still, two incidents on the playground—one immensely satisfying, the other truly puzzling—should have warned me that childhood, like summer, must come to an end sometime. Oddly enough, both events were tied intimately to our redheaded female player, Don.

If there had ever been any doubt about it, Don proved her worth one stifling afternoon late in August. There was a thunderstorm approaching, and the kids, like cattle in the field, could sense it. They were restless and quarrelsome. The ravening eight-year-olds were at their worst, terrorizing the little kids and generally making a pain in the butt of themselves. On one play, Brat threw the ball so hard at a six-year-old, he drove the little boy into the ground.

"You asswipe," Brian yelled at him, helping the little kid up.

"See how you like it!" I said, picking up the ball and throwing it with all my strength at Brat's head.

I popped him good, but he bounced up and flipped me the bird.

That did it. I was about to commit murder and no jury would have convicted me for ridding the world of such vermin. I outweighed Brat by at least thirty pounds and was a good half a head taller, so I could have squashed him like an ant. Brian, however, saved the kid's life.

"It's gonna rain soon," he said. "If you don't kill him, we can still get in an inning or two."

The Game was more important than crime, punishment, or execution, so hostilities were suspended, and play continued.

The air was now a greenish color; menacing gray-black clouds were scudding toward us rapidly, and The Game had a frenzied, feverish pace that set everyone's nerves on edge. At that moment, Brat decided that it would be fun to throw dirt bombs at his own players. He chucked a few at some of the smaller kids on our team. They complained loudly, but the attacks continued. A dozen times I told him to stop, but he paid no attention, making me wish I had killed him earlier.

Then the bellicose Brat made the mistake of his life. He lobbed a particularly hard dirt bomb at Don, catching her on the nape of her neck. She whirled around just as a tremendous clap of thunder shook the ground. I swear she had a hellish green glow in her eyes as she raced from the infield, where she had been pitching, to the outfield, where the obnoxious eight-year-old stood transfixed. Brat saw Death coming for him and she was wearing Bermuda shorts and a pink Izod tennis shirt. She was coming for him and he couldn't move.

What happened next still amazes me: As Don bore down on Brat, the heavens opened up and pea-size drops of rain pelted the parched earth, sending up puffs of dust that looked like the bullet tracks in war movies. Lightning sizzled through the sulfurous air just as Don, her head down, her legs pumping, slammed into Brat like an out-of-control locomotive. He hit the ground with a satisfying thud. But she wasn't through. She picked him up by the scruff of his neck and his Cub Scout belt and hurled him down a small hill that was part of right field. When he landed with an outraged groan, a cheer erupted from the playground.

"I'm gonna tell my mother," Brat whined like the bully he was.

"What? That a girl beat you up?" Don said. "Come on, I'll go with you."

Lying in the dirt, the rain soaking him to the bone, Brat knew he was defeated. The humiliation of telling anyone that a girl had beaten him up was just too much. He struggled to his feet, and with his head bowed, he slouched home to the taunts of "diaper head" and "baby, baby," the worst insults his little victims think of.

Don, her arms folded, a look of unappeasable determination on her face, watched him go. In the rain and lightning, she looked like a red-headed Valkyrie in Bermuda shorts, ready to conduct the players of The Game to a Brat-less Valhalla.

I admired Don tremendously after that and I still do. If I had beaten up Brat, he would only have gotten a shiner, but Don destroyed him totally—his pride, his manhood, his confidence, his arrogance, and his ill temper. Brat later went on to enjoy a distinguished legal career, but it is my opinion that, without Don's fine hand, he would be doing time in Attica. She straightened him out completely.

As August expired in a thick cloud of humid air, and school loomed before us like a hungry mutant ant, we played The Game with an insane intensity that adults would have found troublesome, perhaps psychotic. But we wouldn't give in. We were trying our best to stop time and banish thoughts of school by sheer willpower alone.

Then, right before school began, we were startled by an apparition that suddenly appeared on the playground. It was wearing a white dress with blue polka dots, shiny black patent leather shoes, and it sported a straw hat with a ribbon hanging down the back. A small leather purse was clutched in its white gloved fingers.

It was horrible.

It was ghastly.

It was Don.

The Game ground to a halt while everyone stared in abject terror.

Brian was the first one to recover.

"Get your shorts on and get back here," he said.

None of us had ever seen her wear anything but Bermuda shorts.

"I can't play anymore," Don said.

"Why not?" I asked, still stunned at her appearance.

"Because I'm a woman now. I have breasts."

That was a shocker.

Brat, recently allowed back into The Game, was as baffled as the rest of us.

"Where?" he asked incredulously—as if she might be hiding them in her purse.

"You're such children," Dawn huffed and flounced off the field and out of our lives forever.

Brian and I huddled to discuss this astounding event and to puzzle over the ramifications of this breast business. Unfortunately, neither one of us knew much about the subject.

"Do you think she's really got 'em?" he asked me.

"I dunno," I said. "I didn't get a real good look."

"If she's so worried about 'em, she could wear a catcher's chest protector," Brian said. "That would work."

"I suppose," I said. "But it's like her whole attitude has changed or something."

"It's a shame to lose a good player," Brian said. "Even one that's got breasts."

We were going on twelve and totally mystified.

Chapter 13

DADDY'S GIRL. From the time she was a tiny baby,
Frank sang to Susie many a night. His lyrics were silly,
his tunes were flat, but Susie didn't mind at all.
She only had eyes—and ears—for Daddy.

Song Me, Daddy

I was lying on the couch reading a Hardy Boys book, wondering just when I was going to meet a ruthless smuggler or find a treasure map or have any kind of adventure. So far, at the age of eleven-and-three-quarters, my life had been singularly uneventful—at least by the Hardy Boys' standards.

The television blared in the background and I was keeping an eye on Lassie, who, as usual, was busily rescuing Uncle Petrie from a hole. According to the books I read and the TV I watched, adults were babbling idiots, while children and animals were brave, resourceful, and intelligent. I couldn't help but agree.

Two-year-old Susie was sitting ramrod straight on the floor, totally absorbed in painting herself and the beige carpeting a bright shade of blue. Some of the paint even made it to the sheet of paper in front of her.

I watched her idly, amazed by her concentration. No matter how loudly Uncle Petrie called for help, she kept right on painting. That was the thing about Susie: She lived entirely for the moment. Whatever she was doing right then was the most important thing in the world. She had no real concept of past or future. For her there was only the great now. While I was hoping to match wits with shifty con men, she was intent on painting her fingers blue.

There was a banging in the foyer and I knew my mother was home. I kept on reading, but Susie leaped to her feet like a bird dog suddenly on scent.

"Mama!" she cried, and covered with bright blue paint, she ran to greet Mom with extravagant emotion—as if they had been parted for a fortnight, not a mere three hours.

The two of them engaged in an intricate ballet, Susie attempting to fling herself on Mom and smother her with kisses; Mom trying to spare her coat a coat of paint.

When the dance finished, Mom marched into the living room, pushing Susie ahead of her.

"John, look at this mess," she said, presumably referring to both the carpet and my little sister.

I looked up from my book and grunted. On TV, Uncle Petrie burst into tears at the sight of Lassie coming to the rescue. At that moment, I could have used a bit of rescuing myself, because suddenly I was in trouble.

"It's only watercolor," was not a well thought-out defense.

The next thing I knew, I was on my hands and knees, scrubbing away at the carpeting, while Susie was in the bathtub being scrubbed with equal fervor.

Joe Hardy and his brother, Frank, never had to deal with these ugly domestic details, I knew. They saved their energy for more important matters . . . like finding lost Egyptian tombs. I bet they never scrubbed a carpet in their lives. That was what Aunt Gertrude did. About the only solace I could find was that my father was not named Fenton. Now that would have been embarrassing.

I had just finished my labors and returned to my book when Susie came streaking across the living room, buck naked. Towel in hand, Mom was in hot pursuit, yelling, "Come back here!"

Susie squealed uproariously and dodged around the corner, heading for the kitchen. I hadn't noticed before, but Mom was pretty quick on her feet—for an old person, that is. She caught up to Susie in the dining room and scooped her up in the towel. The two of them were giggling like idiots. At the time I was scandalized by their rowdy behavior, but looking back I realize that my mother thought two-year-olds were absolutely wonderful.

Her feelings on the subject flew in the face of accepted wisdom. The "Terrible Twos" were supposed to be an awful age when a previously tractable baby learned the magic word: *no!* But Mom didn't see it that way.

"While you boys think I'm dumb, incompetent, and dress funny," she told me, "at least Susie still thinks I'm Queen of the Universe."

If Mom was nuts about two-year-olds in general, she was smitten by Susie in particular. From her point of view, two was a time of what she called "perfect love." And it was the only time in a child's life when Mom was the all-seeing, all-knowing supreme being she wished she could be.

I think Susie kept impressing Mom with her own sense of importance, with her need to be needed. It was true that Mom had to wash Susie, feed her, zip her up, trail around behind her, and distract her. And at night Mom's feet would hurt and her back would ache, but the love and uncritical affection she would receive in turn would more than revive her.

Uncritical. That was the key. Unlike me and my brother, Susie didn't care if Mom wasn't thin, stylish, or magnificently coiffed. Susie would just pat Mom's excess padding, bury her head in what should have been her taut tummy, and find reassurance in Mom's well-rounded curves. At one hundred ten or two hundred ten, the pounds didn't matter. Mama mattered. She was the beginning and end of Susie's day.

Susie didn't care how old Mom was or quiz her about what it was like during Colonial times. She didn't notice that Mom's hairstyle was strictly World War II. All she knew was that Mom's hair was a perfect place for sticky fingers and that her mother's less than chichi dress was immune to spills and drips of all kinds.

"Susie's interested in my smile, not my style," my mother said once.

And it was true. She didn't know if she was rich or poor, privileged or underprivileged, and she preferred her own mother to anyone else's. Susie loved her plush animals and push-pull toys and never complained that our car was not sporty or that Brian Thompson had a *real* tape recorder and a *real* TV in his room. In fact, her favorite toy was our canned-goods supply—an area in which we could compete with the neighbors. We had plenty of cans in all sizes.

Susie wasn't forever hounding Mom about other kids' good fortune. She didn't whine about trips to Europe or the Bahamas or demand a new hi-fi, a twenty-dollar baseball glove, or a twenty-five-dollar football helmet. At two, she didn't know anyone who owned a sailboat or had a closet full of expensive clothes or whose mother had two full-time maids. That would come, of course, but petty greed was not a part of her life at the time. About her largest demand was for a Zwieback or a

Lorna Doone cookie. A gift of those items brought a gleam to her eye and a big hug or kiss. You can see why my mother was enamored with Susie's perfect and undemanding love.

Mom also enjoyed being royally received. She must have gotten an inflated sense of her own importance every time she left the house for a few hours. When she returned, Susie would fly to her. Even Mickey Mouse couldn't compete. When Mom opened the door Susie would shriek with joy and climb on her as if she were a tree, all the while showering her with various flavored kisses. My brother and I might acknowledge Mom's presence with a languid wave of the hand or, on special occasions, an inarticulate grunt. Our joy at Mom's homecoming, two hours after she left, was well-concealed.

"The saddest part of having a two-year-old," Mom said, "is that you have them for a mere three-hundred-and-sixty-five days."

She knew that Susie would eventually grow up into a clear-eyed, clear-thinking youngster and would turn a searching gaze on home and Mom and discover that there were many things there that had to be corrected, added, or changed. Mom was braced for the future, but she intended to live it up and appreciate that brief period of perfect love.

It was unusual for Mom to wax sentimental about anything or anyone, but it was obvious that Susie was her favorite child. Far from being bothered by that, Stephen and I agreed with her—Susie was our favorite child, too.

Susie ruled the household with a sticky fist and we were all her willing slaves, catering to at least forty percent of her whims and fancies because we were absolutely in love with her. She was funnier than Uncle Miltie and Lucy put together, if you can image such a combo. She used to keep me and Brian Thompson in stitches when we played the animal-sound game.

"What does a doggie sound like?" he would ask her.

"Woof, woof," Susie would bark happily.

"What does a cat sound like?" I'd ask.

"Meow, meow," Susie would purr.

Okay, here comes the good part.

"What does an ostrich sound like?"

Susie would furrow her brow and bring a finger up to her chin.

Then, after a moment's thought, she would bellow out a hideous screeching noise that would render us helpless with laughter.

"That's right. Good,"I'd say when I had regained the capacity to talk.

We would throw her a few easy ones like cows and goats; then we would inquire about the reclusive duck-billed platypus.

Susie would think deeply about what noise would be appropriate and let out a glass-shattering scream that would have us on the floor, laughing again.

We could keep that up all day, consistently surprised and delighted by her creative interpretations of animals she had neither seen nor heard.

Fortunately for family equanimity, Susie was an equal opportunity charmer. She lavished her affections on Dad as much as she did on Mom. A rather cerebral man with an abstract turn of mind, my father was helpless before the onslaught of this tiny bundle of love. Susie turned him to mush. How she did it was quite simple.

My father liked to sing. Continuously. I don't think he did so because he was musical or he had happiness bursting from his heart. It's my theory that he sang to blot out everything that was going on around him—the chaos of family life. Holding his hands over his ears would have looked silly, so he sang instead. A baby's screams could be neutralized by a few Frank Sinatra ditties; whining children could be eliminated from your consciousness by a medley of 1940s hits; and an angry wife could be canceled out by a bit of light opera.

Like George Burns, Dad never sang a complete song, but rather would warble bits of many songs, stitched together into a monstrous, more or less melodious, melange. He also liked to make up his own words to the tunes he knew—probably because he had forgotten the real words. From the slightly racy,"I'll be *seizing* you in all the old, familiar places" to the downright inane, "I didn't know what time it was . . . so I bought a watch," Dad would drone on all day, ruining the work of many talented musicians and songwriters and effectively shutting himself away from the tedium of everyday life.

We turned a deaf ear to his constant serenade, but Susie had a different reaction. She loved to hear him sing. When her two-year-old world turned gray, she had a ready remedy that was better than any pill.

"Song me, Daddy!" she would demand.

And when he would, with his arms around her, holding her safe in his lap, his bari-tenor-bass voice in her ear, all was right once again.

Dad's "songing" worked when Susie was ill or upset, or had been punished, or had just learned to her horror that it was time to go to bed.

For Susie's benefit, Dad dropped his normal repertoire of old-timey hits and settled on the one tune that seemed to have a therapeutic effect on her—the majestic monotone of the hymn "Rock of Ages." He made up all the words and seldom repeated himself. The big attraction, of course, was that the heroine of all the hundreds of verses was Susie herself. For example:

> *Little Susie, I love you,*
> *With your eyes, your eyes so blue.*
> *Your daddy holds you in his lap.*
> *He will never let you drap.*

Drap? I'm tempted to rhyme that word with a "c," and I'm sure Oscar Hammerstein II would agree, but Susie's face would light up, she would snuggle closer and ask for a second verse, different from the first.

> *My pretty Susie is so sweet,*
> *And she's always nice and neat.*
> *Her hair is golden, blue is her eye.*
> *Please don't chew upon my tie.*

Susie would find that very funny, laugh, and beg for more. Her wish was his command performance, and Dad would continue to make up new verses to the dirgelike "Rock of Ages."

> *Little Susie, you are my dream.*
> *You are sweeter than peaches 'n' cream.*
> *But now it's time to take a bath.*
> *Please don't incur your mother's wrath.*

The odd thing about these silly symphonies was that they were contagious—rather like watching a movie that is so bad, you can't leave. We couldn't wait to find out how he would escape his own incompetence as a versifier. Perhaps it had been a lovely day and now it was time for a cup of "tay" or he might end up excessively sibilant with "now it's time to brush your teeth or you'll smell just like a beetht."

Every night Dad would get himself into some horrendous poetical predicament and attempt to extricate himself by rhyming "weighed" with "sayed" or be forced to substitute foreign words to complete the verse. He would gladly buy her a new dress, but he was "in debt up to my *tête*."

After a few minutes of "songing," Susie would be putty in his hands. Svengali had nothing on Dad. Bath? Let's take it. Dinner? Let's eat. Bed? She was ready.

Mom was impressed and tried to horn in on Dad's territory and sing Susie into compliance. But Susie knew which side of the Rock of Ages was hers. She put a hand over Mom's mouth and said, "Oh, no, Mama, that's Daddy's song."

Feeling she had committed some sacrilege, my mother didn't dare trespass again into a special father-daughter world that had nothing to do with her. A mere mother had to stand tongue-tied and vaguely envious before such affection. Mom had sung in a church choir and she was much better at rhyming than Dad, but that was important to no one but herself. Besides, never in her wildest flight of imagination could she have ever dreamed up:

> *Now you must go to bed,*
> *You have heard what Mama said.*
> *You can see by the light of the moon,*
> *It's time to take off your shoon.*

Not many people can create lyrics like that, and in the interest of civilization, I hope no one else will try—even if those bizarre verses had the power to soothe the savage baby. For Susie, her father's singing was a tranquilizer, sedative, morale builder, and nightly ritual. If we dared to disturb Susie and her troubadour with our talking, she would shush us with, "Daddy's songing me!" And we would quietly slink away, ashamed of ourselves for interrupting. We learned to recognize and respect the magic bond that completely encompassed them during their nightly song sessions. Susie knew that her daddy's songs were just for her and about her only, and if the rest of the family couldn't recognize that, tough. She could.

Unlike the Hardy Boys, I never did capture a gang of bank robbers or solve a mysterious disappearance. I never even had an opportunity to rescue my uncle, who proved to be singularly adept at avoiding dangerous mine shafts. But I did learn a few things about little kids. First off, there are no more eccentric and creative beings on Earth than the members of the one-to-four-year-old set. They have yet to be corrupted by society or homogenized by school and peers. They are true originals who follow their own perverse logic and live in a world of fantasy that the rest of us have long forgotten. They are shining examples of man everywhere born free, but who watch too much TV. They are not miniadults, but a whole separate species to be appreciated for their faults and virtues in a different way from that by which we judge older people. They have much to teach us about love, life, and the workings of the mind—if only we care to listen.

Two-year-olds are a retrograde lot, and I mean that in a good way. Like tiny Victorians, toddlers live in relative isolation, hold unshakable views, receive information from limited sources, tend to weep a lot, and are fearless in telling other people how to live. The problem with our therapeutic, nonconfrontational society is that there are too few Victorians and not enough two-year-olds. Little kids, like their great-great-grandfathers, have no time for blatherskite, detest billingsgate, and don't mind offending anyone with their observations. If you're fat, a toddler will tell you so, but she won't care. If you spank her, she'll forgive you. And even if you're mad at her, she'll try to win back your love with all her heart and soul.

PART FOUR

PROGNOSIS

Death had always intrigued the older generation of my family. They liked nothing better than to hold long, lachrymose conversations about funerals, cremations, burial plots, and headstones. I don't know why they were so fascinated by the subject, but at every family gathering the talk inevitably turned to the Grim Reaper.

With Susie on the verge of being taken to the hospital, I thought it was in extremely bad taste for Great-Uncle William to pick that moment to die. After all, he was only one hundred and two. But bad timing or not, his death brought out the amateur mortician in all the Littells. My Uncle John, Aunt Eliza, and my grandmother descended on us like a black cloud, eager to discuss this latest crisis.

"He was so young," my grandmother said, "or at least young seeming."

Having just returned from a memorial service, my grandmother was still dressed entirely in black silk and wore a hat she must have purchased during the Roosevelt administration—Teddy's, that is. The hat, a baggy shapeless thing, had a long black veil that she pulled down over her pale face. She looked to me like pictures I had seen of Mary Todd Lincoln in mourning—same dress, I think.

"A tragedy," my uncle agreed. For all his sophisticated wit and egg-cracking prowess, Uncle John enjoyed talking about death as much as the rest of the family.

"Yeah," my mother said. "A shame he didn't make it to a hundred and three." Mom didn't share their mania.

"Where are they going to bury him?" my father asked.

"They aren't," my grandmother sniffed. "They are going to cremate him."

"That's nice," my mother said deadpan.

"Nice? Nice? Why, my dear, you don't know what you're saying," my grandmother said, shocked.

"Obviously," my mother said.

"Where are they going to bury the ashes?" my father asked, warming to the subject.

"Not in the cemetery," my grandmother said. "Cousin Emily says that it costs a hundred dollars just to open a grave. She wants to bury the ashes in their backyard, under the rosebushes."

"He never liked their backyard," Uncle John said. "He told me that once. Besides, I think it's illegal. You can't go around spreading ashes anywhere you want. It's not sanitary."

"Perhaps she could spread them around the Botanical Gardens," my father said. "He liked the Botanical Gardens."

"Same problem," Uncle John said. "You can't scatter human remains around like chicken feed. If you could, we'd all be buried up to our necks in ashes, as it were."

"To scatter ashes, you have to open the box," my grandmother said with a slight shudder.

"How big is a box of ashes?" I asked, the genes kicking in. If the guy weighed one hundred seventy-five pounds, that was one heap of ashes.

"About the size of a two-pound fruitcake from Schraffts," my uncle said, indicating the dimensions with his hands.

I looked at him to see if he was joking. He wasn't.

"Like the fruitcake Aunt Amy sends us every year?" I asked.

"The very same," my uncle said. "I suppose you do what we do with it. Keep it until Easter and then throw it out."

I nodded. That was exactly what we did with the inedible fruitcake, but I had never before associated a Christmas tradition with human remains.

"I don't like to say anything," my grandmother said, indicating that wild horses couldn't stop her. "But as you know, I had my brother cremated and I made the mistake of opening the box."

We all stared at her as she carefully rolled the long black veil from her face.

"What happened?" my mother said, intrigued in spite of herself.

"Well, let us just say *they didn't do a very good job,*" she said, enunciating each word.

I had visions of her finding a loose eyeball or two, perhaps a pair of lips, and the odd lung amid the ashes.

"I thought it was just powder," my mother said.

"Not in this case," my grandmother said. "Which is why I'm against cremation in general. I want to be buried on the hill next to my husband."

"I'm sure he'd like that, Mom," Uncle John said. "But I thought you wanted to be buried in Green-Wood Cemetery. Our plot there goes back to the 1810s."

"Green-Wood?" my grandmother gasped. "Green-Wood! Why, there are foreigners buried there. I'd rather be dead than buried in Green-Wood Cemetery!"

My mother and I laughed; everyone else sat stone-faced.

"No," my grandmother continued, unfazed. "I want to be on the hill, and you, John, will be right next to me."

My God, I thought, *she's talking about me.*

"I think you'll enjoy it there," she said.

I didn't think so and decided I had had enough of that macabre conversation.

While my family happily prattled on about "cremains" and the presence of deceased foreigners in Green-Wood Cemetery, I went into Susie's room to see how she was doing. The only good thing about rheumatic fever was that it wasn't contagious and the quarantine had been lifted. We could go into her room at will.

The bad things about rheumatic fever, however, far outweighed the good. Rheumatic fever develops from scarlet fever, which develops from a strep infection. Usually prompt treatment with antibiotics knocks out the disease quickly, but in Susie's case either she or the streptococcus bacteria were resistant to all the drugs the doctor tried. The longer she was in the grips of the disease, the more likely she would develop myocarditis, an inflammation of the heart valves that could be debilitating or even fatal. She was also at risk of arthritis, heart failure, angina, chronic skin disease, and anemia. Unlike many childhood diseases, once you get rheumatic fever, you are prone to get it over and over again.

Susie was lying in bed, dozing fitfully. I felt her forehead. It was warm and bumpy, due to the constant fever and the subcutaneous nodules that had spread across her body. She awoke at my touch.

"I got rheumy fever," she told me.

"So I've heard."

"And I've got a schnake on my tummy."

"A schnake?"

"Look."

Susie pulled up her pajama top and sure enough there was a raw-looking rash on her stomach.

"It does look like a snake," I said, recoiling from the serpentine rash.

"Will you play with me?" she asked.

"Sure," I said. "What do you want to play?"

"Bowling. Will you take me bowling?"

"You have to go to a bowling alley," I said. "And you're not supposed to get out of bed. Besides, have you ever been bowling before?"

"Yes. And I got a three," she said.

"Three pins a frame?"

"Yes. My score was three."

"For the whole game?"

"Yes."

"I'll tell you what," I said. "The moment you get well, I'll take you bowling and we'll see if you can set a new record with a four."

"When will that be?" she asked.

"When you're well."

"I'm not going to get well," she said. "I'm going to the hospital."

"I know."

"I'm scared."

"I know," I said.

I didn't want to admit it, but I was scared, too. Dr. Alexander had been perplexed by her case from the beginning, wondering why the massive doses of antibiotics were having so little effect. The only recourse, he said, was to take Susie to the hospital for round-the-clock care. My mother took this as a personal insult, because she had been caring for Susie around the clock. But she bowed to the doctor's demand. She knew, in her heart, Susie was not getting any better. All of us—doctors, parents, brothers—were at the mercy of a microscopic bacteria that had monstrous consequences on the tiny patient.

"'Night, 'night," Susie said, rolling over on her side.

It was only one o'clock on a cold afternoon, but she was so fatigued and listless she couldn't keep her eyes open. I let her sleep. What else could I do?

Back in the living room, death still held the floor.

"I suppose we could trade you our two plots in Maryland for the one spot in Kensico," Uncle John said.

"What are you going to do with only one space?" my father asked.

"I don't know," Uncle John said. "Perhaps exchange it for a two-holer elsewhere."

Instead of playing the stock market, the Littells had always speculated in real estate, specifically in cemetery plots. Between my father, uncle, and other relatives, they held acres of valuable land in many states and the District of Columbia. If you happened to expire most anywhere in the country, we could have put you up—for a small fee. Had my family built condos on their property, they would have put Donald Trump in the shade. But they remained cash poor, land rich, and death obsessed.

I wanted to yell at them to stop. I wanted to tell them that poor little Susie was in grave danger of joining Great-Uncle William in the rosebushes, but they kept up their dialogue, obviously relishing every bizarre detail, oblivious to anything else.

I don't know if I was suddenly overcome by the family fixation, but I began to think that the worst could happen to Susie. I had saved her life once, but I felt powerless to do it again.

Chapter 14

SUSIE IN WINTER. Susie lived in fear of her blue
snowsuit and preferred more traditional garb.
Here she is standing by the playground where
The Game was played in summer.

Thin Ice

"Help! Help!" Susie screamed, running as fast as her two-year-old legs could carry her. "Daddy hurt me!"

That sounds like the beginning of a TV movie about child abuse, but the reality of the situation was much more prosaic. My father did, indeed, hurt Susie every time he tried to put her in her snowsuit. A man with strong hands, he would tug mightily on the obstreperous zipper and invariably end up pinching her chubby chin. Terrified he would do it again, she would flee from him when he got out her blue snowsuit with the red pompom on the hood.

"Help me, John," she would cry piteously.

So while my abashed father tried to apologize, I would cram Susie into her winter garb and gently zip her up. I didn't care if the zipper went all the way to the top and that left plenty of room for her various chins.

But on one freezing winter day, I was feeling distinctly put upon. Instead of playing basketball that Saturday, I was dragooned into taking Susie to the lake, while my parents and brother went to a school science fair. Stephen had some cockamamy exhibit on display and he wanted my parents to inspect it without having to contend with a rambunctious Susie.

I decided to take the aluminum-and-canvas stroller, not that Susie would voluntarily ride in it unless she was exhausted, but because it was a handy way to carry my basketball and the book I was reading. The Black Torpedo of Doom was, fortunately, exiled to a living death in the basement.

"Sadly come, too," Susie said as we toddled out the door.

"No," I said. "It's too cold for Sadly."

"Sadly come!" Susie yelled. "Sadly come!"

"Let's go," I said.

"No, no, no, no!"

Susie sat down on the sidewalk in protest and began to cry.

"Oh, for God's—" I began. Then I caved in completely because I didn't want to cause a scene in public.

"All right," I said. "We'll get Sadly."

Susie popped up from the sidewalk like a jack-in-the-box, smiling, laughing, and thanking me profusely. After all, Sadly was her best friend.

We made the short, ten-minute walk in a long twenty minutes because Susie, like her buddy Sadly, insisted on investigating every tree, light pole, and fence along the way. But I didn't really mind. I planned to be out in the cold for only an hour or two and I didn't care where I froze. When we finally reached our destination, I knocked on Mrs. Davis's back door, while Susie crawled into Sadly's doghouse to see if he was home.

"Hi, Mrs. Davis," I said. "Can Sadly come out and play?"

"It's so cold," she said, shivering.

"I know, but Susie won't go anywhere without him."

"All right, I'll get him, but don't keep him out too long," she said.

Susie insisted on holding his leash and kept saying, "Giddy up, Sadly." I pushed the stroller, which now contained my basketball, a Perry Mason mystery, a box of dog biscuits, and a bag of people biscuits, compliments of Mrs. Davis. I used the stroller as a cow pony to drive the wandering duo in the general direction of the lake. Every once in a while, Sadly would get it in his head to explore somebody's lawn and drag a protesting Susie with him. Then Susie would get an urge to walk down a side street and drag a protesting Sadly after her. Herding cats must have been be easier.

"I tired," Susie said after what seemed like hours of zigzag peregrinations.

"Okay," I said, taking the basketball out of the stroller. "Hop in."

"No. I ride Sadly," she said.

"No, you can't," I said flatly.

The tears formed and her face turned red. She was about to throw another fit, but this time I was ready for her.

"If you ride Sadly, you'll break his back," I said. *"Crrrackkk!"*

My sound effect got her attention and she stared at me with big eyes.

"Then he'll fall to the ground," I said.

I fell to the ground.

"And howl in pain."

I howled in pain.

"Oh, no," Susie said, forgetting about throwing a fit.

"Oh, yes. You're too big to ride him. You don't want to hurt Sadly, do you?"

"No."

When asking questions of a two-year-old, you have to phrase them in such a way that the natural response—*no!*—means yes.

Crisis averted, we poked along until we reached the lake. *Lake*, of course, is a relative term, encompassing Lake Michigan, Lake Victoria, and the puddle in your backyard. Our lake was of backyard proportions, really just a wide spot in a small river that flowed through town. In the winter it nearly always froze over, affording a good spot to skate or play hockey. Situated around the lake were wooden benches and a lone basketball hoop without a net. We three adventurers were the only ones around. Smart people and animals of above average intelligence were inside enjoying a roaring fire on such a frigid day.

There was some leftover gray snow hanging on, but the lake seemed frozen solid.

"I skate with Sadly," Susie informed me.

"That's not a good idea," I said.

"Why?"

"Look at your feet," I said.

She looked down.

"What are you wearing?"

"Wed boots," she said.

"Now look at Sadly's feet. What's he wearing?"

"His toesies," Susie said.

"You don't want him to freeze his toes off, do you?" I asked, knowing the answer.

"No."

"Because he would hop around and say, 'Oww, oww, oww.'" I hopped around, first on one foot, then the other, shouting my version of a doggie "oww."

Susie clapped her mittened hands at my performance and instructed Sadly to watch her while she "skated."

Like our lake, which wasn't really a lake, Susie's skating wasn't really skating either. What she did was take a few mincing steps on the ice, slide an inch or two, and yell, "Whee!" That kept her entertained for minutes at a time.

I was harder to entertain and watching Susie careering around on the ice was distinctly boring, so I unlimbered the b-ball and took a few shots at the basket. Playing with gloves, on a snow-caked surface, added a new degree of difficulty to the game, and I soon tired of having to chase the ball into the hinterland every time it took a bad bounce. Erle Stanley Gardner's *The Case of the Murdered Minion,* or some such title, offered a better possibility for killing time.

I lured Sadly over to a bench with a dog cookie and made him get off the cold ground. The low-slung basset hound must have suffered terribly in winter, forced as he was to drag his most personal parts through snow of four inches or higher. The wooden bench was much warmer than the ground and Sadly snuggled up to me gratefully.

From time to time, I would glance up from Perry Mason's brilliant closing argument to make sure the blue snowsuit with the red pom-pom didn't stray too far. Then I would slip Sadly another biscuit and go back to the *The Case of the Crashing Call Girl,* or whatever the book was called. I could usually figure out whodunit on page sixteen, but not exactly why. I had to wait two hundred forty pages for Perry to elucidate the motive. Sometimes, of course, I would just flip to the last page to confirm my suspicions and not bother with the rest of the blather. I was just about to cheat when Sadly suddenly stiffened and coughed mildly, his idea of a bark.

"What's wrong, Sadly?" I asked.

He didn't say anything, so I gave him a biscuit and he relaxed on the bench. Then I put the book down and stared out at the lake. All was quiet, there was not a soul around.

No one.

I jumped up from the bench so suddenly that Sadly's head hit the wooden slats with a bang. He looked at me reproachfully with his soulful brown eyes, but I was focused on finding Susie. I scanned the part of the lake where I had last seen her.

Nothing.

I stood up on the bench and made a survey of the area, but all I could see was a lone red dot on a sea of dirty ice.

Before the middle-aged onset of presbyopia, I had perfect vision, but the vision I saw that cold morning was perfectly terrifying. The red spot on the ice was the pompom on the hood of Susie's snowsuit. She was underwater.

With speed born of fear, I raced out onto the lake, seeing for the first time that the ice I had imagined to be frozen solid was actually thin and soupy. It didn't occur to me that I might fall through the ice myself, because I was totally intent on reaching the red spot that seemed so far away.

I ran, as if in a nightmare, my legs pounding away, but everything seemed to be in slow motion. Although it probably took me only a few seconds to get to her, I felt as if I had been running for days.

As I closed in on my target, I felt the ice crack beneath me, and I slid the rest of the way on my belly, reasoning that I might make it if I spread out my weight. Propelling myself with my arms, I covered the remaining distance, making the red pompom my goal.

I inched my way the remaining few feet, finally reaching the gaping hole where she had gone in. Then I reached out, and with all my might, I grabbed the top of Susie's hood and plucked her from the water like an oversize cod.

Blue-faced, sputtering, and crying lustily, my prize came out of the water easily, but now I worried we might both fall back through the thin ice. Still holding her by the hood of her snowsuit, I backed away carefully from the jagged hole where she had gone in, and when I had moved her a few feet, I slung her like a hockey puck toward the shore. She spun and twisted across the surface of the ice and came to a stop some distance away. She struggled to get up, but her waterlogged snowsuit kept her pinned to the spot.

When I was sure she was safe, I gingerly pushed myself backward, hearing the ice crack and complain with each movement. Again, it seemed to take hours to travel a few yards, but as soon as I heard the ice stop complaining, I jumped to my feet and went to poor Susie, who was lying on her back like an overturned turtle.

I picked her up and examined her. Susie's former blue pallor had changed to crimson as she cried and cried.

Good, I thought, *if you're crying, you're breathing*.

With Susie in my arms, I raced as fast as I could for shore. When I got to solid ground, I tore off her snowsuit and wrapped her in my jacket.

"I fall down," she told me in a teeth-chattering gasp.

"You fell in," I said.

"All wet," she said. "Cold."

"Yeah, I know," I said, getting a sudden inspiration. The poor child was shivering and gnashing what teeth she had.

"Here, Sadly," I called, evicting my basketball from the stroller.

He walked over to me, probably expecting another cookie, but I had a surprise for him. I shoved Susie into the stroller; then I placed Sadly on top of her to keep her warm.

"Sadly ride?" Susie asked.

"Yeah."

"Good Sadly," she said, not shivering quite as hard as before.

With the two of them on board, I ran as fast as I could for home. With apologies to Johnny Horton, I ran through the briars and I ran through the brambles, and I ran through the bushes where the rabbits couldn't go. I ran so fast that the hounds couldn't catch me, on down the Mississippi to the Gulf of Mexico-o-o-o.

Actually, I ran across snow-packed sidewalks, up hills, down inclines, and around all obstacles. I ran through parking lots, backyards, and driveways. I ran into pedestrians, intimidated bicyclists, and challenged cars. I ran, jacketless, until I was sweating with anxiety and exertion despite the freezing weather. I even made it up our steep hill in record time, thankful I was not burdened by the Torpedo.

We must have made a comical sight bouncing over hill and dale, me with a mad gleam in my eye, pushing a much weirder science exhibit than Stephen could ever have dreamed up—a basset hound/child hybrid, joined front to back.

Susie, holding Sadly in her lap, urged me to go faster, but Sadly, discommoded by the bumps, coughed his phlegmy bark at each jolt. It seemed to take forever to get home.

I flung open the door to our house and bellowed for my mother, who I hoped had returned from the science fair.

Mom took one look at me, panicked, then regained her composure. "What happened?" she asked in her controlled voice.

"Hi, Mama," Susie said, poking her head out from behind Sadly. "I fall down."

I hauled Sadly from the stroller and extracted Susie from her seat, explaining that she had fallen through the ice. My mother's eyes widened and her mouth tightened at the corners.

"A bath," she said. "A hot bath."

Like the doctors of the Middle Ages, my mother had a tenuous grasp on modern germ theory. In an emergency, she would almost always fall back on her vast knowledge of folk medicine. She knew in her heart that getting cold precipitated a cold and that getting really cold caused pneumonia. Thus the hot bath.

In a trice, Susie was in the tub, complaining bitterly that she wasn't dirty and begging to have Sadly join her in the water. I didn't mind if the basset took a hot bath. In fact, he smelled like he needed one. But my mother vetoed the idea and I led Sadly out to the kitchen to give him an honest-to-goodness people cookie for being such a good blanket.

All the excitement attracted my father and brother, who demanded to know what was going on. I told my tale of disaster and rescue at least five times that day, and I was surprised that, instead of being yelled at for letting her fall through the ice, I was universally lauded for pulling her out alive.

Susie suffered only one ill effect from her plunge: She was put to bed for a nap that afternoon, the victim of Mom's other unscientific belief that naps cured everything from asthma to goiters.

I went back to the lake the next day to retrieve my basketball and book. The air was damp and low clouds foreshadowed the coming snow. I looked out to the scene of our near disaster and found that, like scar tissue, new ice had formed over the jagged hole, erasing any trace of yesterday's crime scene. Susie's sodden snowsuit had frozen solid and was lying where I had flung it, reminding me, an avid Perry Mason reader, of a corpse in the throes of rigor mortis. I picked it up gingerly and tucked it under my arm, realizing again just how lucky we were. If Susie's red pompom hadn't shown above the ice, I wouldn't have reached her in time and she wouldn't have been found until spring.

Chapter 15

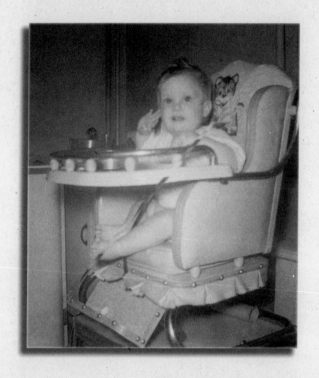

GERBER BABY? Mary thought that if she fed her daughter Gerber's baby food, Susie would eventually look like the infant pictured on the jar. Sound far-fetched? I think not.

Food
Inglorious Food

By the time she was ten months old, Susie was sitting up in her high chair and eating like a real person. What she ate, however, bore no similarity to real food whatsoever. My mother was a devotee of the Gerber Baby Food company and bought all its products religiously. I say religiously because I mean it. Mom had a mystical belief that, if you fed your baby Gerber's, your child would soon look like the kid on the label: beautiful, smiling, and blond. When I pointed out that we were also avid consumers of Uncle Ben's Converted Rice, my mother refused to listen. For her, the label on the Gerber's baby food jar was like the picture of the pretty flowers on a packet of seeds—the label showed the final product.

In those days, baby food came in two flavors: god-awful and not too bad. I watched with great amusement when my mother held her nose and tried to shovel strained liver into Susie's unsuspecting mouth.

"Isn't this yummy?" my mother would say—nasally—as she tried to get as far away as possible from the revolting brown stuff. Susie, however, wasn't fooled. She would spit it out forthwith, her face contorted with displeasure.

The look and texture of the liver was equaled in grossness only by the strained peas. Long before Linda Blair ever thought about throwing up pea soup in *The Exorcist*, Susie had mastered that technique. If my sister could have turned her head around 360 degrees, she would have been a famous movie star.

"Why won't you eat this?" my mother would wail, waving a spoonful of strained veal in the air. "It's Gerber's."

But Susie's mouth would be clamped shut and her head turned at a mere ninety degrees.

Mom was positive that, if Susie ate all those atrocious meats and vegetables, she would become beautiful, intelligent, and talented. The road to being crowned Miss America was paved with baby veal, Mom was sure. And why not? Baby veal had the same taste and consistency as asphalt.

In the not-too-bad category were the tapioca pudding and the strained applesauce. The applesauce was my favorite. Smooth, tart, and utterly delicious, baby applesauce made the adult kind seem coarse, crude, and totally unsophisticated. I would generally pop a jar of it every afternoon after school and share it with Susie. She and I lapped it up with great satisfaction.

I used to get a kick out of feeding Susie and soon discovered there were two methods that worked reasonably well. The first was the long, slow method, which involved an elaborate, time-consuming ritual. Here's how it worked: Once the strained food had been placed in the heated tripartite baby dish, the chanting would begin. As in any ritual, the magic words had to be sung with artistry and feeling—this one in a falsetto voice:

"Knock on the door."

I would rap Susie's forehead with my knuckles to get her attention.

"Peek in."

I would raise her eyelid, causing her to giggle.

"Lift up the latch."

I would place a forefinger under her nose, cutting off her air supply and making her mouth open.

"Walk in."

I would guide the spoonful of god-awful baby food into her mouth. I had to get in and out quickly, or she would bite down on the spoon and refuse to release it.

"Chin chopper, chin chopper, chin chopper."

I would cup my hand under her chin and make chewing motions with her jaw.

Once I had established a rhythm, the exact sequence of the chant became irrelevant. Chin chopping and latch lifting somehow became interchangeable. The important thing about feeding Susie was to mix the order of the god-awful food and the not-too-bad food. Keep the kid confused—that was my motto.

When I grew bored with peeking in and door knocking, I would switch to my patented express-feeding method. I would take a heaping spoonful of baby food and apply it directly to Susie's face, much as a plasterer rough-coats a wall. Then, using the spoon as a trowel, I would gather up all the food and scrape it into her mouth. It was a messy business, but I could usually finish feeding her before she remembered to complain.

My biggest complaint about baby food was the little jars it came in. In those days, you had to pry off the tin tops with a bottle opener, and there was no way to reseal the jar once it had been opened. That meant our refrigerator was always crammed with eighty-five jars of half-eaten baby food. The smell of strained liver, peas, beets, carrots, and who knows what else permeated the rest of the food in the fridge, causing the butter to turn rancid, the lettuce to go limp, and the milk to taste funny. Only the applesauce was safe because I made sure I ate it before it went off.

You can talk about digital computers, sliced bread, and atomic energy, but the screw-top baby food jar ranks among the most useful inventions of the twentieth century—ask anybody who has spent years inhaling essence of strained chicken from an insecurely capped container.

Susie eventually graduated from Gerber's to Mom's food, a dubious advancement. Once she was deemed old enough, my father insisted that Susie join us at the dinner table and enchant us with her sparkling conversation. She tried her best, but I grew weary of her prattling on about her basset hound friend, Sadly.

"Sadly ticks," she said one evening.

"Like a time bomb?" Stephen asked.

"Yes."

"I think you mean Sadly *has* ticks," my mother said.

"Yes."

That was about as sparkling as the conversation ever got, but my father thought it was important to civilize children by teaching them how to dine graciously, even if the food was lousy. Like my mother, he was big on manners. Resting an elbow on the table, chewing with an open mouth, or sporting a milk mustache irritated him beyond endurance. Proper dress at the dinner table was also an obsession with him.

"Always remember," he said on numerous occasions, "your father never appeared at the table without his suit coat."

I guess that was a virtue, and I still remember him saying it, but I have to confess I have been lax about dressing for dinner during the past forty years.

Although she wouldn't have been considered Winston Churchill's rival as a conversationalist, Susie soon got into the spirit of criticizing my mother's cooking.

"This tastes like shark," she said one day. "Ick."

I guess she was right. The pot roast had a distinctly fishy flavor for some reason, though how she knew to equate it to shark remains a mystery to me.

"Eat your shark," my father said.

That was the thing about Mom's cooking: You couldn't really insult it or her. Mom would just laugh, agree, and suggest reservations for tomorrow evening's meal.

As she grew older, Susie was no longer content just to be included at the dinner table. She suddenly became enamored with the idea of passing food—especially food that no one had asked for. The unwary diner, attempting to conduct a civilized conversation, might find his plate heaped to the ceiling with brussels sprouts or discover a stick of butter in his soup. My mother tried to get Susie to ask before she passed things, so throughout a meal she would hound us.

"John, want salt?"

"No, thank you."

"Here's salt. Can I pour?"

"I told you I don't want any salt," I would say forcefully. Two seconds of blessed silence.

"John, want pepper?"

Meals at our house could be exhausting—a triumph of style over substance, of hope over experience.

Many years ago, a friend of mine, who is now a famous novelist, wrote a satire called *The WASP Cookbook*. He wrote it because he had a love-hate relationship with white Anglo-Saxon Protestant women, and he wanted to vent his conflicting emotions. This not-for-publication pastiche lovingly described the silverware, china, crystal, linen, and centerpieces for each recipe. And each of the recipes featured martinis served from silver cocktail shakers and wicker baskets filled with white bread—but no actual food. Unknowingly, he described my house when I was a kid. We were long on the Limoges and short on the lasagna.

Much preferring to dine out, my mother didn't want to have anything to do with cooking. But with three children in the 1950s, she had to bow to the inevitable and produce meals three times a day. Breakfast was easy: cereal and toast, which we made ourselves. Lunch was a bit more difficult: cream cheese and jelly sandwiches on white bread. The problem with cream cheese and jelly is that the jelly (inevitably Welch's grape) leached through the bread while sitting in a hot locker for hours. For years I lunched on sticky purple sandwiches.

Mom also never comprehended the importance of packaging those sandwiches. All the other kids had white sandwich bags filled with an assortment of fruits, raw vegetables, salads, exotic luncheon meats, and delicious pastry. My solitary sandwich would sit, purple and gooey, in the bottom of a vast shopping bag from Macy's. Years of whining never secured me the proper bag, because Mom, like the ladies of Boston, didn't *buy* bags, she *had* them.

So off I would go, an enormous shopping bag containing one lousy sandwich under one arm, and my books under the other, to face the ridicule and laughter of my friends. Even folding the shopping bag into a six-inch-by-six-inch square didn't make it look anything like those pristine, store-bought white bags the other kids had. Just where my mother secured her endless supply of department store shopping bags, I don't know. I do know I was plagued by them until I got to junior high and bought my lunch at the cafeteria. I was the only one in my class who found cafeteria food a vast improvement.

Dinner at our house was always an adventure. My father, who had grown used to bad cooking over the years, was decidedly cool about what appeared on the table. He always made sure he had a shaker of Manhattans and a bottle of wine by his side. He claimed he liked calves' liver and onions, a dish that would send the rest of us fleeing, but he probably just said that to annoy my mother. She agreed with us kids that liver, loaded with tubules and ducts, was pretty disgusting, and if he wanted to eat liver, he should do so in a restaurant. Preferably in Paris.

Although she couldn't cook a lick, my mother was a stickler for table manners. A bottle of milk on the table or a napkin under the chin reduced her to quivering outrage. She taught us about which fork to use, how to indicate when you were done, and how to have good manners when dining in a restaurant or at the odd royal palace, in case we might receive an engraved invitation. (Note to royalty: I'm still waiting.)

To make her point, Mom would produce the twenty-seven-thousand-piece silverware set she had inherited from her grandmother and line up sample place settings that would have baffled Emily Post. How many people, even then, could identify a marrow spoon or a sterling silver tea strainer? She would also make Dad lay out wineglasses and tell us the difference between a Bordeaux glass and one used for Chardonnay. And of course, she regaled us with the old saw about the fabulously wealthy maharaja dining at the court of Queen Victoria. When the finger bowls were passed around, he took a sip out of his. Seeing that, and not wanting to embarrass the maharaja, all the guests, including the queen, sipped out of their finger bowls. In one story, she taught us how to use a finger bowl, and the true meaning of sophistication: being able to deal gracefully with all situations.

Her emphasis on the manners and techniques of dining made me interested in food—especially in where to find some. I was not a particularly picky eater, which was fortunate, because if I had been, I would have starved to death before the age of twelve. However, I was determined to learn all I could.

I was an early veteran of restaurant dining and made it a point to order unusual things on the menu and observe what the other diners were eating. Eyeing the customers, I'd be shocked at breaches in etiquette.

For home cooking, I headed to Brian Thompson's house. His mother was a terrific cook, and his father was an ace barbecuer. They always had lots of good food on the table and were indulgent enough to invite me to dine with them.

Passing up a delicious Swanson's TV dinner one evening, I took refuge at Brian's house because they were having spaghetti and I loved spaghetti—even the way my mother made it. Spaghetti was hard to wreck.

I wasn't expecting anything exotic or unusual, but when Mrs. Thompson brought out a wooden bowl the size of a washtub filled to the brim with spaghetti, I knew I was in for a treat. Although light on sauce, the tub of pasta featured meatballs bigger than a baseball and gigantic mushrooms that looked dangerous. She piled up a plate for me and I was agog. At home, Mom usually served about eleven strands of spaghetti per person. Here, on my plate alone, was more than my mother served the entire family. It was delicious, especially the mushrooms, which rarely appeared at our house because Stephen wouldn't eat them and would carefully pick them out of any dish, murmuring, "Ugh."

I ate so much spaghetti that evening that I could manage only four pieces of bread and a few dozen world-class brownies for dessert.

"Do you eat like that all the time?" I asked Brian after dinner.

"Like what?" he asked.

"Like kings," I said.

"I guess," he said.

Because he dined so well, so often, he had no idea how lucky he was. A week at my house would have convinced him otherwise. I made sure I thanked the Thompsons effusively, hoping to be invited again. Like a dieter who goes on a binge, I was beginning to understand just how enjoyable food could be and just what a rotten concept portion control really was.

After that, I made it my job to canvass the neighborhood to find out what was for dinner and wangle an invitation wherever I could. I spent years being a professional dinner guest and enjoyed every moment of it. From my neighbors, I learned how to use chopsticks, both Chinese and Japanese; how to eat an artichoke; how to tell a compote from a canapé; and how to avoid being burned to death when crepes were ignited at the table. Although I wasn't much interested in the cooking or cleaning-up part, I was an enthusiastic eater. Rather like my mother, come to think of it.

But my epiphany came when I invited myself to dinner at Kim's house. His real name was Kenyon Ingersol Manning Bennett, but he was known by the initial letters of each of his first three names. At twelve, Kim wasn't much to look at. He was a scrawny kid with dark hair and a diffident manner. Somehow, he seemed much smaller than his name. But he was rich. Not just normal rich, but really rich. Or at least his father was. His dad, Billy Bennett, owned oil, cattle, and most of the stocks on the New York Exchange. He once showed me his portfolio, which was the size of the Manhattan phone book. Impressed, I commented on its bulk and he said, "Oh, that's just A to C. The others are over there."

Kim lived with his father, who was a widower, and his sister in a house that looked like the pictures I had seen of Versailles. You needed a bicycle to get around efficiently, especially if you wanted to see all the art treasures: Ming vases; not one, but two Rembrandts; a few Picassos; the odd Modigliani; and an entire gallery devoted to the Impressionists.

Kim, of course, was as completely immune to his surroundings as Brian Thompson was to his family's cuisine. But for me, it was an astounding experience to visit that grand house. For the first—and last—time in my life, I knew what it was like to be rich.

One day, as we were playing catch on the grounds of his house, I noticed that the doors to their vast garage were open and the chauffeur was washing a large black limousine.

"I hear you got a Rolls," I said.

"Yeah," Kim said as if I had asked him if he had a shirt.

"Which one is it?" I asked.

"The one next to the Ferrari," he said.

Oh.

With that kind of wealth, I knew I had to see how the other half ate, so I forced myself on the unsuspecting Bennetts.

Armed with my vast knowledge of dining etiquette, I arrived at Kim's house early one evening.

"Do you want to eat in the dining room or the kitchen?" he asked me.

"Dining room," I said. I ate in the kitchen all the time.

He looked disappointed because he ate in the dining room all the time, but he was a good host and told the butler that we would dine at seven. The butler actually said, "Very good, sir."

"So, you got a cook?" I asked.

Kim looked scandalized. "A chef," he said.

"Good," I said. Chefs, I knew, were cooler than cooks.

"What are we having?" I asked.

"I don't know," he said. "Some kind of lamb."

That sounded all right, I thought. I could handle lamb chops or leg of lamb.

We played a spirited game of acey-deucy, a two-player game that involved matching cards. After a half hour, I owed him seventy-one million dollars. Fortunately, he didn't need the money.

Then I heard a gong.

"What's that?" I asked.

"Dinner," Kim said.

I had never heard a dinner gong before. I was used to my mother threatening to cut off my allowance if I didn't turn off the TV and come to the table—at once! I had to admit a gong was much classier.

Kim and I made the trek from the conservatory, where we had been playing cards, to the dining room, which was at the other end of the house—maybe a mile or two away. On the long march, it occurred to me that, the last time I was in a conservatory, Colonel Mustard was trying to strangle Miss Scarlet with a rope.

When we finally reached our destination, I was awestruck. The dining room was about the size of my entire house. It featured a vaulted roof, exposed timbers, and a giant mural painted on the ceiling. The mural was quite interesting because it featured half-naked ladies cavorting around in the woods. I was so intent on staring at the ladies, mouth agape, that I bumped into a high-backed, leather-trimmed chair.

"Who painted that?" I asked, pointing to the ceiling.

"I don't know," he said. "Some guy in Italy. My dad bought the entire room from a castle there."

I had never heard of such a thing. Nobody bought whole rooms. But the place did look like a castle.

"The table, too?" I asked.

"Yeah. The whole shootin' match," Kim said.

The table, which was ornately carved on the sides, was about as long as a runway at La Guardia Airport and could accommodate the entire New York Yankee baseball team, the visiting team, and a couple dozen fans. Every few yards, stands of three-foot-high white candles poking out of elaborate silver holders cast pools of light not only on the table, but on the miles of ancient tapestries that covered the walls. The ladies on the tapestries were clothed, but they seemed to be having fun helping knights on horseback hunt down deer, boars, and rabbits. In the woven sky, a falcon was about to pounce on a pigeon.

"Wow," I said, thinking I had stumbled upon King Arthur's dining room. "Where's Merlin?"

"Who?"

"Nothing."

At one end of the table, which was centered on an Oriental rug the size of a football field, three chairs had been placed together. Kim stood behind the one at the head of the table and pointed to the seat at his right. I sat down and realized immediately I had made a mistake. So I bounced up again and stood behind my chair.

"Is your father eating with us?" I asked, perplexed by the formality.

"No, he's in Iran," Kim said. "My sister is."

Kim hadn't talked much about his sister, so I didn't know what to expect. In my mind, however, I pictured a tall, older lady, maybe twenty, in a shimmering white ball gown.

I was surprised, therefore, to see a little girl with frizzy blond hair. She was dressed in blue corduroy overalls and clutching a bedraggled doll. She was, she informed me, seven years old and her name was Tish.

Kim helped her with her chair, which weighed about two hundred pounds, then sat himself. Figuring it was safe, I joined them.

"Are you in Kim's class?" Tish asked me, propping her ragamuffin doll up against a crystal water glass. "Why can't we eat in the kitchen? Daddy's not here."

"It's my fault," I said gallantly.

"Daddy's never here," she said, not to me, but to her doll. "We're all alone."

I could stand the loneliness in a place like this, I thought.

"Do you go to our school?" I asked Tish.

"No, I have a tutor," she said. "I don't have any friends."

"Sure you do," Kim said. "You've got me, the staff, and that little girl down the road."

"Okay," Tish said. "One friend."

I didn't like the direction the conversation was taking, so I changed the subject to baseball, a surefire way to make everybody happy. But I didn't have time to compare the previous year's Yankees with that year's, because the butler appeared with a huge soup tureen perched on a wheeled serving cart. Dutifully, he ladled the soup into our waiting bowls.

Quickly finding the correct spoon from the array of silverware in front of me, I dug in. It was delicious, much better than Campbell's chicken noodle, a staple at home.

"This is great," I said. "What is it?"

"Turtle, sir," the butler said mournfully.

That was a shock. I didn't know that those cute little painted turtles that you bought at the circus could be ground up into soup. I had to admit that I liked it, but I also knew I would have to apologize later to my two turtles, Spin and Marty, who lounged around in a plastic container adorned with a fake green plastic palm tree. They would be horrified.

The butler disappeared and a lady wearing a black maid's uniform appeared to clear the table. When she was done, another lady, similarly garbed, brought out the next course: cold smoked trout. I was impressed that she knew how to serve from the left, but I was dubious about the trout. I never liked fish much: It always tasted fishy to me. But this was wonderful because it tasted like smoke and I relished every bite.

While Kim and I talked baseball, Tish mumbled to herself and addressed comments to her doll.

"I know you'd rather eat in the kitchen, Samantha," she said. "But we have a guest."

I was sorry to ruin her fun, but I was anxiously awaiting the next course and I wasn't disappointed.

The butler and the two maids marched out of the kitchen in a V-shaped formation. He was carrying a gigantic silver tray with a domed lid, which he placed on the sideboard. Then, showman that he was, he removed the lid with a flourish.

There, surrounded by greens, was a circle of bones, covered with white paper things.

"The crown rack of lamb," the butler said, probably for my benefit. He knew a rube when he served one.

It did kind of look like a crown, I thought, but how did you eat it? That problem was easily solved, because the butler carved us each two chops and arranged them on our plates. The maids rushed around with silver trays of various roasted vegetables, many of which were strange to me. But following my mother's dictum, I tried some of everything, even though it was difficult to pluck what I wanted from a hovering serving dish, while the maid looked at me, obviously annoyed at having to serve a bunch of kids.

The lamb was rosemary scented, had a wonderful peppery crust, and could be cut with a fork. I scarfed down my two chops and wanted to ask for more. But visions of Oliver Twist kept my mouth shut.

The lamb was followed by an endive salad with a tangy cheese dressing that I later learned was Gorgonzola. Then, with another grand flourish, the butler presented the baked Alaska for dessert. Who ever heard of baking ice cream? Kim's chef must have been from Alaska, I thought.

I was practically licking my plate to get the last of the dessert when the butler arrived carrying a white phone. He plugged it into a jack hidden underneath the table and handed the receiver to Kim.

"Your father, sir," he said.

"Hi, Dad," Kim said, expectantly. "When are you coming home?"

There was a silence, then a disappointed "Oh."

Without another word he handed the phone to his sister and she asked the same question. She had the same reaction to her father's answer and hung up.

"We're orphans, Samantha," Tish said to her doll.

I was sorry about their plight, but I was much more impressed that the Bennetts had phones that could be moved from room to room and were not anchored to the wall, as ours were. In an age before cordless and cell phones, movable phones were on the cutting edge of technology and a wonder to behold.

After dinner I asked Kim what it was like to have a chef at your command day and night. I imagined midnight snacks and crepes suzette for breakfast.

"It's okay," he said. "He cooks anything my father tells him to, but when Dad's not here, he experiments on Tish and me. We just eat what's put in front of us."

Ah, the wealthy, never too rich or too thin. I would have spent all his money on food and drink and been as fat as a blimp.

Thanking everyone, including the butler, the maids, and the chef, I rode my bicycle home. Never had I eaten so well and elegantly, and I was quick to tell my parents what they were missing. They laughed uproariously at my enthusiasm.

"I hope you didn't eat your peas with a knife," my father said.

"We didn't have peas," I said.

"Thankfully," he said, rolling his eyes.

My father was never quite sure about my company manners, and with good reason.

I spent many days at Kim's house, sometimes bringing Brian Thompson with me, but I found that Kim preferred to play at my house. Probably he didn't want to mess up the mansion. Then, a few months after my memorable meal, he and I were hanging around one afternoon when Susie literally assaulted him.

"Kim! Kim!" she screamed, running to him and clasping him around the legs, almost knocking him down.

"Hi, Susie," he said, regaining his balance.

Because he had a kid sister, Kim was great with mine. And although she had a soft spot in her heart for Brian, Susie doted on Kim. More than once, she had asked him to marry her.

"Sure," he said. "Call me in about twenty years."

Susie would beam and ask me if twenty years was next week.

"A bit longer than that," I said. "Just be patient. You're too young anyway."

"Nonsense," my father said. "She's almost three. That's old enough to marry Billy Bennett's son. I'll hold the ladder myself when they elope. Then we can all retire to the life of luxury we deserve."

They never did marry, which is why I'm reduced to writing books instead of spending quality time with my polo ponies. But I can't blame Susie—entirely. She did her best to trap him, even inviting him to dinner that evening.

"Do you want to?" I asked Kim incredulously.

"Sure," he said. "Sounds like fun."

I had never heard my mother's cooking referred to as "fun" before, but Kim and I were working on a school project together and we could finish it up after dinner. I wanted to waste as little time as possible on our assignment: the imports and exports of the Benelux countries.

Does anyone remember the Benelux countries, which were constantly being hyped in *My Weekly Reader* for some reason? For the record, they were Belgium, The Netherlands, and Luxemburg and they were mighty uninteresting places.

I went into the living room and confronted my mother. "Mom, can Kim stay for dinner?" I asked.

"Sure, if he wants to," she said. "But I have a better idea. Why don't we all go over to his house and put the chef through his paces? I could go for some oysters Rockefeller and beef Wellington about now."

"Mom!"

"All right," she said. "Although why anyone would want to eat here if he had an option is beyond me."

"What are we having?" I asked.

"I don't know. What do you want?" she asked.

"Something good," I said.

"We're fresh out of that," Mom said. "Are you sure you can't get us an invitation to his house?"

"Mom!"

"How about spaghetti and meatballs?"

"Great," I said.

"Well, I need a few things from the grocery store," she said.

"Like what?"

"Let's see . . . some tomato paste," she said.

"Okay, Kim and I will go get some," I said.

"And some ground beef," she said, "for meatballs."

"Okay."

"And something for dessert."

"Fine."

"And some crusty Italian bread," she said. "Do you like garlic bread?"

"Love it," I said.

"Then I'll need some garlic powder," she said. "What about a nice salad?"

"Sure."

"Okay, pick up some tomatoes, lettuce, cucumbers, and whatever kind of dressing you like," she said.

"Is that all?" I asked, jotting down the oppressive number of items she had ordered so far.

"I think so," Mom said.

"Good."

"Oh, and one more thing," she said, just as I was leaving.

"What?" I demanded. Would she ever finish?

"A box of spaghetti."

That was the way my mother planned meals—on the fly. What other cook in the world would suggest a meal for which she had absolutely no ingredients? Disgruntled, I went to tell Kim we had to launch a hunting party to put dinner on the table.

"I'd better call my father to see if it's okay," Kim said. "Will you bring me a phone?"

"Sorry, but all our phones are nailed down," I said. "Use that one over there."

He spoke softly for a moment, but when he hung up, his normally dark complexion was ashen.

"What's the matter?" I asked.

"I've got to go home," he said. "Right now."

"Your father won't let you stay?"

"No, he's not home," Kim said. "He flew to Bermuda this afternoon and didn't even tell me."

"Great," I said, wishing my father would take a few days off and fly to Bermuda. "Now you can stay late."

"No," he said. "I've got to go. Tish will worry if I'm not there."

"Stay, Kim," Susie pleaded. But all her charm was not enough.

Visibly sagging, Kim slouched out the door, his head down, mumbling, "He didn't even tell me."

We never did have spaghetti that night. But as I listened to my father pontificating about the state of the world, my mother instructing Susie not to put her fork in her nose, and Stephen rambling on about his life, the semifrozen TV dinner didn't taste half bad.

Chapter 16

VANISHING ACT. From the time she could walk, Susie
was afflicted with wanderlust. And why not? The
neighbors were much more interesting than her
family and they had better cookies. Here she is
making a usual, if undignified, escape.

Wanderlust

By the time she was three years old, Susie had thoroughly conquered our hearts. She sang little songs, danced about endearingly, and if she couldn't spin plates on a stick, she could break them with great regularity. But who cared? We thought that everything she did or said was wonderful. Susie was like having our own *Ed Sullivan Show,* not just on Sunday nights, but every day of the year.

Susie, however, found us as dull as a weekday night in Dubuque. She had discovered a wider world and she was anxious to escape the confines of home and hearth. Every morning she and my father would have a contest to see who could awaken first, while Mom snoozed away. If Susie won, she was out the door wearing her nightgown, or sometimes nothing at all, looking for a neighbor who would feed her. If my father won the race, Susie was content to breakfast with him—then she would shoot out the door to enjoy a snack elsewhere.

One Saturday morning at five a.m., there was a loud knocking at our front door. My mother dragged herself out of bed to find Brian's father, Craig Thompson, standing on the porch, wearing blue silk pajamas and no shoes or slippers. He was unshaven, disheveled, and red-eyed.

"Here," he rasped, thrusting Susie into my mother's arms. Then he stomped off as best he could in his bare feet.

"What happened?" my mother asked.

The answer was somewhat confusing, but a few days of in-depth interviews finally shed light on the incident.

During her predawn perambulations, Susie had decided to see what was doing at the Thompsons' house. Breakfast there, as I could attest, was delicious, and there was always a chance they might break out the brownies. So Susie rang the back doorbell and waited.

The Thompsons had Dutch doors, so when Craig opened the top part, he couldn't see anyone, and slammed it shut. A party the night before had left his mouth dry and his head aching; he was in no mood for pranksters.

The bell rang again and this time he spotted Susie in her teddy bear nightgown, looking up at him expectantly.

"Hi, Cwaig," she said enthusiastically. "How come you wearing your jammies? Why aren't you workin'?"

"Susie, it's five o'clock in the g-d morning. Go home!" Craig managed to croak. "It's Saturday."

Craig Thompson was six-two and built like a linebacker—most people did as he said.

"Cawry me?" Susie asked sweetly.

He did. Like everyone else in the neighborhood, he was under Susie's spell, even if he didn't want to be.

In today's world, a rover like Susie would probably become a statistic, but back then she could—and did—roam about in complete safety. Our neighbors, except for the Thompsons, were mostly old ladies, who found Susie an interesting novelty because she was the first baby born in the neighborhood since the Civil War.

These old parties, the "Battle-Ax Brigade," my father called them, weren't your typical sweet little old ladies. No, they were all crazy. Well, eccentric, I suppose, but I swear many of them would be on lithium today. Cataloging them would take several volumes, but two examples will serve to illustrate my point.

It was a dark and stormy night. (Sorry, I always wanted to use that line.) The wind was howling, the trees were swaying, and the rain sounded like bullets on the windowpanes. I was watching television when the lights went out. In the dark, I could hear my father putting together a compendium of curse words—one of his patented chains of profanity that always delighted me. I wasn't sure what all the words meant, but they sounded really disgusting.

"Frank!" my mother interjected, horrified by his scorching language.

"Where the hell's the goddamn fuse box?" he muttered, crashing into some immovable object. "For Christ's—"

"Frank!"

"Miserable, goddamn . . ." Grumble, grumble, grumble.

I went to investigate and spotted my father in the basement, match in hand, trying to avoid the minefield of junk that was stored down there. In a flickering halo of dim light, I could see my father's pained expression.

"Damn!" he yelled as the match burned itself out on his thumb and forefinger. Now he was pained for real.

"Do we have a flashlight?" he called up the stairs.

Silence.

"Is it too much to ask to have a goddamn, son-of-a—"

The lights flickered on, then went out again.

"Do we have a candle at least?"

More silence, followed by a blast of invectives.

"John, go over to Mrs. Buchanan's house and see if you can borrow a candle before your father has a stroke," my mother said.

"Sure thing," I said, jumping up. I loved going there.

Mrs. Buchanan lived next door to us, in a modest house filled with odd and interesting furnishings. She was old—of course, anyone over fifteen seemed old to me at the time—and apparently she had once been rich. But the Crash of 1929 had reduced her to penury, or at least to a small income. However, her little house was packed to the rafters with the debris of her former life: tiger-skin rugs, suits of armor, giant vases on marble pedestals, enormous oil paintings in gilded frames, and a moose head mounted on the wall of the dining room. The moose's name was Eric and Mrs. Buchanan told me she had shot him in Canada in 1924.

I don't know if she was telling the truth because Mrs. Buchanan tended to be a bit vague and forgetful, but I admired Eric extravagantly. He jutted from the wall, gigantic and magnificent, and took up fully a third of the cramped dining room. Once, he had come equipped with forelegs, but Mrs. Buchanan, in an act of wanton vandalism, had cut them off so that Eric would fit into his new and much smaller quarters. Even if he was an amputee, I never missed a chance to stare at Eric.

It was eight at night when I rushed out into the thunderstorm, wearing my yellow slicker and matching yellow hat. I tried to run between the raindrops, as my mother had suggested, but I failed miserably. By the time I got to Mrs. Buchanan's front porch, I was soaked. A sodden, frayed swing creaked ominously in the wind, rocking back and forth. I could picture ghosts sitting on it. Lightning flashed melodramatically when I rang the bell. The familiar notes of Beethoven's "Ode to Joy" echoed through the house.

After a long wait, with the rain pelting down on me from the leaky porch roof, the door was suddenly flung wide open.

"Yes?"

Mrs. Buchanan wasn't very tall, but she was wide enough to fill the doorway. She was dressed in a kimono that had dragons spiraling up the front. It was bright red to match her eyes, and it made her hair seem startlingly white. In her hand was an oversize martini glass, which appeared to be half full or half empty, depending on your perspective.

"Yes?" she said again, staring uncomprehendingly at the little yellow gnome who had interrupted her nightly cocktails. She hiccuped slightly.

"Mrs. Buchanan," I said, the rain now pouring freely down my back. "My mother wants to know if we can borrow a candle. Our lights went out."

"A candle?" she said, her face deep in thought. She swayed slightly in the doorway, pondering my request, as if I had asked her for the chemical formula of nitroglycerin.

I waited, the rain pouring over and through me.

"Of course!" she said suddenly. "A candle. By all means, you shall have your candle!"

But she didn't move an inch. She just drained her martini glass and asked me if I liked olives.

"Yes," I said, hungrily.

"Delicious, aren't they?" she said, eating all three of the olives in her glass.

"What was it again?" she asked, dabbing her mouth with the cocktail napkin supporting her empty glass.

"A candle?" I said tentatively. I had been standing there so long I had almost forgotten.

"Precisely," Mrs. Buchanan said. "I have a candle and it is in the dining room."

A pause.

"Now, let me see, where *is* the dining room?"

"I'll show you," I said, knowing exactly which of the four rooms on the first floor was the dining room. That was where Eric the moose lived.

"Lay on, Macduff."

"My name's John," I said. Sometimes she forgot.

"How lovely for you," she said, wobbling after me.

It didn't take an expert tracker to spot Eric glaring imperiously from the wall.

"This is the dining room," I said triumphantly.

"Aha," Mrs. Buchanan said. "I believe you're right."

I suppose, in her former life, Mrs. Buchanan must have lived in a mansion with a hundred rooms. There, it might have been possible to misplace the dining room, but not in this little house.

While Mrs. Buchanan was collecting herself, I said a silent hello to Eric. He had a kind, knowing smile on his blubbery lips, as if to say, "Don't I look ridiculous up here?" His wide antlers spread out gracefully from his head, rising to the ceiling. I liked him a lot, but I couldn't help wondering where his legs had gone. Were they in the basement? Up in the attic? Tossed in the trash? Could I have them? It was a mystery only the Hardy Boys could solve.

Mrs. Buchanan was inching around the perimeter of the room. She had to, because the table filled almost every square inch. It was made of mahogany and polished to a mirrorlike shine. When the leaves were installed, Mrs. Buchanan had told me, it could seat twenty-four. Unfortunately, by the time the table had been positioned in the dining room, there was no space left for chairs. The distance between the walls and the table was only about six inches, a tight space that Mrs. Buchanan was attempting to negotiate.

"The very thing," she said, pressed between the wall and the table.

I looked up and saw that she was pointing to the most magnificent candle I had ever seen. It was twelve inches in diameter and at least three feet tall. But it wasn't just a plain candle. It had a Renaissance motif: little golden putti floated up the sides on wax clouds; flowers and vines wrapped themselves sinuously around the base; and at the top, dark blue wax studded with tiny silver stars simulated the heavens. I didn't know much about candles, but I knew this monster was not what my mother had in mind. Even the candles at Kim Bennett's house paled by comparison.

"Do you have anything smaller?" I asked.

"Certainly not," Mrs. Buchanan said indignantly. "You wanted a candle and you shall have *this* candle."

I wasn't about to argue with her, so after a few minutes of pulling and tugging, we got it off the table, and I cradled the behemoth in my arms like a baby. It was as heavy as a log.

With an awkward wave to Eric, I thanked Mrs. Buchanan formally.

"Ta-ta," she said, slamming the door behind me.

As I stood on the porch being buffeted by the wind and the rain, I suddenly realized that I was holding a candle that was probably worth some real dough—maybe even five dollars. So I took off my slicker, wrapped the candle in its waterproof folds, and pushed off into the storm.

When I got home, I was completely exhausted and wet to the bone.

"Why aren't you wearing your slicker?" my mother demanded. Her ability to see in the dark always amazed me.

"I didn't want to get the candle wet," I said.

"For goodness' sake, you could have put the candle under your slicker," she said in her "you dumb kid" voice.

"Not this one."

At that moment there was an electrical crackling from the basement, followed by a few choice words from my father. The smell of ozone permeated the atmosphere and suddenly the lights came back on. My trip had been in vain.

With the smug look of a man who had finally conquered an inanimate object, my father walked up from the basement, glared at me, and said, "Long swim?"

I ignored him and carefully unwrapped my prize.

"Good God," my father said. "What did you do, rob a cathedral?"

"Mrs. Buchanan had nothing smaller," I said and shrugged.

The three of us walked around the enormous candle, taking in its incredible detail. Each of the angels had a different expression and tiny gold wings; fantastic beasts prowled the base; and keeping them company, a naked lady was contentedly eating an apple.

"It's the creation story. That's Eden on the bottom and heaven at the top," my mother said in awe.

We backed away from the extraordinary candle to take in its magnificence.

"I think we've all learned a valuable lesson this night," my mother said solemnly.

"What lesson?" I asked.

"That it is far better for your father to curse the darkness than to light a two-hundred-dollar candle."

Although Mrs. Buchanan was my favorite member of the Battle-Ax Brigade, three other ladies gave her ferocious competition. They were known as the Van Dyne sisters, but they weren't sisters at all, I found out later. They were a mother, a daughter, and a niece, who was always called the Young One. The Young One was about ninety, so that will give you an idea just how old the other ladies were. Interestingly, "the Weird Sisters," as my father called them, were not really individuals, but together formed one three-headed entity.

The Young One was the eyes of the group, but she was stone-deaf. The daughter could hear well enough, but like her mother, she couldn't see very well. The matriarch was blind and deaf, but she did most of the talking, probably out of habit. Until a few years before we had moved into our geriatric ghetto, the ladies had driven a fine 1934 Packard, green in color and about thirty feet long. They would pile into their car every day to take a spin around town. Fortunately, they were ladies of uncompromising routine, so they began their daily journey at precisely two p.m. That gave the police time to clear traffic from their habitual route and to warn women and children of their approach. That was necessary because the Young One believed that the white line painted down the middle of the road was there to be lined up with the hood ornament as she drove the huge car precisely down the center. After their tenth accident, the cops disarmed them by taking away their keys in an illegal, but humanitarian, gesture. The old Packard had sat rusting in their driveway ever since.

Forced to walk, the Van Dyne sisters had developed a peculiar form of locomotion. They walked Indian file, in ascending order of age, clutching onto each other's coats, much as circus elephants march trunk to tail. Dressed entirely in black, with long coats even in summer, the Weird Sisters would take their afternoon stroll about town, then turn around and march home again. You could set your watch by their departure, but you could never predict when they would return. Many days they never made it home at all.

The Young One may have had adequate eyesight, but she had no sense of direction, and at least twice a week she would lead the other ladies to the wrong house. They never seemed to notice that they had barged in on strangers and made themselves comfortable wherever they happened to be.

We were not exempt from their impromptu visits, and I was startled one day to find the three of them sitting in our living room.

"Don't you ever knock?" the Young One said to me in a loud voice.

"Who is it?" the mother asked. "Is it the doctor?"

"No, it's a child."

"Child? Child? There are no children here. Begone!" the mother shouted, much upset.

I ran like hell, not wanting to tangle with those three old ladies, and waited for my mother to get home and gently evict them from the premises. It was unnerving to find them in our house, but after a few years of their unexpected visitations, we were oddly disappointed if we didn't see them regularly.

Mrs. Buchanan and the Van Dyne sisters were just two of the leading lights in an extravagant cast of eccentrics inhabiting our neighborhood. I'll only mention the old man with shoulder-length white hair and no teeth, who sat in his second-story window all day long, shouting obscenities at passersby. And the reclusive lady who received a mysterious weekly visit from a uniformed chauffeur driving a block-long limousine. He walked to her door every Sunday morning and, without a word, handed her a thick manila envelope. My father, convinced that the envelope contained thousand-dollar bills, hatched a plan to waylay the driver, steal the money, and move to South America. But I think he was only kidding.

Into this mad milieu, Susie strode like Alice in her own private Wonderland. She was a friend to anyone who gave her a treat, and in that way, she was much like her canine friend, Sadly.

"Hi, I'm Susie. Can I have a cookie?" was her entree into scores of homes. She knew everybody and everybody knew her. Going anyplace with the child was almost impossible. She would stop friends or strangers on the street and inquire about their "mudders and fadders," their dogs, their cats, their houseplants, their health, their children, and their willingness to invite her to tea. The people she didn't stop would stop to chat with her. It was downright embarrassing to be seen in public with Susie because her fan club was legion. She had lived only three years, yet she knew more people in town than my parents and Stephen and I did combined.

Susie ranged far and wide, and her playmates were those neighbors who would let her into their homes. They thought her most preposterous actions and remarks were funny, and of course, most of them were—preposterous, at least. Any doorbell she could reach, she rang. If a kindly looking person answered, she introduced herself and waited to be invited in. After a cold drink, a cookie, and a spot of conversation, she would leave and try a new place. You can see why a life on the road was so appealing to her. In comparison, home was dull, dull, dull.

In a desperate effort to curb Susie's wanderlust, my mother forbade her to leave the house unaccompanied, but the words didn't really deter her.

"Don't worry, Mama," Susie said soothingly. "I always come home."

And she did—at odd hours.

When Susie finally realized that my mother was serious about curtailing her visits, she made one last mournful tour of the neighborhood, telling her friends she wasn't "'lowed" to come to their homes anymore. That was when the phone calls began. Complete strangers demanded to know what was wrong with them and why Susie wasn't allowed to visit. My mother went to great lengths to appease these irate neighbors, going on about not wanting to bother them or intrude upon them. The neighbors, however, didn't seem very appeased and maintained that they looked forward to seeing Susie. One offended lady even went on the attack and accused my mother of being a bad parent. Stunned, Mom asked the woman what in the world she was talking about.

"It's a well-known fact that your daughter is a musical prodigy," the woman said. "And she must come here to practice because you *refuse* to buy her a piano."

"Refuse to buy her a piano?" my mother said in amazement. "I didn't even know she could play."

The lady on the phone harrumphed, confirming her suspicions that Susie was being raised by a pack of unmusical wolves. Irritated, my mother interviewed Susie at length and discovered she could indeed play, at least a few notes. Before anyone realized what was happening, my mother had ordered a piano and it was delivered to our house, where it took up more room than Eric the moose next door. After two years of intensive lessons, our prodigy could manage to get through the first four bars of "The Alley Cat" and soon lost interest in the musical arts entirely. The piano, like the Torpedo, became a great dust magnet.

The problem with Susie's excursions was that they were as mysterious as the inner workings of the National Security Agency. Mom *thought* she knew where Susie was and what she was doing, but she was never dead certain. To make matters worse, Susie's descriptions of her travels bore only a tenuous relationship with reality.

"I went to Mrs. Fairmont's house today," Susie said once.

"That's nice, and how is Mrs. Fairmont?" my mother said.

"I don't know."

"You don't know?"

"No, she wasn't home, so I went into her house and played dress up all by myself," Susie said.

"What!" my mother sputtered.

Now that she had Mom's complete attention, Susie said, "I didn't really. I went to Mrs. Davis's and played with Sadly."

That sort of behavior would drive my mother crazier than she normally was, and she would worry that perhaps Susie's first version of the story was correct. Then she would sneak out of the house just to make sure that Mrs. Fairmont's door was locked and secure.

Susie's incessant wanderings also tended to make my mother the subject of unseemly gossip, especially when the child would say things like, "Mama *absolutely* adores the gwocery boy and couldn't get along without him." That one had Helen Thompson over to our house in a flash, trying to find out just what my mother was doing with the eighteen-year-old delivery boy. And while she was there, she took the opportunity to see if Mom really ate baloney, peanut butter, and ice cream sandwiches for lunch, as Susie had informed her. My mother protested her innocence on both counts, but Helen had her suspicions for years.

Susie's constant flights had a direct impact on me. Not only was I forced to endure making small talk with her numerous adult friends, but I was also somehow elected kid catcher in our house. My mother would send me out at all hours to find Susie and drag her home. After weeks of this work, I demanded a salary and received a ten-cent bounty every time I brought her home alive. On busy days, I could make half a buck, and soon I learned Susie's modus operandi. I could locate her by following trails of cookie crumbs from one house to another. Open gates and trampled flowers were also a sure sign that Susie, like Kilroy, had been there. I was making money on the deal, but my mother's tolerance was wearing razor thin.

The straw that broke Mom's back came when Mrs. Johnston, a very stout lady from down the street, rang our bell one day. "Oh, hello, Mrs. Johnston," my mother said, surprised because Mrs. Johnston had never called on her before. "Won't you come in?"

"No," Mrs. Johnston said curtly. "I just want to tell you that I was sunbathing in my yard when your daughter ran up to me and said, 'Mrs. Johnston, you're too old to wear a bathing suit.' Then she ran off."

"Oh, I'm so sorry," my mother said, aghast. "What a terrible thing for her to say! I'll punish her severely. I'll—"

"Tut, tut," Mrs. Johnston said, holding up a thick hand to stop my mother's tirade. "I went inside and looked in the mirror and do you know what? The child was absolutely right."

Without another word, Mrs. Johnston turned on her heel and walked away, leaving my mother at the door, gaping. When Mom recovered, she marched out of the house with blood in her eye, determined to find her wayward daughter. She caught up to Susie, and there ensued a scene of violence that made Pearl Harbor seem like a DAR tea party.

Susie was waving good-bye to Helen Thompson and thanking her for a brownie.

"Susan!" my mother thundered.

Susie looked up to see her usually calm mother in a fury. One look at Mom's eyes made her burst into tears.

"Come here, at once!" my mother roared.

Wiping brownie crumbs from her mouth and the tears from her eyes, Susie slowly approached, head lowered in shame.

"How many times have I told you not to leave the house without telling me?" Mom said.

"Twice?" Susie ventured.

"A *hundred* times!" my mother shouted. "You are my little girl and I don't want you out of my sight. *Ever!*"

Never in her short life had Susie been yelled at like that, but what happened next was even more astonishing.

"And just to make sure you remember what I'm saying, I'm going to punish you," said Mrs. Legree.

Susie stared wide-eyed at her, probably wondering what she meant, because in her three years she had never even been spanked.

Mom picked a twig off the lawn. It was five inches long and about an eighth of an inch thick. Then she tapped Susie on the back of the legs with it, sending the poor child into hysterics.

"Don't hit me, Mama!" she cried.

"Never leave my sight again!" Mom said and tapped her again on the back of the legs. "Do you understand?"

Susie, screaming and crying, ran with Mom chasing behind, waving the insubstantial twig over her head like an enraged overseer.

"And just to make sure you understand," Mom said when they got home, "I'm going to keep this switch right here on top of this picture frame. If you ever disobey me again, I'll use it."

The little stick remained on top of the picture frame for months, untouched, but monitored closely by a wary Susie. Her roaming days were curtailed, and she learned to tell my mother where she was going and when she would return. Ensuring her good behavior was easy for a time: Simply pointing at the twig would instantly stop Susie from whatever she was up to.

Then one day, Susie climbed up on the back of the couch and took the twig down from its perch. She handed it to my mother and said, "We won't be needing this anymore."

"You won't ever leave my sight again?" my mother said.

"No."

"All right, throw it away."

Mom didn't know it then, but her words would come back to haunt her.

Chapter 17

PEER DEPRIVED. Lacking neighborhood playmates her
own age never seemed to bother Susie. She enjoyed
her circle of elderly ladies, a middle-aged dog,
and a baby carriage in a pinch.

Don't Ever Leave Me

By not sparing the rod, my mother had spoiled the child—or at least her wanderlust. The command "Don't leave my sight" had worked itself into Susie's brain and she had learned her lesson—perhaps too well. But ever the concerned parent, my mother was not content with compliance. She wanted answers.

"Why does Susie feel the need to run away all the time?" she asked me.

"That's easy," I said. "This is the most boring house on the planet Earth and in the entire galaxy."

"Boring?" my mother asked.

"Nothing ever happens here. Face it, Mom, this is a great place to be *from*," I said, appropriating a line I had heard about Philadelphia.

But my mother wasn't buying the boring argument, and she soon thought she had discovered the *real* reason for Susie's nomadic tendencies. In hindsight, the answer was clear: Susie had no one her own age to play with. The average age of her playmates was about sixty-five.

Mom should have been quicker on the uptake because Susie's third birthday party had been a dead giveaway. What a passing strange occasion that had been.

With her mania for birthday celebrations, my mother had gone to great lengths to ensure that Susie would have a memorable party, but what was most memorable about that party was the guest list.

"Who do you want to invite?" she had asked Susie some weeks before the event.

"Mrs. Buchanan, Carl the butcher, Hank at the grocery store, Helen and Craig, Miss Keller, Mrs. Davis, Mrs. Johnston, and Grandma," Susie said.

"No, I mean children," my mother said.

"Stephen, John, Kim, Brian—"

"No, I mean children your own age."

Susie pondered the question for a moment, then said, "Sadly. He's five."

There has got to be something amiss when your only friend not collecting social security is a basset hound, but Mom soldiered on, inviting the entire menagerie of animals, old ladies, middle-aged couples, my friends, Stephen's friends, and half the tradespeople in town. Entertaining such a disparate group strained my mother's hostessing abilities, but my father saved the day. He kept the crowd of adults occupied by serving copious quantities of alcohol, while Mom supplied two cakes and four different kinds of ice cream. My friends and I ate, while Stephen and his friends played pin-the-tail-on-the-donkey and beat the pants off Susie in the potato race. My mother was appalled, but nine-year-old boys are not known for their sportsmanship.

While the grown-ups were in the kitchen getting hammered, Sadly wandered about the house, looking positively glum. It was probably the conical party hat Susie had forced him to wear. I took the opportunity to adjust his hat while Susie was crying. The nine-year-olds had gleefully eliminated her in the first round of musical chairs.

Into the midst of this confusion, the Van Dyne sisters—the epitome of confusion themselves—made a triumphal entrance. Clutching one another's coats and walking in single file, they plowed through the children and sat silently on the couch. Giving in to the inevitable, my father gave them each a Manhattan, which they drained in a single gulp.

"Those old broads can really pack it away," he said, impressed.

But when he returned with refills, they had hit the trail, looking for their own house. Sadly followed them out the door. I followed Sadly. And my father drank the three Manhattans—gratefully.

We must have made quite a sight as we trudged up the hill. The Weird Sisters, heads in the wind and bent almost double, negotiating the slippery sidewalk, all the while attached to each other like Siamese triplets; Sadly, his party hat tipped at a rakish angle, ambling along behind them; and me, a dumb twelve-year-old kid, armed with a fistful of Oreo cookies to lure Sadly back home. But despite the quality of my bait, it took me almost a half hour to entice the basset back to the house. He probably knew something I didn't, because when we returned, one of Stephen's friends suggested they play pin-the-tail-on-the-Sadly.

My mother quickly put an end to that brainstorm and brought out the cake. We all cheered when Susie blew out the three candles in only four tries. She managed to get most of the cake in her hair and painted the front of her dress with various flavors of ice cream. That's not a criticism. Stephen and his friends looked about the same until Mom brought out a basket of washcloths and cleaned them all up. Wiping my face on the sleeve of my new sports jacket, I commented on how childish and immature they were. I know I was right because a lugubrious Sadly chose to sit under my chair to get away from the madding party and its equally mad guests.

Except for the tears, the mess, and a large stain on the living room carpet, the party was a rousing success. By the time the adults had staggered off and the kids had gone home, Susie was greedily counting her loot. That year she had received four dolls. For most little girls, dolls are an appropriate gift, but not for Susie. Although she professed to like them, she treated her dolls in an abominable way. In the privacy of her room, she would carefully undress each doll and throw their clothes in one corner. Then she would stack the naked bodies like cordwood in another corner, where they would remain, unplayed with forever—or until my mother would dress them up and put them on the dresser. Seeing that, Susie would go through the process all over again. Most of the time her room looked like the scene of an especially gruesome mass murder.

Despite running her own doll abattoir, Susie had a great fondness for stuffed animals. Her favorite was a long, low dog called Morgan, according to the box he arrived in. But Susie quickly renamed him Sadly, after her friend, and when the real dog was not available, plush Sadly filled the void. Her behavior, however, made my father uneasy.

"The child strips dolls and talks to dogs, for God's sake," he said one evening. "We've got to do something before we have to ship her off to the lunatic asylum."

"Do you think Sadly would be allowed monthly visits?" my mother wondered absently, but already she was formulating a plan.

I say formulating because Mom didn't like to rush into things. She preferred to cogitate awhile prior to taking any drastic action. That was why several months went by before she made her move.

"I'm going to send Susie to nursery school," she announced one day. "That way she'll have plenty of children her own age to play with."

"Fine," my father said. "Where?"

"The Jack 'n' Jill Nursery School," she said.

"How twee," my father remarked, rolling his eyes. "How much?"

My mother told him.

"You would think for that price they could afford a real *and* instead of a lousy 'n'," my father grumbled.

But the Rubicon was crossed, and Susie was on a collision course with the educational system. Neither one of them would ever be the same.

Before a child could enroll, Jack 'n' his friend Jill insisted that each kid be given a physical examination, including eye and ear tests. Dr. Alexander signed off on Susie's general health and sent my mother to a private clinic for the other procedures.

Examination day fell on a Monday, and hand-in-hand, Susie and my mother walked into the clinic without a care. They checked in, Mom filled out all the paperwork, and a nurse in a starched white uniform whisked them into the chamber of horrors, which contained eye- and ear-testing machines. They began with an auditory evaluation.

My mother knew this was going to be easy because Susie could hear a whisper from halfway across the house—particularly when it was time for her to go to sleep.

The nurse put a large headset on Susie's head and explained that she was to raise her hand as soon as she heard a sound.

Susie raised her hand.

"But I haven't turned on the machine yet," the nurse said.

Susie lowered her hand.

"Are you ready?" the nurse asked, her hand poised above the dial.

Susie raised her hand.

"No, no, you have to wait," the nurse said, quickly dialing up the first frequency.

Susie just sat there.

"Don't you hear anything?" the nurse asked in amazement.

Susie nodded.

"Then raise your hand so I'll know," the nurse said, turning off the tone.

Susie raised her hand.

"Let's try again," the nurse said.

Susie raised her hand.

"If you just watch her face, you'll know when she hears the sound," my mother said helpfully.

"Please don't interrupt," the nurse said. "Now, Susie, when you hear a sound, hit my knee."

Susie raised her hand.

With a sigh, the nurse turned off the machine and stood up.

"I'm sorry, Mrs. Littell. You'll have to take the poor little deaf girl home," she said, the sympathy oozing out of every pore. "She must be enrolled in a *special* school."

"Now wait a minute," my mother said. "She's no more deaf than I am. Susan! Pay attention to the lady! When you hear a sound, raise your hand. Remember the stick on the picture frame."

With the stick as a carrot, the test proceeded smoothly. Susie was a model of cooperation until the eye test began. She was led to a bulky black machine through which she was supposed to look. Standing on a box to raise her to the proper height, Susie executed a little dance while peering through the viewer.

"This is fun, Mama," she squealed with delight. "It's like TV."

The nurse pushed a slide into place and asked Susie what she saw.

"A boy," Susie said.

"Yes, and what else?" the nurse asked.

"A dog."

"Right," the nurse said, hoping the eye exam would go more smoothly than the hearing test. "Do you notice anything else?"

"Yes," Susie said.

"What?"

"The dog looks like Sadly, but taller," Susie said.

"No, that's not what I meant. Do you see anything else in the picture?"

A long, painful silence.

Finally, Susie looked up with an excited face. "The boy looks like Stephen," she said, giving my mother a beatific smile.

"Never mind who he looks like," the nurse said, the doubt creeping back. "Don't you see a ball in the picture?"

"Oh," Susie said.

"Well, where is the ball?"

"On tall Sadly's back," Susie gurgled happily. The nurse's face clouded over with despair.

"She's not blind either," my mother said helpfully, wondering if the child needed glasses.

The nurse walked around to Susie's side of the machine and spoke curtly: "Susie, you have to look with both eyes at the same time."

Susie had her face pressed to the viewer, but one eye was completely outside the scope.

"Like this," the nurse said, moving her over. It had been the longest ten minutes of the nurse's life, but she wasn't going to give up easily.

"Let's try a new slide," she said.

This one was apparently of a little girl, a wagon, and a kitten.

"What do you see now, Susie?"

"It looks all funny."

My mother caught her breath. Maybe Susie really did need glasses.

Had the nurse been a practitioner of slapstick, she would have applied her hand to her face and done a slow burn, but a true professional in every way, she checked the slide.

"Oh, I'm sorry, honey," she said. "I had the slide in upside down."

Quickly correcting her mistake, the nurse asked Susie what she saw.

Susie stared silently into the machine.

"Don't you see a little girl like you?"

"She's not like me," Susie said. "She's got long hair and I liked it better upside down."

"Susan!" my mother said. "You're not cooperating. Tell the nurse what you see."

"No."

"Let's try another way," the nurse said, putting a card on the wall. The card was filled with rows of the letter E. Some were pointing to the left, some to the right, some to the ceiling, and some to the floor.

"These are E's," the nurse explained. "Tell me which way they are going."

Susie thought that remark was remarkably funny.

"They're not going anywhere! They're standing still," she said laughing. "Right, Mama?"

"Come over here and sit in my lap," my mother said.

Susie complied and was given a sheet of paper to cover one eye.

"Now, look," my mother said. "You see the E's. Which way do the prongs go?"

"Prongs?"

"The ends of the E's," my mother said, taking Susie's right hand and pointing her second, third, and fourth fingers straight out. "Do the points go up, down, right, or left?"

"Left?" Susie guessed.

"You have to *look* at them," my mother said helpfully.

"I can see better without this paper," Susie said.

"Start at the top," my mother commanded.

"All right," Susie said, resigned. "That one goes like this."

She pointed her three fingers to the left.

"That's fine," the nurse said, jumping back into the fray. "Now the next one."

Susie got the next two, but then she came to one with the prongs pointing to the right.

Twisting her right hand like a snake, trying to get it into the correct position, Susie began to sway dangerously in my mother's lap. Mom held her tightly while she finally got her fingers into a complicated inverted arc pointed in the right direction.

"That was hard," Susie said, slumping in her mother's lap. "No more of those, Mama."

After that, the nurse called it a day. Susie passed all of her tests, if not with flying colors, at least with an official imprimatur. Mom always swore that, had the child been deaf, dumb, and blind, the nurse would have ignored the evidence just to get Susie out of her examination room.

Once all physical barriers had been hurdled, and a large check was written, my mother thought the hard part was over. But she was wrong again.

As parents do, my mother had been prepping Susie about the joys of nursery school. She went on at great length about how much fun it was going to be and what a good time Susie was going to have. Mom thought that some children were born to go to nursery school, while others had it thrust upon them. Susie, she believed, was in the "born to go" group. After all, she was a happy, gregarious child who got along well with everyone. Nursery school should be a breeze for her.

But on the first day, the breeze turned into a tropical depression and torrential tears began to fall. Susie raised a piteous face to Mom and sobbed, "Good-bye, Mama," as she reluctantly walked to the little yellow school bus. A passing stranger would have thought that Susie was being given up for adoption or that she was leaving on an extended voyage around the world. But their total separation time would be little more than two hours—less time than one of her usual neighborhood jaunts.

As the bus drove off, Mom waved at the tiny woebegone faces in the window, noting that the saddest one of all belonged to Susie. Wondering if she had done the right thing, my mother waited anxiously for Susie's return. Long before she could possibly expect the bus, Mom was out on the sidewalk pacing up and down. When she finally arrived, Susie raced into my mother's arms as if they had been parted for years.

"How was nursery school?" Mom asked anxiously.

"Tewwible."

"Terrible? Why?"

"I cried."

"Why did you cry?"

"It was tewwible."

Mom waited until after Susie had had her lunch and then she tried again.

"Did you make friends with any nice little boys or girls?"

"No."

"Well, did you play any new games?"

"No."

"Did you paint or crayon?"

"No."

"Then what did you do?"

"I cried. I stood in a corner and cried all day."

About that time, Mom was feeling pretty "tewwible" herself. She wondered if Susie was too young or too inept socially to attend school.

But that was ridiculous, she told herself. Susie should have been having a wonderful time.

That evening she asked my father's advice.

"First day jitters," he said. "Let her alone. She'll adjust. Anybody who can charm dogs and old ladies can get along with a bunch of kids. Besides, how traumatic can playing in a sandbox be, for God's sake?"

Knowing sound advice when she heard it, my mother shipped a wailing Susie off to nursery school for the second day. Less than three hours later, a smiling Susie returned.

"How was it today?" Mom asked, cheered.

The bright smile faded and the waterworks began.

"Howwible," Susie sobbed.

"Why?"

"Nobody pwayed with me. I lied down on the floor and cried and cried," Susie said between gasps and tears.

My mother, who had sworn she would give the school a week before she intervened, crumpled like tinfoil. She picked up the phone and called the school, filled with righteous indignation. How could a responsible teacher allow a child to lie on the floor and cry for two hours?

The teacher immediately took the wind out of Hurricane Mom.

"Susie is a happy, well-adjusted child who has a lot of fun here," the teacher said mystified.

"No tears?"

"None that I ever saw," the teacher said.

Mom didn't know what to believe. Either the teacher was a complete nincompoop or Susie wasn't telling the truth about her time at school. She decided to give the teacher the benefit of the doubt and stick it out.

The next two days were hell on Mom. Each morning Susie would cry upon leaving the house, and when she returned, her face would crumple and she would begin to weep when she saw Mom at the curb. The tales of woe were always the same. Susie didn't participate in any activities, no one would talk to her, and she sat in the corner, ignored and crying.

When Friday rolled around Susie asked how many more days she had to go to school, and when she learned that the next day was Saturday, she seemed to be pathetically grateful. She hugged Mom and said, "Then we can be together all day." That was a surprise because Susie wasn't the clinging type and she kept busy making her rounds in the neighborhood.

"For God's sake," my father said, "if she hates· it, pull her out of school. I'm not paying good money for them to make my daughter cry. If she wants to cry, she can stay home and cry for free."

"But, Frank, you were the one who thought she should go," my mother said.

"If you'll remember, I was the one who thought that spending all her time with the Battle-Ax Brigade would make her preternaturally strange," my father said. "God knows, they make *me* crazy."

The weekend sped by and on Monday morning Susie lay in bed, sleepy-eyed and pouty, asking if she *had* to go to nursery school.

"No," my mother said. "Let's just forget it. You don't have to go."

That morning Susie dawdled over breakfast, but well before bus time, she was dressed and ready.

"I fink I'll go," she said. "Just today."

My mother kept her surprise to herself. "Are you sure?" she asked.

Susie said she was, but when the bus arrived, she broke down in tears.

"You really don't have to go," my mother said.

But Susie, leaking like a broken faucet, grimly boarded the Jack 'n' Jill tumbrel of death and roared off to a day of standing in the corner, crying.

My mother paced around the house for an hour; then she made up her mind. She was going to rescue her poor unhappy daughter and drag her out of that hellhole they laughingly referred to as a nursery school.

Mom, who was an expert at skulking and lurking, drove to the school and parked across the street. Although she didn't have any formal police training, she was a natural for surveillance assignments. With a furtive movement she slid down in the seat to observe what was going on. It was a beautiful, warm day, and all the children were playing in a fenced-off yard filled with swings, slides, and a huge sandbox. Under a shaded arbor, small tables and chairs had been set up for the children to paint, crayon, and work in clay. That was where Susie was, furiously sculpting an odd-shaped objet d'art.

When she had finished her masterwork, Susie showed it to her teacher, who stopped what she was doing to admire it. Together they put it in the sun to dry. Then they spoke together for a minute and the teacher smiled as she laid a gentle hand on Susie's shining hair. Mom was suddenly overwhelmed at the thought she was watching an animated version of *A Child's Garden of Verses*.

With her project completed, the cry-all-day-in-misery girl picked up a long-stemmed paintbrush, and standing at an easel, she began to paint, in bright orange, a series of swoops, dots, and swirls on a large sheet of paper.

My mother walked across the street and entered the school grounds, intent on talking with the teacher. Susie was so busy with her artwork she didn't even notice. Amid the greenery and a border of pink-and-white flowers, Mom fumbled around, trying to explain her presence.

"But, Mrs. Littell," the teacher said, "I told you on the phone she's never cried once while she's been here. Not even on the first day. She's always happy and busy. Look, she doesn't even know you're here."

That was when Susie put the finishing touches on her orange-period painting, looked up, and saw Mom. Suddenly, she raced over, clutched Mom around the knees and burst into tears.

"Why are you crying?" Mom asked. The Jekyll and Hyde transformation had taken only five seconds.

"Because you miss me," Susie sobbed.

"Of course I miss you, but I want you to have a good time."

"When I'm here, you have no little girl to take care of," Susie said, the tears flowing.

"But I *want* you to like school."

"You said you didn't want me to go where you couldn't see me," she cried.

And of course, that was precisely what my mother had said in her effort to quell Susie's spontaneous sojourns.

"Show your mother what you've been doing today," the teacher said, looking as if she felt sorry for Mom.

And at that, Susie's magic fountain of tears dried immediately, and she raced to get her clay bowl and her painting. Then she gave Mom a tour of the school, introduced her to several of the children, and reported proudly that one day she had been in charge of handing out the cookies at snack time. All the while, her face glowed with pleasure and her voice was happy and excited.

Back at home, Mom sat her down for a heart-to-heart talk, about the tenth one they had conducted on the subject of walkabouts.

"When I don't know where you are, I worry," my mother said. "But when I know *exactly* where you are—like in nursery school—I don't worry at all."

Susie's brow creased and she looked as if she wished Mom would make up her mind, but she didn't say anything.

"And another thing," Mom said with a sigh, "when you pretend to be unhappy and cry, then I'm unhappy, too."

Susie looked surprised, as if that were a brand-new thought for her.

"I don't need tears to convince me that you love me," Mom said. "And I love you best."

Apparently the message sank in because, from that time on, all Mom ever got was a casual good-bye wave of the hand and a peck on the cheek. The tears had permanently dried.

"Think how difficult it must have been for her," my mother said later, "putting on an Oscar-winning performance twice a day for a week. I know it was hard on me, her audience, to go through that."

"Does this mean I won't get my money back?" my father said glumly.

"Certainly not," my mother said. "She loves nursery school. I just have to remember not to say 'don't ever leave me' to my little runaway."

PART FIVE

CRISIS

There is an old story about a self-help guru who made millions advising his disciples to repeat to themselves, "Every day, in every way, I am feeling better and better." That was because he believed that all sickness was psychosomatic and that positive thinking could effect a cure. One day a woman came to him and explained that her husband was ill. "No, no," the master said. "He only thinks he's ill." He told the woman to have her husband repeat the mantra, "Every day, in every way, I'm feeling better and better."

The woman returned two weeks later and the guru asked how her husband was. "He still thinks he's sick," she said. When she came back three weeks later, the answer was the same: "He still thinks he's sick."

Finally, two months after her initial visit, the "doctor" asked how the woman's husband was faring.

"Now he thinks he's dead," she said.

That story makes light of the power of positive thinking, and I agree that *wishful* thinking is ineffectual medicine. However, I do believe in a related concept: the power of negative thinking. The guru of that esoteric field is my brother, Stephen. Although he was only eleven years old when they took Susie to the hospital, he had enjoyed a lifetime of thinking negatively and he was really good at it.

A white 1959 Cadillac ambulance had come and taken Susie to the hospital. She was crying, my parents were agitated, and I was hiding in my room. It was wrenching. The only one seemingly not affected was Stephen. He, of course, was made of sterner stuff than the rest of us: He didn't despair—he got mad.

"They can't do this to her," he told me.

"They just did," I said.

"Then I'm going to make her better," he said.

"You're just a dumb kid. How are you going to do that?"

"I may be a kid, but I'm not dumb," he said with the same grim determination he had shown when confronted by the Witch Hazel crisis. "I'll find a way."

While Stephen was pondering his next move, the rest of us began a round-the-clock vigil. We took turns visiting Susie in the hospital in an attempt to entertain her and cheer her up. She was in a room with three other very sick children. I didn't know what was wrong with them and I really didn't want to know. They kept disappearing. I hoped they got well and went home. . . .

The room itself smelled of disinfectant and despair, a potent combination that made me cringe every time I visited. The nursery rhyme characters on the pale blue walls did nothing to relieve the air of sadness that pervaded the ward. The decorations made me think of a troupe of clowns appearing suddenly at a funeral—the height of inappropriateness. This was the least happy place on Earth.

Susie had been reduced to a red, wrinkled thing, lost in a large hospital bed. She lay there hour after hour, trying to be a good girl and do what they told her. My mother was on hand most of the time, but even Mom needed a break. Fortunately, Susie's coterie of eclectic friends made frequent appearances at her bedside. I was there one afternoon when Mrs. Buchanan, swaying slightly, arrived carrying a gift. It was beautifully wrapped in Cartier's distinctive paper and turned out to be a crystal swan. What a five-year-old was supposed to do with a crystal swan, I didn't know, but Susie loved it and played with it as if it were a toy.

"We could always hock it to pay the hospital bill," my father suggested.

"Oh, let her keep it," my mother said. "What's a couple of hundred dollars down the drain?"

With her keenly honed sense of the inappropriate, Mrs. Buchanan had scored a hit as far as Susie was concerned.

Brian Thompson and I would check in on Susie after school. Susie was always glad to see Brian because he was the bearer of good tidings, or at least good brownies, which were strictly forbidden in the hospital. We were there one day when Susie received a special visitor. A nurse came into the ward, got Susie out of bed, and brought her to the window. Three stories below, Mrs. Davis and Sadly were waving furiously. Well, Mrs. Davis was waving. Sadly was looking as if his best friend was in the hospital.

The stream of well-wishers was more or less constant, and included Hazel, who stopped by to bark a few orders at the doctors, nurses, and patients.

"Hazy's not sick," Susie told me when the world's most respected baby-sitter had left. "I am."

I didn't notice any improvement in Susie's condition that first week. In fact, I surmised from my parents' drawn faces that, if anything, Susie was getting worse.

When there is a sick child in the family, everything changes. Normal routines are thrown out and a whole new set of priorities is established. What was once usual, like watching television and playing basketball, was now a rare treat. And what was unthinkable only a month before, like going to the hospital every day, became routine. Everyone's attention was refocused from themselves to Susie.

My parents and I treated the little sick girl as if she were as fragile as Mrs. Buchanan's delicate crystal swan. Stephen, who had more intestinal fortitude than a rogue E. coli bacterium, felt no such compunction. He treated her with boxing, not kid, gloves.

But before he could even begin to put his unspeakable plan into action, he had to get by the guardians at the hospital door. He was only eleven and technically not allowed to visit patients, lest he infect them with some childhood disease. Stephen got around that problem by either lying to gain admittance or, failing that, sneaking in though a side door. If they had known what he was up to, the volunteers at the lobby desk would have ringed the hospital with armed paratroopers to keep him out.

I was privy to only a few of Stephen's verbal assaults, but those I overheard were deplorable.

"Hi, Susie," he said one day while I was by her bedside. "You must really like it here."

"No. I want to go home," Susie said, suddenly on the verge of tears.

"No, you don't."

"I don't?"

"You like it here so much, you'll get to stay for a year," he said.

"I want to go home," Susie cried, hugging her constant companion, plush Sadly.

"If you really want to go home," he said, "you've got to get better."

"I'm trying."

"No, you're not. You like it here and you're never coming home, and I'm going to move into your room and throw out all your dolls!"

"Stephen," I said. "Stop it!"

"That's exactly what I'll do. Throw out all your dolls."

Given Susie's disdain for her doll collection, Stephen's threat wasn't particularly virulent, but it threw Susie into hysterics.

His mission accomplished, Stephen stalked out of the room, leaving me to calm Susie down.

The next day, he returned to continue his work.

"You still here?" he sneered at her. "Your dolls are about to get it."

"Please, Stephen," Susie said piteously. "Don't frow away my dolls."

"Even your favorite, Christmas Carole," he said, naming the one doll that had never been stripped naked and tossed in the corner. "It's your own fault that you're here. I told you before—get well!" Stephen continued, his voice rising from an already high pitch.

I bodily threw him out of the room, amazed and infuriated that he would treat her so. I was about to pound some sense into his head when he raised his hands in surrender.

"Look, John, I don't like to do it," he said. "But as long as everybody treats her like she's sick, she's going to be sick."

"You can't torture her like that," I said, outraged.

"Somebody has to," he said. "I tried it your way and it didn't work. Now I'm going to try it my way. She's my little sister and I don't want her to spend the rest of her life in a hospital bed."

"You're nuts," I said. "And if I catch you talking to her like that again, I'll hit you so hard you'll be in the bed next to her."

"Then you won't catch me," he said defiantly. "But I tell you I'm doing it for her own good."

So while Dr. Alexander instituted a new regimen of antibiotics, Stephen implemented his own twisted rehabilitation program. He claimed he did it because he loved her and I suppose he did. But I knew something about love, and what I knew wasn't pretty.

Chapter 18

ALWAYS A CHARMER. Whether making pot holders
or acting as a beard for John, Susie charmed
everyone she met.

Cupid's Poisoned Arrow

I fell in love for the first time the summer of my thirteenth year, and unfortunately it set a pattern that I have yet to break. I suppose I should have taken the hint: When your inaugural cruise is on the *Titanic*, you should give up transatlantic travel. But thirteen is an odd age and I didn't know any better. In fact, I didn't know anything at all.

The problem with American teenagers—then and now—is that they are totally useless. They have the bodies of adults, the brains of children, and the disposition of hyenas, but they have no useful work to do or any meaningful role to play in society. In the distant past, teens were expected to pull their weight in the family economic unit. On the farm, they had specific functions to fulfill: milking the cows, mowing the hay, tending the livestock, hunting for food. Today, all they do is attend school, which isn't much of a challenge—except when the bullets begin to fly. No wonder so many kids are restless during their teen years—they are lined up on the tarmac, waiting to take off.

I was never in a hurry to grow up because, at every age I reached, I thought I *was* grown-up. It seemed to me that being adult meant, in this order: driving a car, smoking cigarettes, drinking alcohol, and having sex—whatever that was. By the time I was thirteen, I had accomplished the middle two goals, so I knew I was halfway to becoming full grown. I was wrong, of course, and the next month would prove it.

That summer I got a job as a junior counselor at the local day camp. My assignment was to organize the little kids into a softball game. Talk about something I could do! I had seven years of little-kid organizing experience on the kick baseball field, so applying my skills to this new task was a cinch. Besides, softball was my new favorite sport. Everything about the game conspired to make me look good. Unlike hardball, the ball is bigger, the bats are lighter, and even the grounders come at you slower.

I was an enthusiastic shortstop, a position that was impossible for me to play in a real baseball game. I was just too slow. But I did have one peculiarity that made me an ideal shortstop: my arm, or rather my weak arm. No matter how hard I threw the ball, I could never overshoot first base because I just didn't have the power. And although that may sound like a disadvantage, it wasn't. My throws were generally on the money, even if they bounced in the dirt once or twice before reaching the first baseman. Our third baseman, Brian Thompson, could throw the ball into the next county and generally did. The kid playing first would visibly cringe when Brian got his hands on the ball—for good reason. If Brian threw him a strike, his hand would hurt for a week. But if the ball went ten feet over his head, the first baseman would have to spend the next twenty minutes searching the woods for the lost ball. First basemen, naturally, thought highly of me.

I played every other inning, spending the rest of my time trying to teach the kids the fundamentals of the game. At the beginning of the summer, I was a font of knowledge about the strategy, the history, and the mechanics of the game. But the blank stares I received from the six- and seven-year olds quickly reminded me that kids can absorb only small bits of information at one time. So instead of teaching them about the infield fly rule, I tried to show them which way to run if, by some miracle, they hit the ball. Many of them stood rooted at home watching the ball roll away; some would run to third; others would trot out to the pitcher's mound; and still others would simply wait for the next pitch, not realizing they should be legging it to first base.

The first few weeks we looked like the Three Stooges, but the kids were a highly motivated group, and little by little, they learned how to pitch, catch, and hit the ball. By the end of the summer, as I got to know the players and their abilities, I could field two competitive teams that really knew what they were doing.

Our equipment was minimal. We had two wood softball bats: one small and light, the other big and heavy; three softballs: ratty, frayed, and the game ball; and four mitts that must have been left over from Babe Ruth's day. The gloves were for any kid who didn't have one or who had left his at home. I never forgot my glove because I hooked it onto my beaded Indian belt to facilitate riding my bike with both hands on the handlebars.

I was extremely careful with my bike because it was my most valued and favored possession. My previous bicycle had been a Schwinn, a large, clunky two-wheeler that was made of structural steel. It was heavy, slow, and indestructible. By contrast, my new bike was the greyhound of the streets—a shiny black Raleigh with a single white panel over the rear reflector. A lean, mean, totally keen machine, the Raleigh was made in England, and it was the first choice of discerning bike riders worldwide. Imagine, it had three speeds! I kept that bike in my room, fearing that exposure in the unheated garage would damage it. Stephen and Susie were not allowed within ten feet of it, upon pain of death. I had worked long and hard to acquire that bike, and believe me, years of whining, begging, and pleading with my parents had been no easy task. I felt I had earned it, and I didn't want to share it with anyone.

That's why I was appalled when my parents announced they had enrolled Susie in the day camp.

"But she's only four," I said. "She's too young. You gotta be five."

"We have received, uh, a special dispensation in Susie's case," my mother said. "You can give her a ride on your bicycle every morning and bring her home for lunch."

My mind raced furiously. Taxiing Susie to camp presented two major problems. First, after camp closed at twelve-thirty, Brian, a couple of other kids, and I would go over to the school and play stickball. I didn't want to have to dump Susie off first. Second, and more important, I didn't want her on my bike. She might scratch it.

"Won't work, Mom," I said. "I have to be there a half hour early to set up and stay a half hour later to clean up. Susie might drown with nobody watching her."

There was a lazy river nearby, about four inches deep.

Amazingly, my mother bought that story, and I was excused from chauffeuring duties, much to my relief. I didn't give a fig if Susie attended day camp. I just didn't want to chaperon her.

The first week of camp, Susie caused a mild sensation. As the baby of the group, she was immediately adopted by the counselors and campers alike. It was pretty hilarious to watch first graders acting maternal and treating her as if she were an infant. Susie, of course, positively reveled in the limelight and did her best to become everybody's best friend. Groups of little girls would vie for her attention, and more than once, I saw normally stern adults slip her an extra cookie at snack time. Then someone made the mistake of showing her how to make pot holders on a little metal loom, and for the next month, Susie loomed like a loon. I'm sure my mother enjoyed each and every one of the four hundred twenty-seven Susie made for her that summer.

I divided my time between the softball field and the archery range. Now I have to admit that I had been an archery buff for many years. Robin Hood and the American Indians were always favorites of mine, and William Tell was no slouch. But what drew me to the camp's archery range was not men in tights or breechcloths. Far from it.

Her name was Holly and she smelled of lemons. She was blond and wore her hair in a ponytail that flounced in the most intoxicating way when she walked. Her skin was flawless, her eyes were a hypnotic blue, and when she spoke, it was in soft tones that had me hanging on her every word. Holly was tan and healthy looking, and she had breasts—large, beautiful breasts. I hadn't thought much about breasts since Don had announced she was the proud possessor of a new pair. But now I noticed that breasts were everywhere. It was like buying a Pontiac. Before you bought one, you hardly ever saw a Pontiac. But on the way home from the dealer, suddenly you spotted sixteen of them.

In addition to being the epitome of womanhood, Holly was the archery instructor, in charge of teaching beginners how to shoot straight. It was a dangerous job and I worried that some dumb camper would puncture that perfect, tanned skin. The symbolism here went farther over my head than one of Brian's's pegs to first base.

If Holly had one fault, it was her advanced age. She was seventeen that summer and going into her senior year in high school. The gulf between us was only four years, but at my age, she was as unreachable as Alpha Centauri. If I had met her ten or twenty years later, the story might have been different, but I was obliged to worship her from afar.

Well, not from *that* afar. When we took a break between games to slug down a vat or two of purple Kool-Aid, I would sidle over to the archery area and get Holly to give me a lesson. I was a pretty fair back-yard archer, but I presented myself as a bumbling amateur.

"Am I holding it right?" I would ask Holly, knowing I was holding the bow all wrong.

"No, like this," she would say and put her arms around me to show me how to hold the bow correctly and notch an arrow.

I would turn a bright shade of crimson and start to sweat. Then, with her arms around me, she would place her hand over mine and help me draw back the bow. I would take that opportunity to casually nestle my head between her breasts. My knees would get wobbly and I would find it difficult to breathe, but I was in lemon-scented heaven. Or at least I should have been. Mostly I got a headache from the miles of wire that ran through Holly's bra. Like all females of that era, Holly wore "foundation garments"—even under her sporty clothes. It is a lit-tle known fact that all women's underwear, until the late 1960s, was designed and manufactured by the Soviet aircraft industry.

Despite the head pains, I was flying high when gripped in Holly's nonchalant embrace. But like a miser, I indulged myself in this extrava-gant pleasure only twice a week. I didn't want her to get suspicious, although I needn't have worried. Holly had no idea who I was and probably figured I was just another dopey camper. That's the thing about love. A formal introduction helps immeasurably in guiding the course of true romance. I, of course, would have fainted dead away if she had ever called me by name.

"John, John!" Susie cried, racing across the open field.

Suddenly embarrassed, I disentangled myself from Holly's sinuous arms, thanked her with a dry-mouthed croak, and went to see what was the matter.

Susie was wearing her official day camp uniform: blue shorts, white T-shirt, and white sneakers. In her hand was a peculiar object, or per-haps an object peculiar only to camps.

"I made you a yanyard!" she told me happily.

"A yanyard, eh?" I said, looking at a rather lopsided, loosely stitched, red-and-white lanyard.

"You can put a key on it," she said breathlessly.

That was great, except that I didn't have any keys.

"It's beautiful," I said, putting it around my neck.

"Do you want a pot holder, too?" she asked.

"No, thanks," I said. "Mom would be sad. She needs them more than I do."

"I make her one," she told me. Then she raced off to knock out a few dozen pot holders. The kid would have made a fortune doing piecework.

I took one last loving look at my Diana, bow in hand, arms extended, and sighed.

"Hey, Littell," Brian yelled from the softball diamond. "Your side is up. Get over here."

I jogged back to the game and broke up an altercation at second base. Three kids were positive they were playing that position and none of them would give it up. When I had the campers rearranged, Brian said, "Why the hell do you keep going over to the archery range?"

"I, uh, wanted to learn how to shoot an arrow," I said.

"You're a liar," he said. "You already know how. I've seen you."

"Well, I just want to get better at it," I said defensively.

"Then why do you keep shooting over the target or into the ground?" he asked like the steely eyed litigator he would become.

I didn't have an answer for that one, so I told him to go screw himself.

"It's that girl, isn't it?" he said, the light suddenly dawning on him. "That Polly."

"Holly," I said instantly, just as quickly realizing my mistake.

"Ha! It is. You're in love," he said.

"Am not," I answered hotly.

"Are, too," he said laughing.

"Don't tell anybody," I begged.

"You're hilarious, Littell," he said. "You've got about as much chance with her as these campers have beating the Yankees."

I thought he had wildly underestimated the odds, but I kept that to myself. At the same time, I found myself working on a plan.

I was saved wheelbarrows of embarrassment because Brian kept his mouth shut about my pretend love life. He did, however, demand to know the details of the affair—such as it was. When I was ready, I told him my plan.

"She'll never go on a date with me," I said. "But maybe I could buy her a Coke after camp. What do you think?"

"I think you're major league nuts," he said. "She doesn't even know you're alive."

Or my name, I thought. But I liked my plan and I was determined to carry it out.

"What have I got to lose?" I asked.

"Well, let's see: how about your manhood, your self-respect, your ego, your sense of self-worth, your—"

"All right, all right," I said. "I get your point, but I'm going to do it anyway. So screw you."

For the next week, I refined my abstract ideas into a three-part plan of action. Part One was easy. I had to tell her my name, so I invented several variations on the theme. The direct approach: "Hi, I'm John. You're Holly, right?" The indirect approach: "Bill's a great name, isn't it? Too bad my name is John." The oblique approach: "I've got to go to the John, ha, ha. Funny how they named them after me." I tried each one out on Brian and we agreed that the direct approach was best. It only took me a few more days to work up the courage to blurt out my name to her. She smiled warmly and nodded her head so slightly that her ponytail didn't even wiggle much.

Part Two was a bit more complicated because it involved saying more than five words to her—all at the same time. That was a daunting prospect that kept me up at night, practicing. If I had spent as much time trying to improve my baseball game, I would be a retired Yankee by now. But even though I wasn't quite sure what constituted my loins, I girded them up and marched over to the archery range.

"Hi, uh, Jack," Holly said.

Close enough.

"Hi," I said. "Can I shoot a few arrows?"

"Sure," she said, handing me a bow and a handful of arrows.

She stood back and eyed my form critically. All summer I had been lagging it, shooting arrows all over the place so that Holly would have to correct my miserable performance. But on that day, I shot off a bunch of arrows in rapid succession, hitting the bull's-eye every time.

"Wow," Holly said. "That was great."

"I owe it all to you," I said, basking in her approval. "You're the best archery in the world. I mean, you're the best archery *teacher* in the world."

She laughed, revealing a perfect set of gleaming white teeth, which dazzled me. If I was in love before, I was hopelessly lost now.

"'Bye," I said, unable to bear her magnificence one moment longer. "See you next week."

"Keep practicing," she said.

My sudden transformation from clumsy to Cochise was all a lie, of course. I could have put the arrows in the bull's-eye anytime I had wanted. But that was the second part of my plan: making her think I was her star pupil. Of course, I had to backslide occasionally or I would have been deprived of my biweekly hugs. But I was determined to make her feel she was personally responsible for my newfound skill.

"Way to go, Romeo," Brian said later. "I didn't think you had the guts."

"Shows what you know," I said.

"But now you've got to do the deed," he said. "And you don't have a snowball's chance in hell."

Apart from the cliché, he had a point. Now I had to ask her to have a Coke with me after camp. I could feel the words sticking in my throat and my stomach heaving even when I was only at home practicing what to say. That made me keep putting off the day of reckoning.

"Chicken," Brian said.

He was right about that.

I don't suppose I could have ever asked Holly if it hadn't been for Susie, the mad pot holder maker. Growing bored with her craft, she had wandered over to the archery range one day and accosted Holly.

"Pway ouch-a-wee?" she asked.

Holly took one look and fell instantly in love with Susie. Right family, wrong person, damn it. From that moment on, Holly was forever hovering around Susie, showing her how to hold the tiny bow and how to shoot the miniature arrows. With her usual athletic prowess, my sister could miss the broad side of a barn from three paces, but that simply endeared her to Holly even more. I watched them with growing alarm, thinking that their new friendship would somehow wreck Part Three of my master plan.

Brian, however, was more sanguine. He asked me if I knew what a beard was.

"Of course, dummy," I said. "Whiskers on your face."

"No, you idiot," he said. "A beard is like a decoy. Suppose you want to go out with a girl, but you want to keep it a secret. You get someone else to go along. Then it doesn't look like you're actually on a date with her."

"I don't get it," I said, although his explanation was quite clear and almost correct.

"You're *so* stupid," he said. "All you gotta do is ask Holly to go with you *and* Susie. Holly likes her a lot better than you anyway, so she'll probably go."

"You think so?"

"She'd do anything for Susie," he said.

That, of course, was not exactly what I had in mind. My plan was to spend a few minutes alone with Holly, not share her with my kid sister. But desperate love called for desperate measures, and I was prepared to do anything.

H-day fell on a Tuesday. The night before I made my mother press a shirt with a collar and my good khaki pants for me. I shined my black shoes with laces, and just to prove the wet head wasn't yet dead, I loaded up my hair with Brylcreem and plastered it down. In the mirror I looked like a short, greasy tango instructor. Then to make matters worse, I slapped on a liberal amount of bay rum. I was so foul-smelling that plants withered as I passed, animals slunk away in fear, and small children fled before me.

I opted out of the game that day, so I wouldn't get all dirty and sweaty. I already smelled bad enough that the campers avoided me. Finally, with my stomach roiling and the Brylcreem oozing down my forehead, I approached my quarry cautiously. To reemphasize the star-pupil ploy, I slammed a few arrows into the bull's-eye and waited for Holly to notice.

"You really have gotten good," she said in her wonderfully alluring voice. "But what's that smell?"

"Uh," I managed to grunt. "Uh, Holly. I'd like to thank you for helping me and I wondered if I could buy you a Coke after camp. Just to thank you."

There, I had said it. No fissures had opened up beneath my feet. No lightning had fried me in place. However, Holly just stood there, looking at me as if I had descended from another planet. Time to play the trump card.

"Uh, I'm Susie's brother," I said dumbly. "She'll be there, too."

"Susie!" Holly said, bursting into a bright smile. "She's sooo cute!"

"Yeah," I muttered. "Then will you?"

"What?"

"Have a Coke with us after camp. On Friday," I said.

"With Susie? Of course. Sure. Friday," she said, turning to aid a novice who had become entangled in her bow.

I flew back to the softball game, my heart pounding, my mouth dry, and my brain inflamed with thoughts of love.

"I did it! I did it!" I yelled. "She said yes!"

"Really?" Brian asked. "What's that smell?"

"Goddamn really," I said, wiping the sweat from my eyes. "Friday!"

That night at the dinner table, I guess my enthusiasm was all too obvious. Twice, my mother told me to calm down, and then she asked me what was the matter.

"Nothing," I said.

Teenagers are great communicators.

"Well, you're acting as if you had a case of the fantods," she said.

The fantods, or the heebie-jeebies, were described by Mark Twain in *The Adventures of Tom Sawyer*. My mother, because she was originally from Missouri, had appropriated the word in a burst of parochial pride.

"Where's your yanyard?" Susie asked, interrupting fortuitously.

"Your what?" my father asked.

"Yanyard," Susie said.

"That's lanyard," my mother corrected.

"No. I tole you once, I tole you twice, it's *yanyard*," Susie said indignantly. "And you can put a key on it."

"At least it's not another damn pot holder," my father said under his breath. His plate was sitting on one, his glass was poised on another, and his silverware was resting on a third. We were infested with pot holders, which did double duty as coasters and place mats. The plethora of pot holders, however, hadn't done much to improve the food around our house.

The rest of the week passed with agonizing slowness—especially because I was counting down the hours. I had even figured out the number of minutes until twelve-thirty on Friday, but that did nothing to hasten the clock.

I went through the motions of everyday life, but my heart and my mind were with Holly. The incomparable Holly. The plan for my so-called date with her was far from perfect, but I knew that once she got to know me, she couldn't help but return my vast and endless love.

The logistics of this operation were formidable. Once again I had to have my clothes ironed and my hair pomaded with two and a half pounds of Brylcreem. Because of the poor reviews, I decided to skip the bay rum. The problem with that aftershave is that it doesn't smell like rum, but it does sort of smell like a bay—a stagnant, polluted bay. Also, I had to make sure I had at least a buck to spend and I arranged to take Susie home from camp that day.

"Why?" my mother asked.

"No reason," I said.

"Can I ride on your bike?" Susie asked.

"No, you can walk along beside it—if you keep your fingers off it," I said generously.

I didn't tell Susie we had a date with Holly because I didn't want her blabbing. She was incapable of keeping a secret, mostly because she wasn't sure exactly what a secret really was.

On the fatal day, my hands shook and I felt as if I were about to throw up. To my everlasting shame, I yelled at a camper who had screwed up an easy play and made him cry. Brian went legging after the little boy and managed to calm him down; then he told me to go to hell. Or more realistically, to get off the field. As I stalked off the diamond, the little kids cringed and cowered as I passed by. With the words "What's wrong with John?" echoing in my ears, I just wanted to get away from all of them. There were only forty-eight minutes left. That's two thousand eight hundred eighty seconds. I know, because I counted every one of them.

With one hundred eight seconds left, I corralled Susie and told her we were going to have a Coke with Holly.

"Okay," Susie said. "Holly's my friend. We play ouch-a-wee."

I took Susie by the hand and we trudged over to the archery range, with me counting down the last seconds. When Susie saw Holly, she dropped my hand and rushed to greet her favorite counselor. She threw her arms around Holly's tanned and dimpled knees and hugged her. How I wished I could have done that.

"Are you ready?" I asked.

"Ready? For what, uh, Jim?" Holly asked.

"Jack. To grab a Coke with us," I said dumbfounded.

"Oh, I'm sorry," she said. "I'm going to the beach this afternoon with Tim."

Tim? Who the hell was Tim?

"Bye-bye," she said sweetly, giving Susie a pat on the head and me a big wave.

Totally deflated and utterly miserable, I retrieved my bike and watched as this Tim character roared up in a bright red 1957 Chevy Impala convertible with white leather seats. He was wearing jeans and a white T-shirt with a pack of cigarettes rolled up in the sleeve. And he had sunglasses. And his car was totally cool. And it had twin antennae on the fins. And he had a kind of thin mustache. And Holly leaped into the car without using the door. And she pecked him on the cheek. And they blasted off, spraying gravel on me and my dreams and Susie and the Raleigh. And that was the end of my short, miserable love life.

"Where Holly go?" Susie asked.

"To hell," I said.

"You said a bad word!" she informed me.

Even then I realized that Holly wasn't being mean. She just didn't know I existed. I was simply a bit of static in her life, an annoyance to be ignored. Despite my marksmanship, Cupid's arrow had missed its mark by a country mile.

But as I stood there forlornly, the dust coating my greasy hair, it occurred to me for the first time that I wasn't grown up at all. I was just a poky little kid without a driver's license, a car, a mustache, or a pack of Camels rolled in my sleeve.

"Come on, Susie," I said. "I'll give you a ride home on my bike."

"Really?" she said, astonished. She had never been allowed even to touch it.

"Really," I said. "You can ride on it, kick it, scratch it, and get your dirty hands all over it. Who cares?"

My pride, as well as my shiny pride and joy, had turned to bitter gall. After that summer, I walked everywhere I needed to go, and that ultimate symbol of childhood, the beautiful Raleigh bike, joined the Black Torpedo of Doom in the dusty obscurity of the basement—never to be ridden again.

Chapter 19

POOL SHARK. Freestyle, breast stroke, butterfly—Susie couldn't do any of them, but she was positive she would win the camp's annual swimming meet.

A Charming Conspiracy

Although I may have been a loser at love that summer, Susie proved to be a winner in the water—in a way.

Part of my duties as a junior counselor was to herd the kids to a public swimming pool twice a week and make sure they didn't drown. The older campers, who had passed a stringent swimming test, were allowed to jump off the diving board and horse around in the deep end of the pool. Raw recruits like Susie were consigned to the shallow end, where they could thrash about harmlessly. I even took it upon myself to teach the little ones the basics of the Australian crawl. Unfortunately for both teacher and students, playing in the water was so much fun that none of the little kids wanted to learn a thing.

The biggest problem I had that summer, apart from a limp love life, was keeping Susie out of the men's locker room. Although she had a counselor to watch her and to help her put on her bathing suit, Susie preferred that I do it. I suppose that was because I was good at snow-suit zipping. But I had enough trouble making sure the boys wore their trunks, and I didn't have much time to devote to her.

That didn't stop Susie, of course. She would take off all her clothes, sling her suit over her shoulder, and come looking for me. Naked as a jaybird, she would casually wander into the men's locker room and parade up and down until she found me. Scandalized, the boys would leap for the protection of the locker doors as Susie ambled by, giving everyone a cheery "hi." When she finally located me, I would pop her in her suit and return her to her own side of the building.

"You have to stay over there with the girls," I told her.

"Why?"

"Because."

"Because why? I like the way you put on my bathing suit."

"Just do it and I'll give you a Mars bar."

Bribery works temporary wonders with a four-year-old; reason seems unreasonable to them.

At the beginning of the summer, all the campers had been graded according to their ability, and Susie was bursting with pride when she was judged a "rank beginner."

"I can swim now," she told me. "I'm a rank beginner."

"Susie, that just means you need lessons," I told her.

She didn't believe me, but Liz, the swimming instructor, after hours of labor and unlimited patience, finally taught her to float and to paddle a bit. To say that Susie didn't take instruction well was the understatement of the year.

"You want me to put my face in the water?" Susie asked.

"Yes, you have to lie on your stomach in the water," Liz would tell her.

"But I'll get wet."

"I know, but you have to do it."

"I'm too pongy to swim," Susie said.

Pongy was a cross between spongy and pudgy, an apt description of the four-year-old Susie.

"I get out now. All done swimming."

Liz would roll her eyes and glare at me accusingly, as if it were my fault. Liz, by the way, had breasts, too. They were ample and amply displayed in her blue one-piece tank suit. She had quite a set of lungs, I noted, good for staying underwater, I suppose.

Susie's lack of athletic ability, however, was due entirely to genes. She had inherited my mother's odd approach to locomotion through the water. Mom swam just like Esther Williams—assuming Esther Williams had just swum the English Channel twice, put on an Aquacade marathon for Billy Rose, and run twenty miles on her hands. Languid in the liquid—that was Mom's style.

Sliding into the water gently, my mother would float almost perpendicular to the bottom of the pool, looking for all the world like a buoy. Then, with a smooth motion, she would begin a soft sidestroke that propelled her about the pool as slowly as possible without sinking. She made a snail look like a dolphin on steroids. At the end of her leisurely tour, Mom would emerge from the pool, her hair dry and her makeup perfectly preserved. Mom put on a hilarious performance every time she swam. My father, brother, and I could, and did, imitate her perfectly, much to her annoyance.

Given her absolute ineptitude in the water, I was surprised when Susie announced that she was going to participate in the end-of-camp swimming meet.

"I'm going to win," she said.

She wasn't bragging. She was positive.

"Don't count on it," I told her. She patted me on the arm as if she felt sorry for me. In her mind, I was not bright enough to see the obvious.

The top honors for the swim meet were the coveted titles of King Neptune and Queen Neptune, the best swimmers of the year. Both got gift certificates from a local store that had been browbeaten into supplying the prizes. Other campers got ribbons for win, place, and show in the various events. The awards ceremony was held the last day of camp at the log cabin that served as our clubhouse.

With my mother in attendance, the swim meet began promptly at nine a.m. on a Friday. The camp had arranged to have the pool entirely to itself for two hours, so beginning and ending on time was essential. The older kids were put through their paces first and they all did a credible job, much to Liz's relief. Then it was time for the small fry.

"Beginners," Liz called.

"I'm a rank beginner," Susie said proudly, scurrying down to the pool to join the others assembling there.

"Susie, you forgot your cap," Liz told her.

Time was running out.

Susie ran for the locker room, while Liz lined up the other campers in some semblance of order. When Susie reappeared with her red swim cap pushed down over her eyebrows, the games began. Six little girls, including Susie, were poised, ready to leap in and swim the width of the pool and back.

"On your mark, get set—" Liz began. Then she noticed Susie had her hand raised.

"Hold it," she said. "Yes, Susie?"

"Is the water cold?"

"No, it's like bathwater," Liz said, looking at me accusingly.

"Good."

"On your mark, get set, go!" Liz yelled and blew her silver whistle.

Five campers fell into the water in a ragged wave and began beating their way to the other side of the pool. The sixth, Susie, was still adjusting her red cap.

"Go, Susie!" I yelled, waving my arms.

"Hi, John," she said, waving back.

"Susie! Jump in and swim!" Liz cried.

"Okay, Liz," Susie said.

Slowly, and with the utmost care, Susie sat on the side of the pool and inched into the water.

"Brrrr," she said, shivering. "Not baf water."

Susie was just starting out when the other little girls were on their way back, thrashing like paddle wheel steamers. I felt a stab of guilt because it had never occurred to me that Susie had no conception of what to do at a swim meet. I kept forgetting she was a year younger than the youngest of the other kids, and she was essentially ignorant about races and contests.

Susie swam a few strokes, her head resolutely out of the water, Mom-style. Parents and campers were cheering on the little girls aiming for home, but Susie thought the cheers were for her and she stood in the pool to wave back graciously. While she was standing there, the other girls splashed past her, headed for the finish line. Susie joined them, walking the whole way to the starting point.

"Jeez, John," Liz said, helping Susie out of the water.

"Hey, you should have told her what to do," I said defensively.

"Like she listens to me," Liz said, rolling her eyes.

The next event was the dead man's float, in which the campers had to float on their faces to see who could hold that position the longest.

"Now, look, Susie," I said before the whistle blew. "If you want to win, just hold your breath as long as you can."

She nodded vigorously, her red cap bouncing up and down.

At the sound of the whistle, the little girls began floating and so did Susie, but after a few seconds she stood up to see how everyone else was doing. Satisfied that the other children were still floating on their faces, Susie flung herself back into the water. But it was too late. She had been the first up and Liz eliminated her from the contest.

Not at all disappointed, Susie cheered for the other girls from the sidelines.

"Why did you come up so soon?" I asked her.

"How else can I tell if I win?" she said as if she were answering an especially dumb question. Perhaps she was.

Susie did the exact same thing in the back-floating contest, pausing every few seconds to see how the competition was faring. Liz didn't even bother to drag her to the sidelines and just let her go on imitating an aquatic jumping bean.

Disgusted, and not a little embarrassed for her, I wandered away from the pool and took up a defensive position behind the spectators.

"Is that your daughter in the red cap?" I heard a woman say to my mother.

"Yes," Mom admitted warily.

"She doesn't seem to know what to do, does she?" the woman said sympathetically.

"No," Mom said. "But did you ever see anyone more pleased about being last in everything?"

The woman laughed and several other parents joined her. With Mom, they all waved to a beaming Susie, who beamed back enthusiastically. Totally oblivious, she was having a fine time.

The last event of the day was the Jellyfish. The children were told to hold their breath and sink to the bottom of the pool to see who could stay underwater the longest. I knew that the outcome of this contest would be the same as the others, and I cringed when Liz blew the whistle. Two of the six little girls hit the bottom of the pool and immediately popped back to the surface like breaching whalettes. Susie soon joined them to see what was going on. One by one, the win, place, and show kids were named and that was when the crowd turned ugly.

"We've still got ten minutes," Brian Thompson said. "Give Susie another chance!"

"Yeah," I said. "Give Susie another chance!"

"Give her a chance!" a mother from the audience yelled.

"Give her a chance! Give her a chance!" became a chant from the spectators.

Liz looked for guidance. The camp director, faced with an angry mob of parents, nodded his approval.

The crowd cheered lustily, my mother in the lead.

I grabbed Susie out of the water and put my finger in her face.

"One more time," I said. "Hold your breath until you think you can't hold it anymore, and don't come up for anything! Got it?"

"Okay," Susie said, not at all intimidated.

"I'll give you two brownies if you win," Brian Thompson said, encouraging her. He knew about bribery, too. Hey, for two of his mother's brownies, I would have entered the contest myself. I was sure I could hold my breath longer than a gaggle of six-year-old girls, but there was no time because Liz blew the whistle.

The three little girls sank to the bottom of the pool. A few seconds later, one of them bobbed up, but not Susie. The crowd cheered. Then a second head appeared on the surface and she was not wearing a red cap. The crowd went wild. After several tries, Susie had finally understood what she was supposed to do, or she wanted those brownies, I don't know which. But the result was the same. Liz had to bodily haul Susie out of the water to end the contest.

"Did I win?" Susie gasped.

Like the referee in a prizefight, Liz held up Susie's hand, and yelled, "Susie wins!"

By that time, the crowd was delirious. A game-winning home run in the bottom of the ninth could not have received more applause and shouts of approval.

Susie raced from the swimming pool to embrace Mom with a wet, dripping hug and shouted with glee: "I won! I won! I tole you I win! I'm Queen Nepoon!"

My mother wrapped Susie in a towel and hugged her.

"Well, at least you won fourth place in the Jellyfish contest," she said sensibly.

"No, no, Mama. Liz said so. 'Susie wins!' Didn't you hear her?" Susie said as if Mom were slightly deaf or mentally deficient.

"I know, dear. You won the Jellyfish contest. I mean, you won fourth place," Mom said, trying to be reasonable.

"You don't understand," Susie said condescendingly. "I'm Queen Nepoon. Liz said so."

"Explain it to her later," I told my mother.

And we did. For hours. We took turns attempting to tell her what had really happened, but Susie was unshakable in her belief that she had won the entire swimming meet.

The awards ceremony was held that evening at six p.m. Proud parents and friends gathered in the musty cabin lined with animal heads and dusty canoes. It had once belonged to the Boy Scouts, but they had moved on to a more modern headquarters, abandoning it to the camp.

Brian Thompson and I enrolled early-arriving campers in an impromptu softball game before it was time for the awards to be presented. As I was waiting to bat in the second inning, I spotted my father, who had arrived straight from work, wearing a navy blue Palm Beach suit, white shirt, navy tie, and black-and-white wing tip shoes. Despite the heat and the dust, he looked as if he had just emerged from the Stork Club. Maybe he had.

"Hi, Mr. Littell," Brian said from third base. "Do you want to play?"

"No, thanks," my father said. "I'm not dressed for it."

Brian's father, Craig, who had had the foresight to change his clothes before the event, laughed. "What's the matter, Frank? Chicken? Afraid to muss your clothes?" he taunted.

I joined right in the spirit of harassing my poor overdressed father, daring him to take a turn at bat. I thought he never would because Dad was an accomplished indoorsman. He had an unerring instinct for tracking down a decent cocktail party, discovering a new restaurant, and building a roaring campfire with his Ronson cigarette lighter. Although he could sail a boat, cast a fly rod, fire a rifle, and set up a tent, Dad enjoyed none of these activities—perhaps because they were difficult tasks to perform while wearing a Palm Beach suit.

When it came to baseball, however, my father was a player. He enjoyed both watching and participating in the game, though I daresay it had been twenty-five years since he had swung a bat other than to knock out a few ground balls for me to field.

He took the ragging good naturedly—for a while. Then Dad's eyes narrowed and his jaw clenched and I knew something was going to happen. I shut up immediately, always a wise move around my father, but Craig Thompson kept right on chiding him. Finally, like Popeye, my father had had all he could stands, and he couldn't stands no more.

Without a word, he unbuttoned his suit coat and handed it to me. Then he grabbed a bat and set himself at the plate, squinting into the late-afternoon summer sun. Not bothering to roll up his sleeves, he said softly, "Throw it."

The pitcher wound up and tossed the softball to the plate. Like the Mighty Casey, Dad let the first pitch go by.

"What's the matter, Frank? The old eyes not what they used to be?" Craig Thompson said gleefully.

My father ignored him and he ignored the next pitch, too, disdainfully tapping the dirt from his two-toned shoes.

"No batter, no batter!" Craig yelled to the pitcher. "He couldn't hit my grandma's pitching."

Everyone laughed, including me, but my father's face went from grim to neutral as if he had suddenly made up his mind about something. He stared vacantly at the pitcher, not really seeing him.

The third pitch was a fast ball, right down the middle. My father's swing was a blur of power and pinpoint precision. I mean, he crushed the ball and sent it climbing higher and higher into the bright sky until I lost sight of it. And still it went up and up, farther and farther, like a rocket launched from Cape Canaveral. The ball cleared the tops of the trees and was lost forever in the woods. He had demolished the ball, absolutely annihilated it.

My father dropped the bat on home plate, dusted off his hands, and without a word retrieved his coat from me, his astonished son.

"Bring on your grandma," he said to a shocked Craig Thompson.

Then he walked away as cool and elegant as he had arrived, leaving us in stunned silence.

After that display of raw power, the game broke down and, finally, up. Nobody wanted to compete with a shot heard round the world.

"I didn't know your father could hit like that," Brian said.

"Neither did I," I said honestly.

That was the problem with my father: As soon as I thought I had him figured out, he would do something extraordinary. Children want their parents to be boring and utterly predictable. Displays like my father's were unsettling. So it was with a mixture of awe and annoyance that I put away the softball gear for the last time that summer and wandered over to the cabin for the award ceremony.

"Where is your mother?" my father asked me as we were about to begin.

"I don't know," I said. "Susie's probably rehearsing her acceptance speech—like the Oscars."

Then I explained Susie's sincere belief that she had won the swim meet and was about to be crowned Queen Neptune.

"She can hardly swim a stroke," he said when I finished. "They should give her an award for not drowning."

"She floats pretty good," I said.

"At least she doesn't swim like your mother," he said, flicking his hands in perfect imitation of my mother's feathery sidestroke.

I laughed, but was quickly told to shut up by the camp director, who had taken the podium to begin the ceremonies.

As in most camps there were two types of awards: Those that mattered and those that were handed out so the losers would feel good. It was a deceitful thing to do, but the kid who won Best Camper knew that the Good Sport award was a joke. So did the Good Sport, but I suppose he didn't care. Brian Thompson had won the Best New Counselor award, a joke if there ever was one, but his parents thought it was a big deal and insisted on attending the presentation. Fortunately, Helen Thompson came armed with a basket of delicious brownies.

The log clubhouse was dark and damp because it had few windows, presumably because the structure was originally designed to keep the Indians at bay. But after the first twenty awards, the audience was ablaze with children happily waving their red, white, and blue ribbons. Then came the major presentation: King and Queen Neptune were named and came forward to collect their gift certificates. We all cheered heartily, but still no Susie or Mom or Stephen.

"Perhaps your mother decided to keep Susie at home and spare her the humiliation of losing," my father said.

"She'd have to conk Susie on the head and tie her up to keep her away," I said.

At last, the rest of my family arrived in a cloud of dust. Literally, because a gust of hot wind blew Mom, Susie, and Stephen into the cabin. All three were tired and dirty.

"I couldn't get the car started," my mother explained, brushing the dust off her once-white dress. "We had to walk."

"How many goddamned cars do I have to buy to ensure that at least one of them works?"

"Not now, Frank," my mother whispered. Dad could go on for hours about what junk American cars were and how there was no one in the country who knew how to fix them.

"Damn crapola cars," my father whispered back.

By the time my father calmed down and accepted his fate, the Jellyfish awards were being presented. First Prize walked back with her blue ribbon. Second Prize walked back with her red ribbon, and Third Prize walked back with her white ribbon. Then there was a pause and a hasty consultation between the swimming instructor, Liz, and the camp director. I looked at Susie. She was as cool as a dusty cucumber.

"I can't stand it," my mother said to my father. "Maybe there isn't going to be a fourth prize after all."

Then the camp director cleared his throat and said into the microphone: "Susie Littell, Fourth Prize."

Susie jumped up from her chair, her eyes wide, and like a bride marching down the aisle, slowly went forth to claim her rightful prize.

As she climbed the three steps to the stage, a shaft of sunlight pierced the dark cabin and hit her directly. The combination of her yellow sunsuit and golden hair in the shaft of light was ethereal. With the grace of a duchess, she proudly shook the camp director's hand and was presented an enormous royal purple ribbon. It was twice as big as the other campers' ribbons and the only one that was not red, white, or blue. Liz told me later that she had found the purple ribbon in an antique shop and bought it because she had liked the color. She didn't know what it had originally been issued for, but it was so big that it might have been presented to Seabiscuit for winning the Kentucky Derby.

Clutching her ribbon, Susie walked around the cabin, waving her prize and telling one and all, "I won!" The applause was deafening. Susie gladly handed the ribbon around for the others to see. They all turned it over to read the inscription: "Fourth Place, Jellyfish Contest," and handed it back to her, smiling at the littlest competitor.

"I'm Queen Nepoon," Susie told anyone who would listen. She knew she had won and she had the ribbon to prove it.

Amazingly, not one camper said a derogatory word. They smiled and congratulated her. Some of the older boys patted her on her head and told her, "Good job."

My mother was waiting for one of the kids to tell Susie she hadn't won anything except the stupid fourth prize in the Jellyfish, but not one of them crushed her happiness. They all played along.

Susie's victory lap ended in front of the Thompsons.

"I'm Queen Nepoon," she said to Brian. "Two brownies, please."

"But, Susie," Brian said, "you only won—"

"Brian, please," his father interrupted. "If she says she's Queen Neptune, who are we to doubt her? In fact, if Frank Littell can hit a softball four hundred feet without taking off his tie, who are we to doubt anything?"

Helen Thompson produced two large brownies wrapped in wax paper and presented them—royally—as befitted Susie's new status.

"What do we do now?" my mother said to my father. "We'll never be able to convince her that she isn't really Queen Neptune."

"Don't try too hard," my father said. "Look at those children. Not one of them has said a thing. Let Susie enjoy the moment. How many times in her life will she ever be this happy?"

So we never said another word on the subject of Queen Nepoon. We just let her revel in her glory, showing off her enormous ribbon. But the whole atmosphere at the cabin was bathed in a pervasive, benign secrecy. Everyone was in on it except Susie. Strangers smiled at us, and campers grinned at us as we made our departure, and we felt humbled by their unsought kindness.

Due to the unreliability of the American automotive industry, we walked home from the ceremonies at dusk. Susie skipped ahead of us, her happiness complete. If faith could move mountains, Susie's faith could have relocated the Himalayas. She had willed herself to be a winner—and I suppose that is what winners really are. All it took was a charming conspiracy of silence.

CONCLUSION

By her second week in the hospital, Susie showed no sign of improvement. She was listless to the point of immobility and her constant fever was burning the fight right out of her. Dr. Alexander had called in consultants from New York City and beyond, but none of the specialists had anything encouraging to say. Susie was in the clutches of a virulent bacterium that wouldn't let her go—despite the gallons of antibiotics pumped into her tired system.

My parents were distracted and frustrated, not knowing what to do next. I was paralyzed, but Stephen continued his rough therapy out of my sight. His daily demand that she get well, however, was having no effect that I could see. Susie was a wreck—a tiny, shriveled wreck. And she was bringing the rest of us down with her.

My last visit to the hospital had been a painful one. Susie had been lying in her oversize bed looking spindly and insubstantial, her eyes focused on the ceiling. It took me a couple of shakes just to get her attention.

When she finally noticed me, she gave me a wan smile that was full of sadness. I talked with her for a few minutes, but she seemed distracted and unable to concentrate. She even turned down the brownie I had brought for her.

"I'm not hungry anymore," she said.

"You've got to get better," I said.

"I try, but I don't know how," she said. "Can you tell me how?"

What could I tell her about getting well? I patted her on the head and told her that everything would be all right. But neither one of us believed it.

"Why don't they fix her?" Stephen asked me that evening.

I didn't have an answer for that one either.

"Doctors," he sneered. "All they do is make people sicker. It's not fair."

"Yelling at her all the time can't be helping her," I said.

"At least I'm trying to do something," he said. "I'm not just sitting around waiting for her to die."

"Shut up," I said, my usual response to uncomfortable topics.

"There's got to be something we can do," he said.

"Like what?"

"Wait a minute," he said. "I've got a plan."

Uh-oh.

"Who is Susie's best friend?" he asked rhetorically. Then he answered: "Sadly."

"So?"

"If we can sneak Sadly into the hospital, he can cure her."

"That's the stupidest thing I ever heard," I said, and it was. "Dogs can't cure anybody. You've been watching too much TV."

"I know I'm right," Stephen said. "And you can't stop me."

I suppose I could have stopped him with a shot to the snotlocker or ratted him out to my parents, but as I said, I was paralyzed by the continuing crisis.

"Maybe if Susie had fallen into a hole or down a mineshaft, Sadly might be able to sniff her out like Lassie. But dogs aren't even allowed in the hospital," I said.

"*I'm* not allowed in the hospital," Stephen said. "But I visit every day, and if I can get in, so can Sadly."

"How?"

"That's my plan," he said.

I didn't hear anything more about his mysterious plan until the next day when he thrust a piece of lined notebook paper into my hand.

At the top of the page were the words: MY PLAN BY STEPHEN LIT-TELL. The words below, however, were not encouraging. In his school-boy scrawl, Stephen had produced a document that was at once incredibly complex and childishly simple. I read it quickly and shook my head. "Won't work," I said.

"It will, if you'll help me," he said.

In later years, I became an admirer of the worst movie ever made, Ed Wood's *Plan 9 from Outer Space*. Believe me, Ed's *Plan* and Stephen's plan had a lot in common: Neither one made much sense and they were both chintzy productions. Stephen's directorial talent was sorely tested, and his one human actor, me, couldn't emote his way into dinner theater—not even in Tulsa. Sadly, too, as the lead dog, had his shortcomings. Although he was patient to a fault, he really couldn't do much except eat cookies, lie on his belly, and sigh a lot. As the putative star of this mad caper, I would have felt much more comfortable working with a pro like Lassie, but he was high-priced and probably busy in Hollywood. Desperate times, however, called for desperate measures, and we were desperate. Possibly insane, too.

"All right," I said. "If we're going to sneak Sadly into the hospital, we've got to get organized."

I edited Stephen's plan down from a dozen complicated sections involving robbery, murder, and arson, to a few easy steps. Then we put the revised plan into action on a Thursday afternoon at exactly three-twenty-nine. Here's how it went:

1029 Hours Zulu (That's 3:29 P.M. EST for those who don't read Tom Clancy.)

"Where are you going with that?" my mother asked suspiciously as I was sneaking out of the house, a blue-plaid carriage blanket under my arm.

"It's for Sadly," I said. "In case he gets cold."

"What are you talking about?" she asked.

"I'm going to take Sadly to the hospital so Susie can see him," I said. What I didn't say was that the basset hound was going to make an illegal personal appearance in her room.

"That's nice," my mother said. "Tell Susie I'll be over at dinnertime. I wish she would eat more. She's so thin."

"Yeah," I said, slinging the blanket over my shoulder like a serape and getting out of the house as quickly as possible. I had gotten away with Step One and I didn't want to press my luck.

Step Two was easy enough. I had no problem convincing Mrs. Davis to lend me Sadly for the afternoon. As usual, she gave me a bag of biscuits to keep him happy and a bunch of Oreo cookies for Susie. So armed with dog and blanket, munching an Oreo, I set off for my fateful rendezvous with Stephen.

1104 Hours Zulu

"This place gives me the creeps," I said.

"It's only the morgue," Stephen said nonchalantly.

We were in the basement of the hospital, walking down a dim, dank corridor that contained dead bodies and sleeping interns. We had entered the building through an unlocked window behind a row of hedges. Convincing Sadly that he wanted to be manhandled through a window had taken a lot of muscle and half a bag of biscuits. He didn't like the gloomy basement any more than I did.

"You do this every day?" I asked my brother.

"I have to," he said. "I'm too young to get in."

As we crept down the corridor, every noise made my stomach lurch. I had seen enough horror movies to know that this was the kind of place discerning monsters preferred.

"Are you sure this is going to work?" I whispered as we neared the elevator.

"All you have to do is wrap Sadly in the blanket and pretend he's a baby. Susie's room is next door to the baby ward and there are always people there carrying babies around in blankets. No one will notice."

We got into the elevator and Stephen said, "You've got about thirty seconds to get him ready."

I threw the plaid blanket over Sadly and hoisted him onto my shoulder. Stephen adjusted the blanket so that the dog's head and feet were neatly tucked inside its folds. Sadly looked like a big, ungainly baby, but he took this latest humiliation with good humor and hardly squirmed or complained at all.

"Here we are," Stephen said when we reached the third floor. "Remember—just follow the plan."

1111 Hours Zulu

Once the battle begins, however, the most artfully laid plans often go awry. Ours certainly did. As I was sneaking through the hospital, trying to look as if I belonged there, I suddenly encountered an unforeseen obstacle—our neighbor Mrs. Buchanan. She was wearing a long, rather tired-looking mink coat and her hat was slightly askew.

"Hello there, young man," she said, grabbing the railing attached to the wall for support. I was sophisticated enough to observe that she had obviously just returned from a marathon liquid lunch.

"Hi, Mrs. Buchanan," I said, gripping Sadly tightly, hoping he wouldn't bark.

"I was just visiting young Miss Van Dyne," she said. "Pleurisy, you know."

I didn't.

"Is that your sister?" she asked, nodding at my struggling bundle of joy.

"Uh, yes," I said.

Sadly groaned.

"My, she doesn't sound at all well," Mrs. Buchanan said.

"That's why she's in the hospital," I said, recovering brilliantly. "Well, I've got to go."

"Oh, let me have a peek at the dear little thing," she said, coming toward me.

As I turned to run, Mrs. Buchanan swiped at the blanket with her gloved hand and snatched away Sadly's cover.

Sadly blinked, frowned, and drooled.

Mrs. Buchanan gripped her heart and staggered backward, a look of pure horror on her suddenly ashen face. Quickly, I covered Sadly's head. He woofed. Mrs. Buchanan woofed. I woofed, trying to cover up Sadly's woof.

"My," Mrs. Buchanan said, holding on to the rail for dear life, "she certainly is sicker than the last time I saw her. You'd better get her back to bed."

"'Bye," I said gratefully, loping off down the hall.

When I rounded the corner, I paused to catch my breath. My heart was racing and I felt as if I was about to faint, but the plan had been saved by a combination of very bad eyesight and a half dozen luncheon martinis.

"Wake up, Susie," I stage-whispered. "I've got something to show you."

The crumpled little figure in the bed rolled over and stared at me for a minute.

"What?" she asked.

I put Sadly on her bed and, with a flourish I had learned from Kim's butler, I whipped off the blanket to reveal Susie's best friend.

They stared at each other for a moment, neither one of them believing what they were seeing. Then Susie threw her arms around the startled dog and planted a big wet kiss on his head. Sadly licked her face and glad to be free of the blanket, he yawned, stretched, and assumed his usual position, lying on his belly, his paws stretched out in front of him.

For the next ten minutes, Susie carried on a conversation with the immovable Sadly, asking him about his food, his friends, his doghouse, his toys, and his general outlook on life. Sadly woofed quietly at the appropriate intervals, encouraging her to continue. She told him about her "rhumy" fever and how much it hurt and how she wanted to go home. He seemed to agree with every word she said. She patted his back and kissed his face and told him he was the best dog in the whole world. He agreed with that, too.

I gave Sadly a biscuit to keep him interested in Susie's monologue and I was amazed to see her snatch it out of his mouth and gnaw on it. Sadly looked insulted, but resigned, so I handed Susie an Oreo and gave him back his slobbery biscuit.

In the space of only a few minutes, Susie's transformation had been astounding. Her eyes were sparkling, not dull and leaden; her face was animated, not sad and pained; and her voice sounded happy, not hoarse and mechanical. Not only that, she was hungry again and bolted down three Oreos and half a dog biscuit. She was a different child from the one I had visited the day before. I liked this Susie a whole lot better than the other one.

Stephen broke up old home week by poking his head through the curtain and telling me it was almost dinnertime and that we had better get going. Susie, of course, begged for Sadly to stay, but Stephen said we'd bring him back the next day and swore her to secrecy.

We retraced our steps to the dark basement and crawled out the window. I reattached Sadly's leash and said, "I hate to admit it, but I think you were right." Stephen smirked knowingly.

That evening, when my mother returned from the hospital, she was full of good news.

"Susie's the best I've seen her in weeks," she said happily. "She ate her entire dinner and she laughed at a joke I told her and she wanted her hair brushed. Those new antibiotics Dr. Alexander prescribed must be doing wonders."

"Doctors," Stephen sneered under his breath.

"But there was one problem," my mother continued. "As good as she looked and as well as she acted, I think she must be hallucinating."

My father looked up from his Manhattan.

"She swore to me that Sadly had been in her room and that she had talked to Stephen, who had told her not to tell anyone," Mom said.

I about choked on the mashed potato portion of my turkey TV dinner; Stephen's face turned the same color as the spuds.

"She must have confused seeing Sadly through the window with an actual visit," my father said reasonably. "Poor child."

"I suppose," my mother said. "But she seemed so positive."

Despite our promise, Stephen, Sadly, and I never made another clandestine visit to the hospital. There was no need. Susie began to improve markedly. Her fever went down, her rash cleared up, and she got restless—a sure sign that she was on the mend. My parents and Dr. Alexander assumed that the new course of treatment had worked the miracle, but Stephen and I didn't believe it. Susie began to get better the minute she was reunited with Sadly. Coincidence? I think not.

Today, of course, dogs are routinely used in the treatment of sick children and adults. Animals seem to have a soothing and therapeutic effect on patients, but in 1961 dogs were anathema to the medical profession. Stephen's inspired guess about Sadly was decades ahead of its time. His constant hectoring, too, must have helped Susie to escape the hospital. Who among us could stand to be harassed day and night by an eleven-year-old fanatic determined to cure us?

When, at last, we had Susie back home safe and sound, Stephen gave her a stern lecture, prohibiting her from ever getting sick again. That was a sentiment we could heartily agree with: We loved her too much ever to be parted again.

Susie had been an unexpected gift that had shaken up our bland, established little family and made us realize that there was something in the universe beyond ourselves. She may not have been the most beautiful baby ever born, or the most talented, or the most brilliant, but there was never a little girl who was more adored by her family and an odd assortment of friends. Susie enchanted us from the beginning and kept us captive with her immense capacity to love, her generous nature, and her wide-eyed wonder at the world around her. When we almost lost her at the age of five, we recounted our blessings and considered ourselves fortunate indeed.

Afterword

I'm a sucker for a happy ending, but Susie's complete recovery ruined a good story. In a paroxysm of creative genius, I pictured a frail little girl pathetically wasting away to nothing. I planned a final tear-stained chapter that would have had the nation weeping tears of anguish—tears that Oprah would have found irresistible, inviting me on her show to relive the loss of my baby sister amid buckets of new tears. Unfortunately, Susie took a dim view of that idea. She even turned down a massive bribe ($212.00, the entire contents of my savings account) to move to Brazil for a year while I promoted the story of her tragic, Camille-like demise. That journey would have been necessary because I didn't want her popping up hither and yon like Elvis. But in the end, I was forced—reluctantly—to tell the truth.

Everyone claimed that the new wonder drug had saved the day, but I still don't believe it. I think it was a combination of Sadly's influence and Stephen's constant bullying that cured her. In his youth, Stephen could heal the lame, the halt, and the incontinent simply by yelling at them. Today, as an MBA, Stephen is still yelling at people, this time about their finances or in my case, the lack of them.

Amazingly, there were no other reported cases of scarlet or rheumatic fever in the county for decades. And even more amazing, Susie never developed the post-fever heart problems we worried about so much. She grew up to be a healthy adult, mercifully free of the terrible damage she could have sustained. Susie may not have been Queen Nepoon, but she was a winner. And she still has the purple ribbon to prove it.

Susie lives in the suburbs of Chicago with her husband, Charlie, and two beautiful daughters, Betsy and Anna, and a dog named Bandit. Bandit, by the way, is no Sadly. I knew Sadly, and believe me, Senator, that dog is no Sadly.

In later years, I would sometimes find Sadly sitting under a lamp-post in the village. He would be scrutinizing the passersby with a dole-ful eye, looking as if he would burst into tears at any moment. Using a Tootsie Roll as bait, I would lure him home. Then I would yell at the new generation of kick baseball players, telling them to be more care-ful and always lock the gate to his yard.

Kids. They never listen.

But Sadly kept escaping, and of course, the inevitable happened. On one of his treks, poor Sadly was hit by a passing car. Although the driver rushed him to the vet, it was too late for the old basset hound. Sadly died in the arms of his owner, Mrs. Davis, who had been notified by phone.

There was much mourning among the kids who had known and loved Sadly. And there was much speculation about his old-age wan-derlust. The players unanimously declared that they had always locked the gate behind them but their track record belied their claims. My own theory was that Sadly was out searching for his best friend and confidante, Susie. She was much older then and was busy with school, her friends, and being a kid. She just didn't have the time to play with him anymore. Sadly must have been the loneliest dog on the planet without her.

My mother died in 1975, followed by my father three years later, making us rather aged orphans. Fortunately, my father held on long enough to see Susie graduate from college, but my mother never had a chance to dance at Susie's wedding, a wish she had long held. They did, however, find out about our covert operation to sneak Sadly into the hospital. Stephen, driven to distraction by my parents' fawning praise of Dr. Alexander, blurted out the whole story about six months after the fact. My father was appalled, but my mother, with her pen-chant for folk medicine, saw the connection. She was also glad that the drugs Susie had taken hadn't damaged her brain, making her see things that weren't there.

As for me, I rode my bike without a helmet, I went swimming with-out a lifeguard, I spent years playing without adult supervision, I roller-skated without body armor, I watched television and movies until my eyes hurt, I never played a video game, I never went to a mall, I read books my teachers thought were inappropriate, I never heard of sunscreen, I ate fried foods, I liked whole milk and butter, I drank an ocean of soda, I smoked cigarettes, I blew up frogs with M-80s, I climbed trees without a safety harness, I scaled rocks with my bare hands, I excavated for kryptonite, I rode in the front seat of cars sans a (safety) belt, I thought an air bag was someone who talked too much, I wrote a novel, I visited Mafia hangouts, I put my fingers in electrical outlets, I stood on one leg for two hours, I knocked out half my teeth sleigh riding, I jumped in mud puddles wearing my school shoes, I left the house without my jacket, I sipped the dregs of leftover martinis and Manhattans, I got so filthy one bath was not enough, I fell in love with an older woman, I shot arrows in the air, I didn't shoot my eye out with a BB gun, I played cowboys and Indians, I listened eagerly to real rock and roll, I didn't have a doll named GI something, I never got a cramp, I stepped on cracks, I slaughtered ants, I mashed fireflies, I played with toy guns and shot real ones, I told dirty jokes, and guess what? I survived to the age of thirteen—and beyond, even.

OSHA, the EPA, and the myriad regulatory agencies involved in controlling children's behavior would be sore amazed and somewhat steamed that the billions they spend every year to "save the children" could have been used for something more productive—like rutabaga research perhaps.

But my horrifying childhood was a product of the times—the long Eisenhowerian afternoon—an era of unprecedented freedom for children. I presume we will never see its like again and that's sad for the kids of today. They will never know what it is like to be left alone by their parents, their teachers, and their two-hundred levels of intrusive government. (Note to kids: Those bicycle helmets make you look dorky. You would have been laughed off the playground in my day.)

I just hope that somewhere—in a dusty cornfield or a dirty urban alley—a bunch of kids grab a ball and invent their own game. It should be a game that requires long minutes of arguing about the rules and long hours of playing. It should be a game open to anyone from five to twelve; a game that tests the varied abilities of the players; a game that evolves constantly; and a game where tears of shame can be averted by the granting of an extra strike or two.

And it would be nice to think that somewhere nearby a little girl and her best friend, a droopy basset, are keeping a critical eye on The Game, while sharing intimate secrets only the two of them can understand.

Postscript

I don't know if you believe in reincarnation or not. I never did—until the last time I visited Susie in Chicago. The wind was blowing, the snow was falling, and the temperature was hovering in the teens. It was June, I think.

Susie picked me up in her new car, a shiny black Lincoln Navigator, which is a gigantic SUV, only a bit smaller than a Greyhound bus. I almost had to reach over my head to open the door, but what I saw inside made me laugh out loud. There was Susie, all five feet four of her, perched high above me in a command chair worthy of Captain Kirk. She peered down from a lofty height and asked me why I was laughing.

"Even after all these years," I said, "you're still riding around in the Black Torpedo."

Old perambulators never die, I guess. They are just recycled into sports utility vehicles.

Acknowledgments

This book could not have been written without the help, advice, and criticism of my sister, Susie. She threw herself into the project with abandon, practically abandoning her husband and children. Susie did the picture research, uncovered obscure notes my mother had made, and reminded me of long-forgotten stories. She jogged my memory and jogged down to Fotomat for umpteen copies of picture number 4A. All I can say is thanks, and I hope that the final product is worth the gargantuan effort she put into helping me with the book.

All children say and do cute things, but it is the rare mother who writes them down. That's why I'd like to thank my mother for having the foresight to collect stories about Susie, some published, many unpublished, and hand them down for me to plunder.

I would also like to thank my ace word processors, Carolyn Parqueth and Diane MacFarlane, who do more than just type. Diane is a computer genius who has helped me recover from the Blue Screen of Death, and Carolyn constantly noodges me to work harder and produce more copy, quicker. Without these two ladies' encouragement, I'd still be thinking about Chapter 1 and trying to get my computer to work.

And finally thanks to my editor, Audrey LaFehr, whose deft direction made this book possible.